"Paul Farrell gets inside the pyche of investors to show them how to build a winning portfolio for a lifetime. In his book, *The Millionaire Code,* Dr. Farrell reminds us that investing has nothing to do with hot stocks and five-star mutual funds. Instead, he reveals to us that becoming wealthy, both spiritually and financially, means first discovering our inner compass, then boldly proceeding in that direction on our road to success.

Paul Farrell has a keen understanding of the struggles we face when trying to make sense of the hype of Wall Street. As a result, most investors are unable to emotionally embrace simple principles that they intellectually know to be true. *The Millionaire Code* shows us how and shows us the way. The only thing left is for readers to act on his message. His book not only helps us become better investors, it challenges us to become better people!"

Bill Schultheis
Author, *The Coffeehouse Investor*

"When it comes to financial and career advice, one size does not fit all. Paul Farrell shows that knowing yourself leads to both happiness and wealth. Determine your personality code and follow a path to wealth designed especially for you."

John R. Nofsinger, Ph.D.
Finance Professor, Washington State University
Author, *Investment Madness*

THE MILLIONAIRE CODE

16 PATHS TO WEALTH BUILDING

PAUL B. FARRELL

WILEY

John Wiley & Sons, Inc.

Published by John Wiley & Sons, Inc., Hoboken, New Jersey.
Published simultaneously in Canada.

For general information on our other products and services, or technical support, please contact our Customer Care Department within the United States at 800-762-2974, outside the United States at 317-572-3993 or fax 317-572-4002.

Wiley also publishes its books in a variety of electronic formats. Some content that appears in print may not be available in electronic books.

For more information about Wiley products, visit our web site at www.wiley.com.

Library of Congress Cataloging-in-Publication Data:

Farrell, Paul B.
   The millionaire code : 16 paths to wealth building / Paul Farrell.
      p. cm.
Includes index.
   ISBN 0-471-42616-4 (CLOTH)
   1. Wealth–United States.   2. Millionaires–United States.   3. Success in business–United States.   4. Investments–United States.   I. Title.
   HC110.W4F37 2003
   332.024'01–dc21   2003001699

Printed in the United States of America

10 9 8 7 6 5 4 3 2 1

To
Dorothy,
the love of my life.
The best is yet to come!

CONTENTS

ACKNOWLEDGMENTS

First and foremost, a very special thanks to my literary agent, Gene Brissie. His guidance, encouragement, and uplifting spirit have been there every step of the way. To Debby Englander, my editor at John Wiley & Sons, another special thanks for seeing the vision of *The Millionaire Code* and for making it a reality. To Chris Furry of North Market Street Graphics, who added her magical touch and transformed the rough manuscript into a real book. And all along the way, this terrific trio had the backing of a team that made the work come alive: Greg Friedman and Alexia Meyers at Wiley and Vicky Dawes and Mary Jo Fostina at North Market Street Graphics.

Also, I owe a debt of gratitude to all the wonderfully creative men and women at CBS MarketWatch who have been my extended family for many years and have given me the opportunity to stretch my wings as a journalist, especially David Callaway, Thom Calandra, Chris Pummer, Alec Davis, Anne Stanley, Tom Bemis, Barb Kollmeyer, Deborah Adamson, Barbara Costanza, Jeanne Stewart, Chuck Jaffe, Jonathan Burton, Paul Erdman, Paul Merriman, Craig Tolliver, Marshall Loeb, Irwin Kellner, and, of course, Larry Kramer, whose leadership and vision turned our little online financial news service into a broad-based media powerhouse. What a thrill being on this adventure with all of you!

And my thanks to several incredible mentors who opened me to the road less traveled: Joseph Campbell, an extraordinary man who taught me about *The Hero with a Thousand Faces* and *The Power of Myth;* Carl G. Jung, the spiritual grandfather who spoke to me across time in his *Memories, Dreams, Reflections;* Bill Wilson, who taught so many of us in The Program how to live the impossible dream one day at a time; my dear friend Calvin Holt, whose serendipity was so much more than a chic restaurant in Manhattan and a magical dance mediation class in Soho; and most of all, my beautiful wife, Dorothy Boyce, a brilliant psychotherapist, who is my best friend, companion, confidant, teacher, and cheerleader. Nothing would be possible without her love.

PART 1

INTRODUCTION: UNLEASH THE MILLIONAIRE WITHIN YOU

A NEW WAY OF THINKING ... GETTING RICH IN SPIRIT AND IN FACT

> In the story of Sir Galahad, the knights agree to go on a
> quest, but thinking it would be a disgrace to go forth in a
> group, each entered the forest, at one point or another, where
> they saw it to be thickest, all in those places where they found
> no way or path.
> Where there is a path, it's someone else's path. Each knight
> enters the forest at the most mysterious point and follows his
> own intuition. What each brings forth is what never before
> was on land or sea: the fulfillment of his unique potentialities,
> which are different from anybody else's.
>
> Joseph Campbell

Do you want to become a millionaire? Seriously, do you *really* want to become a millionaire? Okay, I'll show you. It's much easier than you think—*because once you know "the code" you're headed in the right direction.*

Discover the Power of the Code: Unleash the Millionaire Within

There's no mystery to becoming a millionaire. Anyone can do it. Take, for example, the unassuming utility company maintenance man making a modest salary over a 36-year period. He lived below his means, even buying clothes at thrift shops, yet enjoyed watercolor painting, ballroom dancing, traveling, and investing. And left $3 million in stocks and real estate to charities.

Or the copier salesman in a small town who took over a small store of his own. He worked seven days a week, took few vacations, raised two children, bought some real estate, and invested the maximum in retirement savings. At age 41 he sold the shop for $1 million and continued working for the new owners. Or the doctor who raised four kids and still managed to retire with almost $2 million.

And how about all those steady American workers–schoolteachers, city librarians, police officers, nurses, and lab techs–who retire on a nice combination of resources from a pension, 401(k), Social Security, a few stocks, bonds, and funds, a low mortgage, and some real estate?

The Only Real Way to Become a Millionaire

Actually, the most difficult step on the road to becoming a millionaire is the first step. And the first step is not just "getting started," as most experts will tell you (although that's a big one). *The first step is making sure you're pointed the right way–your way. Most people aren't!* Most people have trouble getting started because they haven't figured out which way is their way.

All too many people are headed in the wrong direction, going nowhere fast. Or they arrive in the wrong place too late, traveling somebody else's path. Or, frustrated, they give up before they even get started.

And that's what this Millionaire's Personality Code is all about, helping you discover the only real way you can ever become a millionaire–*your way.*

No Shortage of Formulas Out There

You already know about the mechanical one-size-fits-all cookie-cutter formulas for getting rich, making big bucks, and wealth building. In fact, I bet you're like many other Americans who have a small but well-stocked library with many of the same how-to books I've collected over the years.

You're probably already familiar with some of the most popular ones: *The Millionaire Next Door; Ordinary People, Extraordinary Wealth; Eight $teps to $even Figures; 9 Steps to Financial Freedom; The Millionaire Mind; Getting Rich in America; The 401(k) Millionaire; Rich Dad, Poor Dad; You're Fifty, Now What;* and the list goes on and on.

On top of that, I bet you that the last time you were poking around a newsstand you saw at least one magazine with a cover story telling you exactly how to make a million bucks so you can retire comfortably some day.

Sound familiar? I have a big box of these old "how to become a millionaire and retire" issues from *Fortune, Business Week, Kiplinger's, Money, Forbes, SmartMoney, Mutual Funds, Newsweek,* and *U.S. News & World Report.* You've seen them, too. After you've read enough of these books and magazines, you know they all say the same thing, over and over again. They are like New Year's resolutions and popcorn, quickly forgotten.

Information Overload—Confusing and Overwhelming

There's no big mystery about how to become a millionaire. You can easily find tons of information in libraries, bookstores, periodicals, and online.

So here's the big question for you: If we have all this fancy ultrasophisticated information, *why are there are so darn few millionaires in America?* Why are there only 8 million in a nation of 283 million people? That's less than 4 percent of the population.

Very simple—the reason there aren't more millionaires in America is not because you and I lack the information. We know we have all the formulas, tools, databases, newsletters, methodologies, and software we'll ever need on budgeting, saving, investing, and all the other tricks essential to becoming a millionaire.

The problem is, we have too @#%& much information, not too little!

Looking for Love in All the Wrong Places

You have all the books and magazines you'll ever need telling you exactly how to follow some simple set of rules or steps, even guaranteeing that if you do you'll become a millionaire and retire happy as a clam.

But in this new age of information overload, all the formulas, rules, and steps go in one ear and out the other, as my grandpa used to say. Our attention span rapidly fades. For so many of us, the cookie-cutter formulas don't feel right—so we're off looking for the next new book, hoping it will fit who we are.

That's right, as wonderful as it all sounds, most investors tune out most of the information because somehow—no matter how good things look on paper in that book or magazine—it just doesn't fit your personality!

Why 90 Percent Are Going in the Wrong Direction

So, what's the problem? The problem is that there really is no one-size-fits-all, cookie-cutter approach to becoming a millionaire.

As a result, *the vast majority of Americans trying to become millionaires are doing it the wrong way*—doing it someone else's way, using formulas that just don't fit with their true personality. Or worse yet, they get frustrated, give up, and do nothing.

No wonder we have so few millionaires. Studies by such respected organizations such as the American Association for Retired Persons (AARP), Employee Benefit Research Institute (EBRI), Economic Policy Institute (EPI), Consumer Federation of America, and the U.S. Bureau of Economic Analysis tell us that only one in three Americans are saving enough to retire comfortably and that the average American's portfolio is less than $100,000 at retirement, including home equity. Many Americans may never be able to retire, let alone become millionaires.

Wall Street's Not Your Friend

Wall Street's money managers have most Americans believing that Wall Street gurus can beat the market and that you can't win without their superior intelligence. Wall Street spends over $15 billion annually for marketing and advertisements to keep you dependent on this illusion.

Yes, it's a big hoax: Several research studies confirm, for example, that Wall Street's actively managed mutual funds charge excessive loads and higher fees, even though Wall Street firms consistently underperform the top no-load funds run by an independent fund company like Vanguard.

No wonder Wall Street hates to see books come along like *The Four Pillars of Investing,* in which Dr. William Bernstein, a neurologist and money manager, bluntly says that Wall Street operates with the "ethics of Bonny and Clyde," and they do it under the cloak of legitimacy, disguised as a trusted friend. Yet study after study consistently proves that Wall Street's money managers charge more for their services and return less to investors.

The fact is, Wall Street money managers don't give a hoot about you personally. Oh, they will smile and pretend, but Wall Street's primary goal is to increase assets under management and gain control of your money so they can charge higher account fees and expenses, book more earnings, and increase profit margins—at your expense. You can do better without Wall Street.

Yes, You Are Unique—Trust That Still Small Voice

The problem goes back to the culture of Wall Street and the entire financial services industry, including fund companies, cable news networks, and best-selling gurus, magazine writers, and newspaper editors.

Like sheep, they go along with the Wall Street myth, either focusing on one-size-fits-all, cookie-cutter approaches to getting rich and becoming a millionaire, or confusing the issue with lots of information so that Main Street will, by default, turn to Wall Street for advice.

Occasionally, however, a still small voice will scream inside your head "But wait, I'm unique."

And you're right—you are unique. Your brain is wired differently. Your DNA and your genes point you in a special direction, down a road less traveled that's off the beaten path—and on your path.

It should come as no surprise that you'll naturally resist all the mechanical how-to formulas you've read over and over again in Borders and Barnes & Noble.

Find the Path Made for Your Unique Personality

That's where *The Millionaire Code* comes in. This book is designed to help you understand why you're different (and why it's okay to be different!) and to help you discover the only real way you can ever become a millionaire—*your way*.

There is no one-size-fits-all, cookie-cutter formula to becoming a millionaire. None. Life would be less of a struggle if there were. But as we all discover sooner or later, what worked for your father or mother, for your siblings or best friend, is probably wrong for you. Even what your well-intentioned teachers, mentors, coaches, or favorite uncle think is best for you may be wrong.

In fact, research studies show that the vast majority of college graduates aren't working in their major field of study. Moreover, studies show that most graduates will make at least three career changes in their lifetime.

Like it or not—you've got to find the path that fits you and you alone.

To Thy Own Self Be True—Period!

The only real mystery—if there is one—is discovering the real you and the millionaire within you. We've heard this great challenge so often since ancient times.

Writing in the *Tao Te Ching* 5,000 years ago, Lao Tzu tells us to "follow your true nature." Twenty-five hundred years ago, Plato repeated the message: "Know thyself." Down though the ages, great mystics of all faiths tell us to "listen to the still, small voice within," for there lies the truth of our being.

Get in touch with the real you and your mission in life—and then your unique path to getting rich in spirit *and in fact* will become obvious.

America's 42 Million Millionaires in Training!

You can avoid the false starts and increase your odds of becoming a millionaire by *first* identifying your unique personality code—yes first, *before* you start saving and investing and all the rest of the stuff you need to do to accumulate a million bucks.

Know your code, and get into action, and you'll join a powerful yet quiet subculture in pursuit of the new American Dream—retiring as a millionaire.

Statistically, we know there are already 8 million millionaires in America. That's about 3.6 percent of the total population of 283 million people. Some experts predict the number will grow to as many as 50 million American millionaires by 2025.

That means that today we could have as many as 42 million Americans on the path to retiring as millionaires. Of course, inflation will have some impact on the results. But however you look at it, there are roughly 42 million millionaires in training in America today, searching for the best way to capture this new American Dream.

The New American Dream: Discovering Your Path to Financial Freedom

What's the best way for you? It's probably *not* what your boss says you're great at. Not something that's one of the latest top 20 hot career fields in America. Probably not something you score well on in some standard tests. And it's likely not even the job you've been doing for a few too many years:

- *Shifting into high gear:* You could be one of the 35 percent of Americans who are already building a nest egg—but you just want to accelerate things and retire early.
- *Running on empty:* Maybe you're doing all the right stuff (at least what seemed like the right stuff years ago). You're making a good living, but you're unhappy with your life and feeling as though you've been wasting time in the wrong career.
- *Happy, but broke:* Maybe you are doing exactly what you want to do, perhaps fulfilling your life's mission helping the handicapped, but you're not making much money, or you'd just like to find ways to better fund the work. At least we can help confirm that you're doing the right thing.
- *Still searching:* More likely, you're one of the 65 percent of Americans who really aren't doing much about becoming a millionaire,

very possibly because you haven't discovered the real you, your mission in life, the millionaire within.

Whatever the case, something tells you it's time to get in touch with your secret millionaire's personality code, time to get in sync with your true self, time to get in the millionaire's spirit, now, today.

How to Get the Most out of This Book

We know there are 16 unique millionaire personality profiles. We have The Code and you can easily self-test to find yours. That's the first step: Get in sync with your personality type.

If you want get the most out of this process, work your way through the four parts of the book:

Part 1. "Introduction: Unleash the Millionaire within You." Get an overview of the background, history, and science supporting personality profiling, why it works and how we have taken this powerful tool to the next step, profiling the 16 millionaire personalities.

Part 2. "Test Yourself and Discover Your Unique Millionaire's Code." Here is a simple self-test that will help you identify the four distinguishing factors in your Millionaire's Code, along with an analysis of how you can use any ambiguities to transform your life, going in a whole new direction and becoming a millionaire in spirit and in fact.

Part 3. "The Four Temperaments in Millionaire Profiling." One of the screening tools used by personality profiling experts is the four temperaments, which give an added perspective into the depth of your personality, serve as an introduction to the 16 personalities, and show you how to take advantage of your assets on the path to financial freedom.

Part 4. "The 16 Millionaire Personality Codes." Once you take the test, you have your unique four-letter code and are pointed in the right direction. Each profile summarizes the distinguishing character of this personality type, what makes these people tick, and how they are most likely to become financially successful in the world and become personally fulfilled because they are living out their true destiny.

Once you know your type, your code, your personality, you can then focus all your energies on your true mission in life, on why you are here. Know the code and you'll increase your odds of becoming a millionaire and achieving the new American Dream—the financial freedom of living the life you were destined to live.

Different Strokes for Different Folks

Each of the 16 millionaire types will reach their goals in their unique way. Each will make their decisions differently, each capitalizing on their strengths differently and managing their weaknesses differently.

Stick with us and you'll discover the right way for you. Each millionaire personality type sees and responds differently to the tasks facing them as they accumulate wealth. Our test will help you discover your millionaire code so you can get on track to becoming a millionaire and enjoy your trip. We'll also include principles and tools to help each type maximize strengths and manage challenges on the way to this new American Dream.

* * * * * * * *

My life course is totally indifferent to money.
As a result, a lot of money has come in by doing what I feel I want to do from the inside. If you do that, you are doing things that attract money, because you are giving life and life responds in the way of its counterpart in hard coin.
If you follow your bliss,
you will always have your bliss,
money or not.
If you follow money,
you may lose it,
and you will have nothing.

Joseph Campbell

2

HISTORICAL OVERVIEW: UNLOCKING THE SECRET OF THE MILLIONAIRE PERSONALITY

> The great events of the world are, at bottom, profoundly unimportant. In the last analysis, the essential thing is the life of the individual, here alone do the great transformations take place, and the whole future, the whole history of the world, ultimately springs as a gigantic summation from these hidden resources in individuals.
>
> Carl G. Jung,
> *Modern Man in
> Search of a Soul*

What is the secret to your personality? Unlock *that* secret, know who you are, the real you, and you just might have a fighting chance to fulfill your destiny and achieve wealth beyond your wildest dreams. Know thyself. Know the secret to *your* personality!

"My life has been permeated and held together by one idea and one goal," wrote Carl G. Jung in his autobiography, *Memories, Dreams, Reflections,* "namely, to penetrate the secret of personality. Everything can be explained from this central point, and all my works relate to this one theme."

Jung wrote those words in his eighties, looking back over a rich life in which his research and writings shifted the entire field of psychology from the study of sickness and psychopathologies in mental institutions to developing an understanding of the inner workings of healthy minds.

Imagine, an entire life focused on one central theme, penetrating the secret of personality. In a way, all of us, you, me, and our neighbors are—*consciously or unconsciously*—also searching for the secret to our own individual personalities.

Think about it for a minute: When you cut to the chase, isn't your entire life also focused on penetrating the secret of your personality—on discovering who you are, why you are here, and whether you are fulfilling your destiny?

Even the Great Jung Had to Break from His Father

Jung's *Psychological Types* was published in 1921 and even today remains the core work used for all subsequent studies of personality. Before Jung's work hit the streets, the conventional wisdom of psychological gurus worldwide was that the masses of people were basically all alike and all driven by a single motivation in life, for example, Freud's focus on the satisfaction of our libido.

In contrast, Jung's work focused on the differences between personalities. His book was "the fruit of nearly twenty years' work in the domain of practical psychology," and "sprang originally from my need to define the ways in which my outlook differed from Freud's and Adler's," which focused on the common elements.

The emphasis Jung places on his motivation for writing *Personality Types* is interesting and significant. Freud, 19 years Jung's senior, was for many years his mentor. Freud became a dominant father figure in the younger man's life, heavily influencing Jung's early works. He often referred to Jung as his adopted eldest son, his crown prince and successor.

As he approached his midlife transition at age 40, however, Jung realized how fundamentally different his views of the human personality were from his mentor's. It was painful emotionally. Jung broke free to develop his own personality, separate and unique from the personality Freud, the strong father figure, was trying to mold for Jung.

The Struggle to Become Your Own Personality

Does that sound close to home, perhaps something you've experienced in your lifetime? What we see here between these two legendary giants is a classic example of a rather common human drama—the controlling influence that so many parents and teachers, mentors, clerics, and author-ity figures of all kinds exert over each of us.

The relationship between Jung and Freud clearly grew out of mutual respect, admiration, and affection, at the beginning. But as time passed, the student's own personality emerged, distinct from his teacher. At some point, such choices become quite simple, though all too often culminat-ing in painful separations.

The choice, nevertheless, is clear and simple: You either surrender yourself and live your life as others define your personality, or you decide to break free and assert your own personality, letting it emerge and grow in the direction of your destiny.

Eventually, we are all confronted with choices like this. Some people become their true selves while still children, some when they emancipate from their parents' home as teenagers and go forth as adults. Others do not choose until a major loss or midlife crisis. Still others not until late in life—or never. Everyone must decide for themselves: *Are you your own per-son, or a clone?*

This conflict, of course, is inevitable, because Jung also discovered that the preferences forming our personality become evident early in life, in childhood, as if they're genetically locked in our DNA. Of course, the science of genome technology was unknown at the time and not part of Jung's analysis. But today the idea that personality is biogenetically encoded in our DNA is a highly plausible concept.

Are Your Decisions Controlled by Your DNA?

Jung's groundbreaking *Psychological Types* was based on a fundamental principle "that every judgment made by an individual is conditioned by his personality type."

We are conditioned? Yes, some mysterious force—your personality, perhaps hidden in your DNA and genes—is conditioning, guiding, direct-ing, perhaps even secretly (and unconsciously) controlling how you see the world, what kind of information you decide is important, and the very processes you use to make decisions and live every day in the world.

Moreover, like most people, you're probably somewhat unaware of how profoundly your personality type controls you from deep within your unconscious mind. You may use phases like, "The devil made me do it," or "The other part of me took over," or "I couldn't help myself."

When this happens, there may well be "another you," a repressed part of your personality, hidden under a false "you" that's trying to please your parents, for example, and the source of internal conflicts and anxiety. Arguably, you aren't responsible, or in the extreme, you might even say that since your personality predetermines your choices, none of your choices are freely made.

The truth is, even if you don't understand why you act the way you do, you are still responsible for your behavior. Although you may be vaguely aware that other people do, in fact, think, feel, and behave differently from you, unless you know more about personality differences, you're stuck, unable to pinpoint why others are different, wishing that they would be more like you.

Progress, of course, comes when you change, and when you better understand personality types, beginning with Jung's basic typology.

Jung Began with Eight Personality Types

Jung's research uncovered a structure of eight separate personality types, which still have relevance today. First, he discovered that each of us has a natural tendency toward extraversion or introversion. Second, he saw that each of us operates using four functions, which Jung says "correspond to the obvious means by which consciousness obtains its orientation to experience":

1. *Sensation* (i.e., sense perception) tells us that something exists.
2. *Thinking* tells you what is.
3. *Feeling* tells you whether something is agreeable or not.
4. *Intuition* tells you whence it comes and where it is going.

Jung further believed that we gather information with either our senses or our intuition and that we make decisions using either objective thinking or our subjective feelings. In order to develop the framework for his personality types, Jung first differentiated between the Extraverts and the Introverts:

Extraverts prefer the world outside themselves—drawing their energy through interacting with the external world. They have lots of friends, like to socialize and talk to people, and even think out loud as a way of working things out. They love telephone conversations, meetings, and group-think, and they tend to avoid private time. Their view of the world is objective, focused on things and people, cars, sports, family, machines, the home—things external to them.

Introverts are the opposite—energized by their own inner world. They enjoy their own company, time alone, reading and thinking quietly, working things out *before* going into the real world with other people. They have a few close friends with intimate relationships. They are great listeners, preferring to avoid group meetings and long conversations. They live in their heads and enjoy a clearly subjective view of the world.

Jung saw these two attitudes as mutually exclusive. That is, while we all can and do swing in and out, back and forth between the two ways of being, the two don't occur at the same time. Moreover, each of us has a natural tendency to prefer one or the other of these two attitudes.

Your Four Functions: Thinking, Feeling, Sensation, Intuition

Jung also observed that people naturally preferred one function over the other three in gathering and processing information, what he called the *principal function*. No doubt you have people in your life that fit each one of these traits to a tee.

Some personalities are rational thinkers, while the emotions of others control their thought processes. As well, others rely heavily on their five senses—sight, sound, touch, smell, taste—in contrast to people who rely primarily on intangible sources to tell them what's real, often not knowing where the these intuitions come from.

Here's an overview of Jung's eight combinations of the two attitudes (Extraversion and Introversion) and the four functions (Thinking, Feeling, Sensation, and Intuition) showing how the eight combinations are expressed in the behavior of individual personalities:

1. *Extraverted Thinkers*. According to Jung, this personality type is best exemplified by an economist or a scientist such as Einstein—people who use their rational minds to learn about the objective world. They rely on cold, hard logic and theories to explain reality in an impersonal way.
2. *Introverted Thinkers*. Introverted Thinkers are the philosophers, theoretical mathematicians, existential psychologists, and others who prefer the pure reality created in their inner world. They have little interest in whether others accept their ideas and may appear cold and emotionless because they place little value on feelings—theirs or those of others.
3. *Extraverted Feeling types*. These people rely heavily on their emotions and as a result often turn from passionate love to intense anger as their feelings run hot and cold. They are attracted to the

latest fashions, styles, and fads of the moment, always searching for some new turn-on. Celebrity entertainers like Jay Leno and Madonna fit this profile.

4. *Introverted Feeling types.* There's an air of mystery about this personality, often exhibited in composers, musicians, poets, and monks, individuals who have deep feelings, but keep them deep inside, where they live in the quiet of their souls. Although on the surface they may appears pensive, even depressed, they are quite balanced and self-sufficient within themselves.

5. *Extraverted Sensation types.* This personality type is exhibited by the world's hardheaded realists, unconcerned about the past or future or the meaning of things. They are totally absorbed in what's happening right now and want to enjoy the full range of sensual pleasure in work and play, often jumping into dangerous challenges. Speculators, athletes, entrepreneurs, and other risk takers fit in here.

6. *Introverted Sensation types.* These people isolate themselves from the external reality, which they find mundane and boring compared to the exciting sensations of their inner world. They may seem aloof, haughty, and rather quietly amused with people, preferring to express themselves in abstract expressionism or surrealism.

7. *Extraverted Intuitives.* According to Jung, individuals with this type of personality jump from project to project in search of new adventures, yet often move on to something new before completing the previous thing. Yes, they are unstable, but they can be great promoters of new businesses. However, they hate routine and become bored easily, so they may not be the best candidates as ongoing caretakers of the new business, for example.

8. *Introverted Intuitives.* Here are the mystics, visionaries, and clairvoyants, the daydreamers, eccentrics, and misunderstood geniuses all searching for some special union with the other world. They may be out of touch with everyday reality and unable to share their inner experiences, because they also have difficulty understanding the strange world they inhabit.

Jung recognized that the eight personality types were extreme cases. Most people are a mixture of extraverted and introverted, possibly shifting back and forth. They also use all four functions in varying degrrees.

Notwithstanding the gray areas, hybrids, and overlaps, Jung definitely saw that we do have preferences. His research made it clear that people tend to favor one of the four functions more than the other

three, and they also tend to be either more extraverted or more introverted.

Myers-Briggs Personality Types: The Secret Four-Letter Code

"Synchronicity," wrote Jung, "is the meaningful coincidence of two or
more events, where something other than the probability of chance is
involved." Well, there was clearly a synchronicity between Jung's powerful spirit and that of two women on the other side of the world.

While Jung was doing his research on personality types in Switzerland
for two decades leading up to the publication of *Personality Types* in 1921,
an American woman, Katharine C. Briggs, was also independently
exploring and classifying the differences in human behavior.

The story goes that her work on types became particularly intriguing
when in 1918 her 21-year-old daughter, Isabel Briggs Myers, an idealist,
married a tough-minded left-brain lawyer. Here was someone unlike anyone else in the family, someone who provided a challenge to her work in
typecasting.

When the English translation of Jung's *Personality Types* appeared five
years later, Katharine turned to Isabel and shouted, "This is it!" And with
that, the two women began their incredible collaboration.

World War II added considerable impetus to their work, as they saw
an increasing number of mismatches and increasing frustrations between
individuals and their jobs in the war effort.

As a result, they set out to create a scientifically verifiable psychological test based on Jung's theories of personality preferences. Their
work led to the groundbreaking Myers-Briggs Type Indicator (MBTI) in
the 1950s, which remains today the standard for personality preference
testing.

Isabel Briggs Myers published a book on the MBTI in 1962, the year
Jung died. Today, the Myers-Briggs Type Indicator is the world's leading
test for personality types, with over 2 million people tested annually
worldwide. The test is professionally administered and evaluated by
trained professionals and consists of 16 separate and unique personality
types.

Keirsey's Four Temperaments: A Shortcut

Dr. David Keirsey ushered in a new popularism to the field of personality typecasting in 1984 with the publication of his work, *Please Understand
Me,* which, along with his 1998 update, has sold over 2 million copies.

In part because use of the MBTI test was restricted to trained professionals for a fee, Keirsey and others began developing their own personality tests and their own descriptions of personality types, along with suggested career opportunities, relationship and parental advice, and other information helpful in the interactions between a particular type and the other 15 personality types. Other popular works worth special note include *Type Talk* and *Type Talk at Work* by Otto Kroeger and Janet M. Thuesen and *Do What You Are* by Paul D. Tieger and Barbara Barron-Tieger.

While Keirsey built on Jung's work and the Myers-Briggs 16 personality types, he added two new key elements to personality typecasting: (1) a much longer historical perspective and (2) the concept of Temperaments, a shortcut that narrowed personality types down to four primary groups with similar characteristics. Fortunately, his approach has proved to be extremely helpful and popular for the average Joe and Jane America by bringing typecasting to Main Street.

Noteworthy is the fact that Keirsey's work traces the roots of personality typecasting back before the time of Jung and the Myers-Briggs team. Keirsey goes back through history to study many theorists, from ancient Greece's Plato and the physician Hippocrates almost 2,500 years ago to Paracelsus, a Viennese physician in the sixteenth century, and later, philosophers Rousseau in France and Kant in Germany—all of whom divided people into four categories similar to his four Temperaments.

You will also notice similar four-part divisions in such diverse areas of world culture as astrology, Eastern religions, primitive Indian rituals, and also in interpretations of the four gospels of the Bible. Throughout history, philosophers, sages, and physicians have tried to understand the human personality; although there are major differences, a simple four-part structure is the common thread.

Keirsey's Four-Part Synthesis of the History of Personalities

Keirsey observed this common thread repeating throughout history, beginning with the four Temperaments first identified by Plato as the four main personality types, or characteristics, exhibited by humans: We are either *Guardians, Artisans, Rationals,* or *Idealists.* We explore the four primary personality types in detail in Part 3.

Keirsey not only adopted Plato's four Temperaments, he also layers them over the 16 Myers-Briggs personality types to create both a four-part shortcut set of four personality types and a basis for his descriptions of the original 16 personality types. From a historical perspective, the Keirsey-Plato four-part structure and the Myers-Briggs 16 personality types are important as a starting point in understanding how you can tap into the millionaire within you.

New Science of Behavioral Finance Disputes "Rational Investing"

While Keirsey was uncovering links to the past, the emerging new science of *behavioral finance*—the study of the mysterious world of the psychology of investing—was adding new insights to personality typology.

In the past few decades, both academics and professional money managers have begun exploring this new region of the human personality, totally reversing the long-held conventional wisdom of Wall Street's gurus—that investors are rational.

This new reality was dramatically underscored in 2002 when Daniel Kahneman, a Princeton psychologist, won the Nobel prize for Economic Sciences. Apparently, Kahneman and many other psychologists have been telling us the truth for years—*that investors are actually very irrational.*

For example, investors buy at the peak of a bull market when greed and euphoria run wild. Then they sell at the bottom when fear and panic are rampant. Either way, they lose. In *Investment Madness,* Dr. John Nofsinger, a behavioral finance expert, writes:

> All people (even smart ones) are affected by psychological biases. However, traditional finance has considered this irrelevant. Traditional finance assumes that people are rational and tells us how people should behave in order to maximize their wealth.

Behavioral finance psychologists dismiss rational investment theories. Their research indicates that investors are anything but rational. All too often, investors act as if controlled by a little saboteur locked deep in their brains, a saboteur overriding their rational thinking functions. Fortunately, such insights from the behavioral finance field are beginning to impact not only economic and investment theory, but the psychology of personality types.

New Neuroeconomists Exploring Hot Spots in the Brain

Even more recently, the medical profession has stepped in, reinforcing what the psychologists and economists are discovering about the personality of the investor. This new science is called *neuroeconomics,* a marriage of brain science and economics—*the new science of irrational investing.* There were less than 50 of these new experts at their first conference in 2002, but their research is enormously promising.

Using magnetic imagery, they can actually see the brain in action, as hot spots, using new technologies. In reporting on their work for a *Wall Street Journal* article, "This Is Your Brain. This Is Your Brain On a Surging Stock," Sharon Begley wrote:

> When people anticipate rewards, the fMRI shows, the circuits that switch on are the very ones that go wild when you anticipate a delectable chocolate truffle, sex, or (in the case of addicts) cocaine.

With that auspicious beginning, you can bet this new science of neuroeconomics will be adding incredible insights to the work on personality types in the near future.

Some Personalities Are More Vulnerable

Meanwhile, one interesting example of the merger of psychology and medicine with personal finance and investing can be seen in the work of Dr. James Gottfurcht, president of Psychology of Money Consultants. His anagram, RAPIDS, was developed to remind investors of six traps that are sabotaging our decisions about money. As you review these, consider how some personality types may be more vulnerable to these traps than others:

1. *Rationalization.* We hate anything that contradicts our expectations and belief system. We hate negativity so much that our minds work overtime to explain it away. We'd do anything to avoid changing—such as hanging onto our illusion of the technology revolution in the postmillennium market collapse.
2. *Avoidance.* Investors regularly make bad decisions (e.g., buying at the top and selling at the bottom). In down cycles we delay decisions, hoping against hope for a reversal of fortune—such as hanging onto a tech stock down 50 percent and still falling. Inaction converts little losses into bigger loses.
3. *Projection of blame.* Refusing to take personal responsibility is costly. "Whether you win or lose, you are responsible for your own results. Even if you lost on your broker's tip, an advisory

service recommendation, or a bad signal from the system you bought, you are responsible," said Jack Schwager in *New Market Wizards*.

4. *Idealization.* Trust no one. You cannot. Blue chips fail. Talking heads babble. Nobody really understands the economy. Fund managers rarely beat indexes. Fund data is old and misleading. CEOs manipulate earnings. Wall Street has failed us. You are on a ship of fools, afloat the illusion of a rational market.

5. *Denial.* When we can't rationalize away bad news, we simply block it–anything to avoid making more risky decisions. For example, facing a collapsing market means not only selling dogs, but making other major decisions: admitting we made fundamental mistakes, rethinking our entire investment strategy, and selecting new securities in an unfamiliar world.

6. *Splitting.* At some point, usually after the shock of a big loss, you may have a moment of awareness and an overwhelming sense of failure. The guilt may be so great that you overreact, acting in haste and without a plan, selling everything and swearing off investing in the market ever again. And as the shock wears off, hopefully you can then develop a more conservative strategy.

Behavioral finance experts see all this is a natural reaction of the human brain riding a psychological roller coaster. We cannot help ourselves. A strange mixture of greed, invincibility, and fantasy creates the bubble in our minds on the up cycle. Then sets us up to cascade down the rapids with unfortunate negative financial consequences.

The Secret May Be No Secret—to You

Unlocking the secret to your secret Millionaire's Code is really no big secret. If you really want to find it, trust me, you will.

I am not referring to all the magic tricks, tips, and tools that will help you accumulate a million bucks by the time you retire. The mechanical formulas are easy to find. They're well known, and you need only follow them, one, two, three. Of course, that's the catch, so few actually do follow them.

One thing I am quite sure of: Unless you know your personal Millionaire's Code, you will be handicapping your destiny–not just sabotaging your chances of retiring as a millionaire. That is, whether you accumulate your million or not, you won't be truly happy unless you are in sync with the millionaire within you.

* * * * * * * *

I am really no different from any of you. I may have more money than you, but money doesn't make the difference.

Sure, I can buy the most luxurious handmade suit, but I put it on and it just looks cheap. I would rather have a cheeseburger from Dairy Queen than a hundred-dollar meal. . . .

If there is any difference between you and me it may simply be that I get up every day and have a chance to do what I love to do, every day. If you learn anything from me, this is the best advice I can give you.

Warren Buffett

JUNG'S FOUR-STEP DECISION-MAKING PROCESS FOR THE MILLIONAIRE WITHIN YOU

> Most of us believe that money-making is a game that is
> played with forces outside ourselves, forces such as the
> economy, the stock market, interest rates, the Fed,
> government policies, employment statistics and the like.
> But as you move along a spiritual path and begin to get a
> taste of the power of your invisible self, you discover that
> money-making is merely a game that you play with yourself. . . .
> Authentic power comes from your soul, that magical place
> that is always within you.
> Money is not a goal unto itself.
> If you chase after it,
> it will always elude you.
>
> Wayne Dyer,
> *Real Magic*

Once again—do you want to be a millionaire? Yes, of course. But remember, there's a lot more to being a millionaire than just making money, getting rich, accumulating stocks and bonds, and collecting things and gadgets and toys from Sharper Image, Best Buy, and Tiffany's.

Your goal is to discover who you really are—*the millionaire within you*—and fulfillment of your mission in life. If you know that, the rest of the journey falls into place easily. If you try to bypass the inner journey and chase after canned formulas in "how to become a millionaire and retire rich" books, you will miss the best part of life!

We know we already have 8 million American millionaires, with another 42 million millionaires in training working toward the magic number. On the other hand, we also know that of the total of 283 million Americans in all, more than 80 percent aren't even headed in the right direction and therefore can't possibly end up with $1 million in assets.

As far as we can see, the main reason there are so few millionaires in America is simply because there is no single best system on how to become a millionaire—at least not one that'll work for everybody. Yet the bookstores and magazine racks are loaded with books and magazines that pretend to have *the* magical one-size-fits-all cookie-cutter formulas.

As a result, the vast majority of Americans who are serious about becoming millionaires are going about it the wrong way—either using formulas that just don't fit with their natural personality, or worse yet, when they work this or that formula, they wind up frustrated and give up, abandon their quest, and do nothing.

Both Personality Types and Decision-Making Processes

Therefore, the purpose of this book is rather simple: to help you identify the real you—that powerful millionaire deep within you—and tap into that resource *before* you do any financial planning, budgeting, saving, investing, or anything else dealing with money. Otherwise, you could be doing all the right things with your money according to some canned how-to-get-rich formula, moving fast, but headed toward the wrong target.

How do you know whether you're headed toward the right target for you? Know your code, the Millionaire's Code that fits you. That code describes not only our personality types, but also our natural process of making life decisions, including financial decisions.

For example, we've already taken a brief glance at Jung's original structure of eight psychological personality types: two attitudes (Introversion and Extraversion) combined with the four functions (Sensation, Intuition, Thinking, and Feeling).

Jung's Strategic Decision-Making Process

At first glance, all we have is a static checklist of eight personality combinations, which is helpful once you know your Millionaire's Code and can jump to your combination and learn more about yourself. However, we are missing the dynamic setting. Jung actually did a lot more than just create a laundry list of personality types. He created a simple but effective strategy for making decisions. Let's take a close look at Jung's system so that you can understand the easiest and most natural way for you to make decisions about your money, finances, and investing.

A SERIES OF NATURAL STEPS

We know that Jung described the four functions as a balanced set of two opposites: First, either you have a dominant thinking capacity using logic, reason, and analysis, or you're more of a feeling person. You rely more on one or the other in your daily life, at work, with family, and in social situations: You're a rational thinker, or your emotions run the show.

Second, Jung says you will lean more heavily on either your *sensory perceptions* of the world (tangible evidence you can touch, taste, see, or smell about people, places, and things around you at work and at play) or on your *intuitions* (those gut instincts that come to you out of the blue but that you can't pinpoint how or why you know what you know).

So, you're either a Thinker or Feeler. In addition, you trust either Sensory information or your Intuitions—either/or.

JUNG'S FOUR-STEP DECISION-MAKING MODEL

Actually, Jung outlined for us a perfect four-step process, a model that fairly well describes the way people make decisions under the best of circumstances. True, you may be more of a hard-nosed Thinker-Sensor, for example, and as a result, you may tend to ignore or downplay information about feelings and intuitions. Conversely, you may be too much into emotions.

Nevertheless, Jung laid out a rather neat model for making creative decisions. Here's how this process works—and how your process might work when you're operating at your peak:

Step 1. Sensing: Collecting Basic Facts Using Your Senses

You spend all day every day getting sense impressions, thousands of them. Letters, reports, calls, magazines, television, spouses, kids, bosses, experts, amateurs—you name it—information is coming in all the time. Information from the senses: seeing, hearing, touching, smelling, and tasting. Practical stuff, facts, specifics, details, and raw data that relates to comparable information from the past. Your brain is recording these sense impressions all day long, about a lot of things, observing, collecting, and storing rather than interpreting.

Step 2. Intuition: Speculation, Alternatives, Interpretation

What does all this information mean? All day long you're also, consciously or unconsciously, sifting through all the facts, figures, and data crowding into your mind. Your brain is assigning priorities, meaning, and connections between isolated information within the bigger picture you've created for your world. Where facts are missing, incomplete, or sketchy, your mental processor will fill in the blanks, so to speak—using your imagination to speculate, invent, and predict future results, often without any rational analysis, because you just *know*.

Step 3. Thinking: Logic, Objectivity, Rational Analysis of Options

At some point, you move beyond the facts and intuitions. Your brain says you have a decision to make. Maybe a deadline, a client, an offer, a problem. Maybe it's buying or selling a stock, making a marketing presentation, or deciding which new business opportunity is the best for the company. You define the problem. Set priorities. Analyze data using logic, rational tools, and preset, objective criteria. Nothing personal, you're just thinking through the decision.

Step 4. Feelings: Subjective Relationship to People, Society, Values

Whether before, after, or parallel with the decision-making process, subjective reactions and emotions kick in. Everyone has a set of values, beliefs, integrity, and conscience that guides them in making decisions. What's right or wrong, in the eyes of God and yourself? How will your family, associates, and community be affected? Will they benefit or be hurt? Whatever the source, we all know when a hot button taps into our emotions: We're excited and nervous; our breathing quickens; we focus on the matter; and our thinking may be impaired.

Decision Making in the Real World

In fact, we're making decisions all the time, whether it's to pick up donuts on the way to work or to accept a new job offer. Lots of decisions, all day every day.

Our brains are high-speed supercomputers working full-time, jumping around between all four functions, constantly picking up new data, comparing it with past experience, reacting emotionally, speculating on the future—yes, no, maybe.

While this four-step decision-making model is sequential in an optimum world, in the real world of information overload, with multiple decisions to be made, your brain may start anywhere in the process and be using all four functions, as Jung called them, in and out of sequence, over and over and over, jumping back and forth.

HOW YOUR BRAIN MAKES DECISIONS NATURALLY

Keep this four-step decision-making model in mind, because each of us does have a natural inclination to favor either our thinking processes or our feelings, either hard facts or our intuition.

As we favor one over the other, and this is crucial, *we naturally tend to ignore, minimize, and even dismiss the other functions.* This isn't bad, it just is. This is the way the millionaire within you works. It's your DNA code, your personality type in action; it's how your brain operates, semiautomatically including and excluding information in the process of making decisions out there in the real world.

Remember, Jung's four functions are not merely a set of static ways your brain works; the four functions are steps in the decision-making model your brain uses all the time. You need to understand which of your four functions are strongest and which take a backseat so you can consciously compensate and balance all of the functions and improve your decisions.

* * * * * * * *

On the other end of the spectrum
from *not* having a plan is someone
who gets lost in their plan.
It's easy to become focused,
even obsessed with your plan or your goals.
You can become so engrossed in your plan that
you forget to enjoy the process . . .
A successful life is
achieving a balance
between these two seemingly
different messages.

Richard Carlson,
Don't Worry, Make Money

PART

TEST YOURSELF AND DISCOVER YOUR UNIQUE MILLIONAIRE'S CODE

CHAPTER 4

THE MILLIONAIRE'S CODE: TAP INTO THE SECRET POWER WITHIN YOU

> Before it incarnates,
> each soul agrees to perform certain tasks upon Earth.
> It enters into a sacred agreement with the Universe to accomplish
> specific goals. . . .
> It may be the task of raising a family,
> or communicating ideas through writing,
> or transforming the consciousness of a community,
> such as the business community.
> It may be the task of awakening the awareness of the power of love
> at the level of nations,
> or even contributing directly to the evolution of consciousness on a
> global level.
> Whatever the task your soul has agreed to,
> whatever its contract with the Universe,
> all of the experiences of your life
> serve to awaken within you
> the memory of that contract, and
> to prepare you to fulfill it."
>
> Gary Zukav,
> *The Seat of the Soul*

How do you know when or whether you're in sync with the real you? Are you off track and don't know it? Here's a simple test designed to help you uncover the four-letter code that identifies your personality type and the millionaire locked deep inside you.

The code system is essentially the same as Jung described it, although, as you'll see, the Myers-Briggs team has added a fourth dimension, creating 16 personality types (compared to Jung's original 8 types).

You'll find several popular versions of the basic test in the works of Keirsey, Kroeger, Tieger, and others, all similar and each one resulting in a four-letter code that describes your personality type. Each of these tests is, however, a shortcut. My advice is, take the Myers-Briggs test and have it evaluated by a professional. The experience is well worth it.

Your Genetic Personality Code— Can It Be Altered?

Your four-letter code shouldn't change over time. However, you might find it helpful to confirm your code by taking another version of the test in one of the other basic texts. The results should be the same each time, but doing the reruns forced me to see myself in a new light.

For example, you might find, as I did, that you tend to move back and forth between two personality types. Knowing that tendency in your personality may help you understand why you excel in doing certain things but have trouble with others.

Take the Test—Discover Your Millionaire's Code

Here's my miniversion of the classic test. It's very simple, without any lengthy technical explanations. In each of the following four pairs, pick the one word in each pair that best fits your preference in daily life.

1. *Extravert or Introvert? What's the source of your energy?* Do you interact with the external world outside of you–or do you prefer your inner world of thoughts and ideas?
2. *Sensor or Intuitive? How do you gather information?* Do you prefer hard facts that your five senses can confirm–or would you rather work from abstract ideas, concepts, and theories?
3. *Thinker or Feeler? How do you make decisions?* Do you prefer being objective and impartial–or are you more subjective, taking into account the impact of your decision on other people?
4. *Judger or Perceiver. What's your daily lifestyle?* Do you like to have your days known and scheduled–or do you prefer a more spontaneous lifestyle, keeping your options open?

Whatever you do, please do not pick the one that you think other people (family, friends, coworkers, social friends, bosses, etc.) are *expecting* you to be, either at home, at work, or socially. That is not the real you, the millionaire within you, the person other people want you to be to serve their needs.

Pick the personality characteristics that best capture the real you when the facade is stripped away. The way you prefer to be when the pressure's off and you don't have to impress anyone at work or in social situations or conform to what they want you to be. Look inside, get back to basics, admit to yourself who you really are, not who "they" want you to be. Uncover the millionaire within.

And remember, although few people are all one way or the other, you will discover that you have definite preferences, leaning more one way than the other.

Bottom line: There is no right way, no wrong way—*there is only your way.* And the four-letter code will reveal the millionaire within you and point you in the direction of financial freedom, happiness, and a full life living out your destiny.

* * * * * * *

Be nobody but yourself—
in a world which is doing its best,
night and day, to make you
like everybody else—means
to fight the hardest battle
which any human being can fight;
and never stop fighting.

e.e. cummings

CHAPTER 5

TEST THE FIRST LETTER: EXTRAVERT OR INTROVERT (E OR I)?

*I*s your source of energy the outside world or from within you?

This first personality preference isn't as clear cut as you may think. For example, as many as three out of four of us are Extraverts. So Introverts are at a bit of disadvantage, a minority living and working in a world dominated by Extraverts–where they may be forced into functioning as Extraverts.

Further complicating matters for you is the fact that in the everyday impersonal world of business and commerce, there is considerable pressure for an Introvert to fake being an Extravert, thus becoming a closet Introvert in order to function "out there," interacting with other people. This is not to say that you should abandon this role, only that you should be aware of the life you are living and consciously choosing it.

For example, Carl Jung was a man of the world. His life was filled with lectures, consultations, and writings. An Extravert? Listen: "Solitude is for me a fount of healing which makes my life worth living," he once wrote in a letter. "Talking is a torment to me, and I need many days of silence to recover from the futility of words." In fact, later in life he spent half his time in the solitude of his lakeside retreat, a structure he built with his own hands.

Search your soul and identify the real you, not the one who is performing for others. What really turns you on? We know there's a millionaire within you–what turns it on, and where does your best energy come from?

Extraverted Types

You just love being with people, talking, and thinking out loud.

If you're a true-blue Extravert, your energy comes from the world around you, so much so that when you're alone you're probably looking for opportunities to get out and interact with people in any way you can. This is essential to your way of being real.

You Extraverts *genuinely love people,* in business, socially, and with the family. One way you show it (and others know it) is that you are a great talker. You *love letting us know what you're thinking*—at business meetings, social gatherings, birthday parties, and dinners out.

In fact, you *enjoy striking up conversations* with anybody—coworkers, neighbors, kids, bosses, or strangers on the street. The action and interaction energizes you and makes you feel alive.

YOU THINK OUT LOUD, SO JUST START TALKING!

Oh, you'll listen on occasion, but even then you're waiting for the next pause in their conversation to tell people all about some great ideas you have, and you often *jump in even before you know exactly what you're going say.* In fact, talking out loud helps you work things out.

Hopefully, you know that's who you are—really are. It's essential that you know this business of *interaction with people* is crucial for your personality type. You need people as *sounding boards to help you think out loud and process your ideas.* Trust it, use it, do it.

Because a large majority of people are Extraverts, they add to the *competitive spirit* in business, constantly trying to *verbally dominate* a meeting, one-upping each other in an effort to control the group mind. Here again, remember that this is how Extraverts work things out, so passionate dialogue should be seen as just another way for Extraverts to be Extraverts!

Introverted Types

You find peace in your own private world.

My grandmother was an Introvert. I remember her baking bread in the kitchen, stuffing dough in an old cast-iron stove. I'd listen to her talking out loud to herself and ask why. So's I can get to know all the people, she'd say with a knowing smile. And she loved all of them.

If you're an Introvert, you really love spending time alone because you genuinely *enjoy your own company* and the wonderful world that you have created in your head. Interacting with people in impersonal business meetings and large social occasions just isn't your cup of tea. Why? Because you've got a better idea, and you'd prefer exploring it by yourself.

If you have a choice, you'll be reading in your den, browsing through a bookstore, sitting in a movie, puttering around your garden or tool shop, maybe hiking the backwoods—any old excuse to *spend time by yourself, alone.*

You *carry your private inner world around* with you, and quite frankly, it's more interesting than dealing with bosses who put too much value on group participation or interacting with crowds of those superconversational, attention-getting Extraverts who keep trying to impress you or draw you into small talk.

Oh, you're likely to have a *few close friends* and loved ones who really understand the fascination you have with your inner world, so you'll let them in on occasion. But even then, you need to retreat and recharge your batteries by yourself. You need to go back into your mind where ideas energize you.

LISTEN TO THE STILL SMALL VOICE—TALK TO THE CREATOR

If you are forced to interact with people, chances are great that you'll be the one *listening rather than talking.* When you do talk, you may just be asking questions to get them talking again, or making uncomfortable small talk, or if you're lucky enough to find someone interesting, taking the chance to listen and learn something new.

You prefer to *work things out in your head* and on paper before exposing your ideas to the world, and even then you'll avoid the spotlight if at all possible. In business situations, you may wind up taking a backseat to the Extraverts, who thrive on group dynamics.

If you really are an Introvert, you need to honor this personality preference. If you try to fake it as an Extravert, the internal friction will dissipate your energy and reduce your effectiveness as a moneymaker and decision maker. It's likely that you'll be frustrated with your career and your life, sensing that something may be missing—a *rich, vibrant inner life of your own creation.*

TALKING TOO MUCH VERSUS NEVER SAYING ANYTHING

On occasion Extraverts can be a real pain in the ass for Introverts and vice versa: One wants to dialogue, exchange ideas, and work things out. The other wants to work things out in his or her head first. Each must learn to understand the differences in their personalities, but Introverts must step out of character and clearly state their needs.

Whether you're an Introvert or Extravert, your core trait is natural—*neither one is better than the other*—and it will be expressed in everything you do, directly or indirectly, so don't deny it, go with it!

Both Extraverts and Introverts need to understand and honor their true personality, because it will show up in things they do all day long—most importantly in their choice of careers and how they deal with money (planning it, making it, spending it, and investing it). If you're out of sync with who you are, you'll not only miss your destiny, the journey won't be as much fun.

CHAPTER 6

TEST THE SECOND LETTER: SENSOR OR INTUITIVE (S OR N)?

Where do you get your information—concrete facts or intuitions?

We all know the business world needs Sensors, lots of them, to fill endless jobs that require handling facts and figures—programming, data processing, project scheduling, document storage and retrieval, automation, inventory control, cost estimating, numbers crunching, research, systems analysis, and so on. Computers deal in numbers and data, in and out. The best e-mails are short and factual. Business lives on facts, "just the facts, ma'am!"

Once again, it may be a bit too easy to assume you're a Sensor. You may actually be an Intuitive pretending to be a Sensor in a world of Sensors. After all, Sensors outnumber Intuitives by at least two to one.

True, Intuitives are naturally more interested in the forest than the trees, the big picture rather than details. But in order to function in a high-tech world dominated by numbers and Sensors, a true Intuitive may find it necessary to talk the language of the Sensor, or even to suppress his or her natural talents.

The truth is, neither one is better than the other. Moreover, while we all use both talents, our natural inclinations will lean more one way than the other in how we process information. Know which one is the real you. You'll be a lot happier when you acknowledge who you really are and build on it in your career and personal life.

If there is a problem, it's not your coworkers, boss, or partners. The problem is likely to arise because you're trying to act like someone you're not or work at a job that doesn't fit your personality type. You're trying to be a Sensor when you're an Intuitive, or vice versa.

Sensor Types

"Stop speculating, just give me the facts."

Remember the classic *Dragnet* television series? Detective Sergeant Joe Friday is a true Sensor. We've all heard him interrogating a crime witness: "The facts, ma'am, just the facts." No maybes. No speculations. No "on the other hand, it mighta been." No guesswork, just the facts.

For over two-thirds of the population, this preference comes naturally; they enjoy working with numbers for their own sake. There's an odd, comfortable sense of security that comes from working with *tangible evidence, facts, details, and concrete information.* In fact, they place such a high value on doing things the traditional way that any new ideas and innovations had better have some practical near-term returns.

Sensors also *work best when they're in the moment, here, today, this minute.* That's their comfort level. Here and now. They'll take care tomorrow when it gets here. You can't do much of anything about yesterday; that's water over the dam, so let it go and move on. There's enough to do today, in the present moment.

When Sensors ask, "What time is it?" they don't want a vague answer like, "About half past three." When *they ask a specific question, they want a specific answer.* Otherwise, they become frustrated. Of course, real Sensors may never ask the question—they're probably wearing a precision chronometer with a stopwatch and multiple time zone indicator, accurate to a hundredth of a second.

IF YOU CAN'T KICK THE TIRES, YOU'RE JUST GUESSING

Sensors are hands-on people, not abstract thinkers. They have no illusions about people. They are realists with an inherent *need to see, hear, touch, taste, and smell the world around them.* Give them specifics, details, numbers, maps, outlines, schedules, how-to lists, programs, operating manuals, step-by-step plans, and schematics, and you have a happy person.

If you're a Sensor, you prefer dealing with *concrete information that you can confirm* by seeing and reading a document or getting a detailed account directly from a witness, a scientific report, a lecture delivered by an expert, or by physically working on a building under construction.

If they don't have the right data, *rather than speculate,* Sensors are likely to insist on doing *further research and experiments* to get the information they need to fill in missing pieces. Sensors are happiest when they are living life to the fullest, experiencing life today, right now, when what they see is what they get, no more, no less. When it's gone, it is gone. They enjoy it while it lasts.

Intuitive Types

"Don't confuse me with facts—what does it mean?"

The Intuitive's mind loves abstractions and sees life from a theoretical perspective. *Facts have no value by themselves, they must have meaning.* The facts must fit into the bigger picture, the one in the Intuitive's head. An Intuitive will look at the same computer reports, lab numbers, sports data, or crime statistics as a Sensor, for example, and the Intuitive's brain automatically shifts into search mode, asking, "Where does this fact fit? What does this new information *mean?"*

In order to get the attention of an Intuitive, every bit of information must have some meaning in the larger scheme of things; otherwise, they're random and irrelevant. Facts are threads in the whole cloth, links in the overall network, pieces of a much larger puzzle—and it's the *mysterious world* of patterns and theories, schemes, networks, and conspiracies that *fascinates the Intuitive.*

TRUST YOUR GUT INSTINCTS AND LISTEN TO THE INNER VOICE

Even before they see the evidence, Intuitives are already scanning for *alternatives, new and improved solutions.* They constantly question reality and traditions, looking for unusual *patterns and possibilities,* asking about the relationship between this piece of data and everything else they know. Once something new has been mastered, they get bored and move on to the next new thing.

Experience teaches Intuitives to *trust their inner voice* rather than the cold hard facts, which are often incomplete and misleading. They are the innovators, inventors, and visionaries who rely first on their *gut instincts, insights, imagination, intuitions, and other kinds of intangible* sources of information. Facts are incidentals that later prove or disprove their theories.

In fact, Intuitives are *likely to discount and even dismiss facts* that disagree with their intuition. Of course, it is also likely that Sensors may dismiss the Intuitive's work as unsupported, lacking sufficient evidence.

BOLDLY GO WHERE NO ONE HAS GONE BEFORE

While the Sensor is most comfortable living in today, the Intuitive prefers *being out there in the future.* In fact, the Intuitive's brain automatically operates like long-range radar, constantly scanning the world in search of facts to confirm and expand what they already intuitively know about the universe beyond this world. The *Intuitive is Captain Kirk of the Starship Enterprise,* while the *Sensors are sitting at Mission Control on Earth.*

Of course, we know most people use both intuitions and sensory perceptions in collecting information. However, Jung and others tell us that everybody tends to rely more heavily on one way of processing information than on the other. That's just the natural way our brains, or inner computers, work. Our brains are governed by our unique genetic DNA code, learning one way or the other.

Remember, neither one of these preferences is better than the other, only different—you are who you are. You're one of a kind. Know yourself, the real you. Have confidence in your natural preferences, and you'll improve your chances of harnessing the power of the millionaire within.

CHAPTER 7

TEST THE THIRD LETTER: THINKING OR FEELING (T OR F)?

*H*ow do you analyze and make decisions—objectively or subjectively?

Did you know that today's *New York Times* has more information in it than a person would get in a lifetime 500 years ago? As if that isn't enough, you're being bombarded with new pieces of information thousands of times every day, from television, radio news, billboards, online sources, business reports, and other sources.

You are an information collection and filtering machine that's in operation every minute of every day, often to the point of overload. There's no shortage of information. The problem is, *how can you filter out the noise, isolate the important stuff,* and use it to make decisions?

Once you have to make a decision, *the process narrows and you become focused.* You have choices, options, alternatives. At some point, something tells you it's time to make a decision, to choose between alternatives, even though you may change your mind later.

You also know that the failure to make a decision becomes a decision when options disappear. For example, when you delay making an offer on a house you love, someone else buys it.

SOME WOMEN ARE FROM MARS, SOME MEN FROM VENUS

As you think about how you make decisions, ask yourself, *what criteria do you value most?* Don't let cultural stereotypes fool you. Yes, two-thirds of all Thinking types are men and two-thirds of all Feeling types are women. But Jung's terms are a bit misleading.

In fact, both men and women have rational as well as emotional characteristics. The real difference is in the criteria and values used by each gender in making decisions. Correction! It's the criteria *you* use! So ask yourself, when you make decisions, are you *more objective and impersonal or more subjective and empathetic?* Some clues follow.

Thinking Types

Do the right thing, and don't take it personally.

If you're a typical Thinking personality type, you want to make the right decision. In the purest sense, a Thinker acts like a courtroom judge, because your personal feelings are not as important as *doing what's right, what's fair, what's just, what's moral, what's legal, what's good for society and the country.*

Your measuring stick is *objective impartiality,* and you mean it, so help you God. Your decisions are "nothing personal." You believe some *greater good* is the standard governing your decisions. If possible, you will cite *authorities and do research to analyze and prove the correctness* of your decisions—professional experts, legal precedents, famous books, statistical databases, scientific studies, elders, or the Bible.

NOT A PERSONAL PREFERENCE—A UNIVERSAL LAW

Moreover, in your mind, being impartial, detached, logical, or rational is *not simply a personal preference* of yours. That's an important distinction. True Thinkers will tell you that objectivity is never just a personal preference. They believe Feeling types have subjective preferences that shift according to their emotional temperature. Thinkers, on the other hand, believe they are *doing the right thing,* acting logically, objectively, and rationally according to principles of a *universal law that's above personal preference.*

Feeling types, of course, will take issue with the decision-making processes used by the cold, calculating Thinkers. They believe that Thinkers *ask too darn many questions* that they come across as *critical and uncaring,* when it's more of a defense mechanism to *hide your emotions* and keep Thinkers and Feelers alike from penetrating their defense mechanisms and discovering their vulnerabilities.

Moreover, impersonal probing questions often do make Thinking types come across as judgmental around business associates as well as family and friends. On occasion, they'll react, let loose, and let you know that you've turned into a cold, insensitive machine once again.

KNOW THYSELF; BE TRUE TO WHO YOU ARE

In fact, you really are a good person who's not only being true to your personality profile, you really do believe you're doing the right thing. You have to. You place quite a bit of value on making decisions fairly and objectively, because that really is the only way you can live your life, being true to yourself.

Otherwise, you feel as though you're compromising some eternal values that govern everyone equally. When you compromise your principles, you feel guilty and inadequate.

Yes, you do go overboard on occasion, and yes, you can be a bit too coldhearted, too logical, too objective, too impersonal, and you know all that doesn't work well with people, especially those close to you. But trust me, that's just the price of being a Thinker—that's the real you.

Feeling Types

Everything's personal, do what's right for the people.

When a feeling personality type makes a decision, it's not only personal, it's very personal to you and to the people being affected. In short, people weigh heavily in the equation when you make decisions. *Society's specific rules and regulations often take a backseat,* because they just are not as important as the people involved and the impact a decision will have on them. As a result, when you make decisions, you use *subjective* criteria.

It's not that you aren't rational, because you are. *You just use different criteria.* It's not that you don't use logic and objective reasoning in coming to your conclusions. You do. And it's not that you don't believe in the law of the land and a universal law—you just believe that people come first in the eyes of God, which often leads you into *careers in the service industries.*

YOU GOTTA HAVE HEART: MILES 'N' MILES 'N' MILES OF HEART

You care a lot how other people feel, because in the world you see, everything is personal. People matter more than facts, rules, and assets. You just *cannot make decisions on the cold, hard facts alone.* Yes, you use them. But when you finally choose between alternatives, your emotions guide the outcome of your decision.

As far as you're concerned, the world would be a better place if more people looked at it your way. There is far too much tension in the world.

So you tend to *avoid conflict and competition,* even hesitating to voice your opinions for *fear of offending people.*

When you do speak up, even if you are expressing some strong views about issues that matter, you may temper your remarks with an apology if you feel you've created any hurt feelings. Yet something tells you it's all worthwhile. The *world would be a better place if we had more harmony* in business, social, and personal relations.

LEARN TO BE OF SERVICE WITHOUT SACRIFICING YOURSELF

Your friends may tease you for being *too caring of others' needs, often at the expense of your own needs,* even when you know people are taking advantage of your good nature. Whether you're male or female, those tough-minded Thinkers will often call you Feeling types too soft, or wishy-washy, or irrational, or overly emotional.

In business, you're likely to become skilled in the language of Thinkers, to fit in and *protect yourself in the world of dog-eat-dog competition.* That facade may help somewhat. But when push comes to shove, your values must either be honored or you feel the inner conflict. A better solution is to *find a career that pays you to be who you really are, a people person.*

In your heart you know that your values often push you to the extremes of people-pleasing. But you're also aware that that's who you are and that being of service makes you happy. Still, you're constantly trying to *strike a balance between the two, between taking care of everybody else and caring for your own needs*—often asking why nobody seems to care about your needs.

In the end, neither one is better than the other. Feeling and Thinking types are just different, and somehow the world has created an odd balance in the supply of both types. Together they work to harmonize businesses, families, and the world around them. Problems arise in relationships only when people are out of sync with themselves. The important thing is for each to honor their natural preferences while respecting the unique qualities of the other.

8

TEST THE FOURTH LETTER: JUDGING OR PERCEIVING (J OR P)?

Is your lifestyle organized and structured or open-ended and flexible?

You already have three of the four links in the Millionaire's Code. First, you prefer living in either the external world of people, places, and things or your private inner life. Second, you know how you prefer processing information about the world: You either want to stick to the hard facts, or you rely more heavily on your intuitions about how pieces of information fit into the bigger picture. Third, the process by which you make decisions is either objective and impartial or subjective and personal.

This fourth link in the Millionaire's Code focuses on how you prefer living during the day. From morning to night, what kind of lifestyle makes you most comfortable?

You'd think these two people are from different planets: The *Judging character* gets mighty uncomfortable when things aren't locked down and organized in advance, the sooner the better. The *Perceiving type* is just the opposite: They have to hang loose, can't stand structure, keep looking for new information, checking out new alternatives, delaying decisions until the last minute, then do the job in a flurry of activity.

Judging Types

You set goals, organize now, start early, and stay on schedule.

Being a Judger doesn't necessarily mean you're judgmental about people, places, and things. You may be, but it really means that you have a definite need for a *well-organized life, planning everything in advance.* Keeping your options open makes you uneasy. You need structure.

Your motto: Plan ahead, beat the crowd, do it now. In fact, Judgers are happiest when their lives follow a set routine, because that gives them a *sense of security in knowing what comes next.* You need the structure, and that's what you like to see in the people around you.

Your *appointment book may be the best clue to your lifestyle.* You probably have the business day completely set in advance, such as meeting times, calls to make (along with telephone numbers), reminders of things to follow up on, and personal notes, such as when to take kids to soccer and ballet, important anniversaries or birthdays, flowers to buy, cleaning to pick up, time at the gym, and perhaps a bunch of neatly placed yellow Post-it notes or business cards stuck in as priority reminders so you can *efficiently handle today's tasks.*

FEEL PRESSURED? TAKE CHARGE NOW

Modern life is hectic enough—there's always too much to do and never enough time or money to get everything done. There are only so many hours in the day, and once they're gone, you lose them. You *feel pressured all the time.* You don't like the feelings. The solution? *Take control of your life, be very disciplined, set goals, targets, deadlines.*

Because of all this, you've learned to be decisive at work and at home. You're a *good decision maker* because you don't like uncertainties hanging over your head; indecision unsettles you, making you nervous. Besides, it just wastes time to think and rethink decisions when all you have to do is *take charge,* do what it takes, resolve the matter, lock down the decision—and then move on to the next problem.

Your head is constantly barking orders, instructions, directions, detailed *plans for each day, each week,* your next business trip, summer vacation, the next medical exam, family visits, and a plan for retirement. In addition, you already know the best method to accomplish the task in the most efficient way.

IN LIFE'S RACE, YOU WIN IF YOU DO THE JOB RIGHT

Knowing this about yourself, you generally *prefer working on projects,* analyzing systems, scheduling tasks, monitoring progress. Projects have definite objectives, beginnings, and completion dates, and that gives you a much needed *sense of accomplishment.* Corporate America loves dedicated, hardworking employees like you, and these traits also make for successful entrepreneurs.

True, on occasion you make decisions prematurely. But knowing this about yourself, you've probably also *developed a knack for getting necessary research and analysis done early and fast* so you can make quick decisions.

You'll also *hang in tenaciously* with any decision you're responsible for, even when new information suggests a better solution. Why? Because you *don't like making changes* in preset plans—in fact, you just don't like change, period. You need loose ends resolved; they make you nervous. In the extreme, this attitude makes you *too rigid and dogmatic,* with a demanding "my way or the highway" attitude.

The pressure of living this way can create tension in your relationships, too. When something isn't working according to the plan that is locked in your mind, or when new information pushes you off schedule, or when things get delayed and life is up in the air, you may snap at your coworkers, spouse, or anyone else who brings you unexpected news, even if they're only a messenger.

Perceiving Types

Free spirits keep all their options open to the last minute.

The Perceiver is a *free spirit.* While the Judger feels more comfortable with an organized life and a structured schedule, Perceivers are just the opposite. They get *uncomfortable with rigid organizational charts and fixed schedules.* They need to *keep their options open,* often until the last minute. However, once the pressure's on, watch out: They're a fireball of energy heading for the goal line.

Watch how the two types approach projects. Judgers love getting a head start. They can't wait to get into action. Perceivers, on the other hand, are slow to start, even arriving late to the first meeting—but when the chips are down, they are *great sprinters,* carrying the team across the finish line.

What's going on between these two totally opposite characters? Nature definitely wired the genetic codes of these two birds radically different. Just remember, neither is better than the other.

Put two extremes to work on the same team and the Perceiver is bound to see the Judger as *too darn rigid, critical, and intolerant.* And the Judger will accuse the Perceiver of being an *indecisive, unfocused procrastinator.* Sound familiar? I'll bet you've gone to one of these extremes or the other at least once—we all have some of both traits in us.

SOMEWHERE OVER THE RAINBOW—ANOTHER NEW OPPORTUNITY

You've already met the Judger, now let's take a closer look at the Perceiver. Keep in mind that the term *Perceiver,* which originated with Jung, remains the glue that holds together all work on personality types even today. Being a Perceiver doesn't mean you're unusually insightful or perceptive about the world. It simply means you *love generating alternatives.*

Perceivers generate alternatives in part to delay making decisions. Decisions make them uncomfortable. Judgers need to make decisions in the present. Perceivers look ahead with *an eye for the future,* excited about the possibilities out there, and *yet, paradoxically, they prefer enjoying the present* moment while it lasts, unconsciously knowing they can figure out the future and deal with it when it arrives and the pressure is on.

In the extreme, this trait is simply procrastination, but it is also gives you *time for diversions* along the way—smelling the roses, casual lunches with old friends, having fun—*while the unconscious mind does its magic* in the background, quietly *coming up with the best possible solution* for the task at hand.

REAL WORLD OF FIXED DECISIONS IS AN IMPOSSIBLE DREAM

Fundamentally, the two types are philosophically, psychologically, and genetically in different galaxies: *The Perceiver simply doesn't believe in the kind of tightly controlled world the Judger tries so hard to create. Perceivers believe that's all a big myth,* created by the Judger's anxiety, fear, and imagination. This basic difference is locked deep within the two genetic codes and is guaranteed to create endless friction between the two.

At some deep level, the Perceiver knows that everything is fluid and will remain so—that *goals are moving targets* and decisions are unstable. Inevitably, new information will arrive, and past decisions will no longer be the best ones for the job. They never are; that is the cycle of life.

PROCRASTINATOR OR PROPHET, THE SEARCH NEVER ENDS

Perceivers often *hold off until the last minute,* collecting new information, coming up with new alternatives, analyzing and reanalyzing options—*until the pressure is so great that a deadline slaps them in the face* and a decision is unavoidable.

Even really good Perceivers may *try to avoid making decisions at the eleventh hour* by restructuring the project, setting new goals, or arguing that some *new information points to an alternative or even a totally new project.* But keep this in mind: They may be right, because there really are times when no decision is the best decision, even if it makes Judgers (who can't stand such indecision) extremely uncomfortable.

In spite of all the delays and endless searching, when Perceivers uncover what they finally conclude is the right answer, they will lock onto it with absolute certainty, accepting no distractions and dazzling everybody as they work obsessively to come up with an incredible presentation of the solution.

HAVE FUN EXPLORING—LIFE IS ONE BIG CREATIVE ADVENTURE

Perceivers see *life as a creative process,* and it's the process rather than the end product that they enjoy. They really need to enjoy what they're doing while they're doing it in order to come up with the best possible solution. They *love exploring the future, searching for new possibilities, and encountering the unexpected and the unknown.* It all turns them on.

Regardless of their specific career paths, these people are happiest when their work, family, and social lives give them lots of opportunities to adapt to the constant stream of new information, keep a *flex schedule, go with the flow* (including unrelated diversions), change their minds, be the *spontaneous* member on the team—and also *play around like a kid* if necessary, because they know *that's how they often end up generating the best possible creative solutions.* In short, they really do function best when they can keep their options open and have fun doing what they're doing.

In the best of all possible worlds, *we all need some balance* between these two traits, capitalizing on our dominant preference in a healthy way. When we get off track and *go too far into an extreme position* either way (i.e., too rigid or too indecisive), it is more than likely that someone around you, maybe a coworker or spouse, will react and confront you and help you get back to a more balanced state.

Keep an open mind, but *don't try to fake it and be someone you are not.* If you do, you will be *working against your natural instincts and sabotaging your destiny.* Whether you're naturally a Judger or naturally a Perceiver, simply honor that character trait and get in sync with the millionaire within you.

CHAPTER 9

DISCOVER THE REAL YOU IN THE "X-FACTOR" OF YOUR MILLIONAIRE'S CODE

> Everyone has a purpose in life, a unique gift of special talent to
> give others. . . . Sit down and make a list of answers to these two
> questions: Ask yourself,
> if money were no concern and you had all the time and money in
> the world, what would you do?
> Then ask yourself: How am I best suited to serve humanity?
> Discover your divinity, find your unique talent, serve humanity
> with it, and you can generate all the wealth you want. When your
> creative expressions match the needs of your fellow humans, then
> wealth will spontaneously flow from the unmanifest into the
> manifest, from the realm of the spirit
> into the world of form.
>
> Deepak Chopra,
> *The Seven Spiritual*
> *Laws of Success*

By now you should have a pretty good idea of who you are and what your four-letter Millionaire's Code is. There's also a good possibility that three of the four are fairly clear in your mind and one may be a bit fuzzy. Let's call this the *X-Factor* of your code.

This is a very healthy sign, actually a gift. You're probably going through a very important life transition, and this lack of clarity may be a key piece of the puzzle, pointing the way through the jungle. Please take the time to explore this particular piece. Go deeper and more will be revealed.

Unlocking the Secret of This Mysterious Little Gift

Perhaps you are on the fence about whether you're an Introvert or an Extravert. Maybe you really enjoy spending a lot of time alone, reading, gardening, and working with tools. Maybe at work you enjoy spending a lot of time working things out in your head.

On the other hand, maybe you often find yourself in the public eye, as a speaker and seminar leader, making business presentations, writing about public issues, working with groups, and engaging in outside activities, all of which make you think you're an Extravert.

As another example, you could also be on the fence because you are fantastic with numbers and facts and analysis and make a great living in the financial world, so think you've always considered yourself a logical, rational Thinker.

But in the past few years you feel empty about the financial world. Your career has lost its meaning and is boring. Your therapist has you in touch with your feelings. You become overly emotional about man's inhumanity to man. You even think about buying a bed-and-breakfast in Vermont, or starting a landscaping business, or becoming a therapist, or writing a novel—anything to escape the old life and the old you, even though it pays extremely well.

EVERYTHING WAS GOING WELL—THEN SOMETHING HAPPENED

You have been living the life you assumed was right for you because it was all part of a particular profession, business, or career you've been doing for maybe 20 years. You became your job. You did the same thing over and over because that's what people do to make a living, right?

For a long time you convinced yourself that you were an Extravert and enjoyed it, or a master Thinker, because that was your job, and, over time, you became that job. You just never questioned it much—until recently.

LOST IN A DEEP, DARK FOREST, WANDERING

Maybe you became a doctor, a lawyer, or an engineer because your dad was one, or because a school counselor suggested it, or because a best friend was doing it, or because it sounded like a great way to make money after you got a degree. It probably even worked for a long while. But now, maybe 10 or 20 years later, you're unhappy, on shaky ground, not really sure what to do next.

Even if you have some ideas of what you'd like to do, you aren't quite sure it's right, or whether you have the talent, or where to start, or whether you really have the guts to throw away all you have invested in the career you've built over many years. In short, you're on the fence and it's been going on for a painfully long time. The career your old self built over the years no longer fits.

When in Doubt, Take a New Test, Keep Searching

If you're really serious about getting the right answer about the real you, here's one way you can check yourself: Take another test. Uncovering the right answer is too important not to take another one. Besides, my guess is that if you're on the fence, this has also been going on for some time, so a few more days won't matter.

Get in the car and drive to your local bookstore. Buy one of the other key books in the personality field and take one of the tests–Keirsey, Kroeger and Tieger are all first-class resources. Or find a good career counselor and take the Myers-Briggs test. It's your life you're dealing with, the most precious thing you have. The only one you'll ever have. And it's passing quickly. This is no rehearsal. Let's get serious and get it right.

Another suggestion: Go off alone this weekend. Meditate on the apparent division. Then write a long essay. Answer this question: If money weren't an issue and you had all you needed, which type would you prefer being? Focus on the pair of opposites that you're most unsure of, then on the other three. Finally, take one of the other tests.

NO FUN, BUT YOU'RE OKAY—TRANSITIONS ARE A GIFT

My guess is–nothing's wrong. You may, in fact, be on the border line between the two because you're going through a major life transition, finally waking up and becoming aware that you've been living a dual life. Loss of a loved one, a job change, health problems, or an extraordinary failure can also force us to review our life's direction.

It happens to the best of us, even to Carl Jung. The famous doctor thought he had some kind of immunity. After all, he was a trained professional. He had been analyzed himself. He had helped thousands through transitions. He knew what to expect. Yet he was in shock when a major transition hit him extremely hard in his late thirties, at times leaving him deeply depressed, even suicidal. It lasted for years.

That's what transitions are like from the inside–too long, too confusing, and too painful. For most of us, transitions unfortunately take much longer than we expect, as we pray for relief.

Let Go of the Old Self and Emerge as a Winner

It's no surprise that one of the four letters in the Millionaire's Code is a toss-up when you're in the middle of a major lifestyle transition, which is a rather common reason for exploring how your personality type impacts your financial life. You wake up one day and you wonder:

- Am I really an Introvert faking it as Extravert, or the opposite?
- Am I an Intuitive disguised as a Sensor, or is it the other way around?
- Could I be a Feeling person masquerading as a Thinker, or vice versa?
- Or am I a Perceiver acting as a Judger to impress the boss?

Whatever the case may be, you are trying too hard to be something or someone you are not. You have been off track and out of sync with your true self for a long, long time, and you are finally becoming painfully aware of this discrepancy in yourself and ready to move on.

Now you have an opportunity to take the ambiguity as a very special gift, a hidden compass pointing to a new direction. If you take time to uncover its meaning locked inside the missing or gray letter of your Millionaire's Code before continuing down the path, you will substantially increase your chances of reaching your goal. (See Table 9.1.)

Table 9.1   Your Personality Code

Which one in each of these four pairs is the real you?
Take the test and record your four-letter code below.

Extravert	Introvert
Sensor	Intuitive
Thinker	Feeling
Judger	Perceiver

Above all, trust the X-Factor—it's a great gift that will empower you!

PART

THE FOUR TEMPERAMENTS IN MILLIONAIRE PROFILING

THE MILLIONAIRE TEMPERAMENTS: A SHORTCUT TO THE MILLIONAIRE WITHIN

> People differ so . . .
> Contrary to everything that
> modern psychologists tell you,
> I am convinced that one can acquire knowledge,
> one can acquire skills,
> but one cannot change his personality,
> Only the Good Lord changes personality—
> that's his business.
> I have four great children,
> and I can assure you that by the time
> they were six months old,
> their personalities were set in concrete . . .
> you are not going to change the basic structure.
> It is much more important that in
> this age of psychology people
> tell the kids that
> what you are matters, and
> your values matter."
>
> Peter Drucker,
> *Psychology Today*

Retiring a millionaire is easy, right? Go to any bookstore and you'll find tons of books, such as *The Millionaire Mind* or *The Millionaire Next Door*, loaded with all kinds of rules, tools, and tips on how to retire a millionaire.

Seriously, simple compounding will turn your IRA and 401(k) into $1 million during a normal working career. At least, that's the message in the popular literature. Still, the vast majority of Americans never become millionaires. Why? Because if rules, tools, and tips were all we needed, we'd all be millionaires.

But we aren't. America has only about 8 million millionaires. And only a third of America's 94 million investors, or about 30 million, are saving enough to retire comfortably. These are the serious ones that I call the "millionaires in training." They don't have the money, but they are working on it.

The Only Way Is Your Way

The reason there are so few American millionaires is simple. There really is no one single best system on how to become a millionaire that works for everybody. Yet the shelves of bookstores are filled with books and magazines telling you that they have *the* magic bullet, the one-size-fits-all, cookie-cutter formula that's perfect for you. You no doubt have a bunch of them sitting around the house—books you've collected in your quest to do the right thing so you can achieve the new American Dream of accumulating $1 million by the time you retire.

And yet, like so many other Americans who are serious about becoming millionaires, you may be going about the job the wrong way—either using formulas that aren't right for your particular personality or trying various formulas that leave you frustrated, so you give up and do nothing. How can you avoid getting off track? What should you do?

Discover the Real You *Before* You Spend Another Nickel

There is a better way to approach the job of becoming a millionaire. *Before* you do any financial planning or budgeting. *Before* you put a nickel into a saving account. *Before* you invest in your first stock or mutual fund.

In fact, *before* you buy a new home, purchase life insurance, start a business, take a vacation, or do anything dealing with your financial affairs, look inside and find out who you really are, your Millionaire's Code.

Otherwise, you could be doing all the right things with your money according to some canned how-to-get-rich formula—moving fast, but headed toward the wrong target.

How do you know if you're headed toward the right target for you? Know your code—the Millionaire's Code that fits you. That code describes our personality types and also our natural process of making life decisions, including financial decisions. You might also call it the "Happiness Code." Because if you don't know who you really are, then with or without $1 million, you won't be fulfilling your destiny in this lifetime, and you won't be happy.

Narrowing the 16 Personalities into Four Temperaments

I'm sure it'll come as no surprise to you to hear that typecasting is not an exact science, in fact more an art than a science, for a number of reasons. The experts tend to assign slightly different meanings to the key terms. They use different testing methods. Often, their egos result in some good-natured competition.

For example, the original personality types created by Carl Jung in 1921 were expanded over the years by the Myers-Briggs team. Jung considered the Extravert-Introvert function one of the most significant in developing his system of eight types, an essential to typecasting people along with the Sensor-Intuitive and Thinking-Feeling functions.

Myers and Briggs added the Judging-Perceiving function to distinguish their typology, but they stayed true to Jung's structure and his emphasis on the importance of the Extravert-Introvert opposition.

Later, Keirsey arrived on the scene and took issue with both Jung and Myers-Briggs. In the updated version of his book, *Please Understand Me II*, Keirsey says,

> While Jung considered the distinction between extraversion (E) and introversion (I) as the most important of his dimensions of personality, I think of it as least useful in understanding people and predicting what they'll do . . . the Myers' E-I scale is badly flawed because she inherited Jung's error of confusing extraversion with observation (S) and introversion with introspection (N).

KEIRSEY GOES DOWN A SLIGHTLY DIFFERENT PATH

The original Jung shortcut focused first on the way people collected information—concretely as a Sensor or conceptually as an Intuitive—and second on their decision-making criteria, Thinking (objective) or Feeling (subjective).

However, in his own research, Keirsey discovered that the individuals in two of the Myers-Briggs groupings didn't have much in common: the Sensor-Thinkers and the Sensor-Feelers.

Keirsey says his historical work (going all the way back to Plato) helped him "see that Myers' four 'SJs' were very much alike, as were her four 'SPs.' Bingo! Typewatching from then on became a lot easier, the four groups—SPs, SJs, NFs and NTs—being light-years apart in their attitudes and actions."

The names of these four personality groupings have changed throughout history. Keirsey calls them Artisans, Rationals, Idealists, and Guardians. We refer to them as Freelance Creators, Systems Masterminds, Pathfinders, and Guardians of the Establishment to reflect the way each defines *wealth* and *getting rich* in the Millionaire's Code.

THEY'RE WORKING IN THE BUSINESS AND FINANCIAL WORLD

The distinction is subtle but important in the popular interpretations of personality types as they developed in the past 20 years. If you are interested in the historical and technical background of this competition between these dedicated experts, I strongly urge you to read Keirsey's book, which is clearly the best from the past couple decades.

Oddly enough, Keirsey's classifications do make sense and mesh with our experience in career counseling. However, even though he strongly dismisses the importance that Jung and Myers-Briggs gave to the Extravert-Introvert function, Keirsey writes extensively about the eight Extravert personalities as distinct from the eight Introvert personalities. So the Extravert-Introvert function is still quite important to Keirsey, as well as to Jung and Myers-Briggs, which has also been my experience.

My guess is that most people will probably recognize these differences as the kind of good-natured competition you'd expect between respected, strong-willed experts, although not something that demands much more of the average reader's attention in order to discover the millionaire within.

ANOTHER WAY TO LOOK AT THE MILLIONAIRE WITHIN YOU

To help you better understand your Millionaire's Code, let's take a closer look at the four general personality groups. You already have your four-letter Millionaire's Code. Now, quickly scan through the following four two-letter combinations to see which group you fit in.

(SP) Freelance Creators (Sensor-Perceiver)
    ESFP, ISFP, ESTP, and ISTP
(NT) Systems Masterminds (Intuitive-Thinker)
    ENTJ, INTJ, ENTP, and INTP
(NF) The Pathfinders (Intuitive-Feeler)
    ENFJ, INFJ, ENFP, and INFP

(SJ) Guardians of the Establishment (Sensor-Judger)
  ESTJ, ISTJ, ESFJ, and ISFJ

For example, my four-letter code is INFP, one of the Pathfinder (N-F) group. If your code is ESTJ, you are in the general category of the Guardians of the Establishment (S-J) profile. An ENTJ would be a System Mastermind. And if you are an ISFJ, you are one of the Freelance Creators. (See Table 10.1.)

My choice of the names of these four personality groups builds on the four names Keirsey and Plato used, adding my experiences on Wall Street and in Corporate America as a banker and executive, my work in the technology and counseling fields, and my appreciation of modern culture through film and television. As you read on, I urge you to jot notes in the margins that draw from your own experiences in the real world—lots of notes!

Fuzzy Name Tags for Real People in a Foggy World

A couple words of caution are in order. Don't get too hung up on the descriptive names used here. As Humpty Dumpty says to Alice in *Alice's Adventures in Wonderland,* "When I use a word, it means just what I choose it to mean—neither more or less," as indeed we all do, all the time.

So be forewarned—the name tags on these four groups, as well as the names of the 16 personality types, may easily apply to some of the characteristics and traits in the others.

That's simply a fact of life, isn't it? All of us often use popular terms that in fact are rather fuzzy, which often happens when you're trying to include or exclude large numbers of people under an umbrella term or word, such as *liberal* or *conservative.* Often, the vast majority of people are somewhere between the extremes of language labels. In the end, the only descriptive name tag is the one you finally pick that feels right for you.

Table 10.1

Guardians Sensor-Judgers (SJ) 40%	Artisans Sensor-Perceivers (SP) 40%
Masterminds Intuitive-Thinkers (NT) 10%	Pathfinders Intuitive-Feelers (NF) 10%

If any of these labels seem too inaccurate for you, my advice is to simply use the nondescript four-letter code, as Myers and Briggs prefer. Frankly, I'm more comfortable using the NF term to describe myself, because Pathfinder does tend to suggest that the other types aren't searching for their mission or path in life.

On the other hand, many of the other authorities prefer using the term *idealists* for the Pathfinders. However, because there are many people of high ideals and morals among the other three groups, the term may be less than acceptable to everyone. Don't get hung up on the name tags.

HYBRID PERSONALITIES ALSO FOG UP OUR NAME TAGS

You may have a split personality, so to speak, and belong in two of these basic groups, as I do—maybe all the time or perhaps because you are going through a life transition, as discussed in Chapter 15.

Or, like me, for example, perhaps your brain operates differently under stress, switching from a dominant Thinking to a dominant Feeling mode, which moves you from one whole group of four to another and from one of the 16 types to another. We'll dig into this interesting condition later, after you've had a chance to review the difference between these four personality groups.

Let's see how this exploration of the four main "Temperaments," as Keirsey calls them, can help you confirm and refine your Millionaire's Code and put you on the best path to become rich—in spirit and in fact!

* * * * * * * *

It's never too late
to be
what you could have been.

Mary Engelbreit

11

FREELANCE CREATORS: SENSOR-PERCEIVERS (SP)

You become what you believe.
Not what you wish or want
but what you truly believe.
Whatever you are in life,
look at your beliefs.
They put you there. . . .
I believed I belonged to someone
or something bigger than myself,
my family or even Mississippi.
I believed I was God's child.
Therefore,
I could do anything.

Oprah Winfrey

FREELANCE CREATORS

- Entrepreneurs and Promoters (ESTP)
- Entertainers and Performers (ESFP)
- Master Craftsmen (ISTP)
- Directors and Composers (ISFP)

Different as day'n'night, that's what you'd have to say about these Freelance Creators and their cousins, the Guardians of the Establishment, even though they're both Sensors. As we've already seen, Guardians place a high value on security, safety, and a structured lifestyle and often find what they need in large, established organizations.

Free Spirits of the World

The Freelance Creators, on the other hand, are totally the opposite. They love their freedom and thrive on a life of action filled with surprises and demands for instinctive, spontaneous responses—and they hate being tied down by any kind of establishment systems.

I call them *Freelancers* because they are truly life's original free spirits and *Creators* because they have within them a powerful energy that can explode in a flash of inspiration. These people love life and they spend a lifetime searching for ways to drink in every minute of it.

At the extreme, Creators will risk everything—*including their lives at times*—in order to tap into that inner something that turns them on. Life really is an adventure, and experiencing that adventure lets Creators know they're alive, doing what they were born to do and fulfilling their destiny.

Fiercely Independent:
"I've Gotta Be Me!"

If Creators had a theme song, it'd have to be Frank Sinatra's "My Way" or Sammy Davis's "I've Gotta Be Me." If they needed a classic hero, one of the more expressive examples would definitely be Zorba the Greek, with his hearty, wild claim: "To be alive is to undo your belt and look for trouble!"

Freelance Creators are fiercely individualistic, living for themselves—quite the opposite of those duty-bound Guardians who spend life devoted to serving the establishment, the corporation, the community, society, the greater good, or some divine authority. Neither, of course, is better than the other. You are what you are; it's in your genetic structure.

Ask them and they'll tell you they're not just taking big risks for the hell of it or because it's a good-paying job—*because often the compensation doesn't match the dangers to their life, health, and assets*—but because they just love the thrills and chills and spills of going it alone, of being freelancers who experience and create something new and unique to them. They live to experience life to its fullest.

Awaken the Hero Within:
Tell the World You Are Alive!

Of course, not all the Creators are daredevils like Evel Knievel, Special Forces officers, firefighters, and ER physicians. But we do know that most of them are drawn to their work because of the adrenaline rush that comes from being in the thick of the action.

Many also get their excitement from such diverse careers as coaching sports teams, promoting real estate deals, composing music, and directing films. The thrill of creating something bigger by tapping into their unique talents makes them feel alive, as the creative process works its magic in that moment.

This need of the Creators has deep subconscious, even spiritual roots, beyond momentary pleasure trips, coming from a force often only faintly sensed and understood. The everyday world can become boring and monotonous, with people viewed as faceless entities. Joseph Campbell sees life as a search to "find the force within you," to awaken the hero within you, to become as one with the Creator, fully alive, creating your own life. In that moment, you "find yourself." That is the goal of the hero within—and the true goal of the Creator's life quest.

Sensors—Information Is a Turn-on That Says "I Am Alive!"

While these two groups of personalities—*Temperaments,* as Keirsey calls them—have much in common because both are Sensors, the contrast between the Guardians and the Creators is enormous—peace versus passion, security versus freedom, safety versus risk. Let's take a closer look at these two quite different personality types.

Even in this common area of collecting information, there is a major difference between Guardians and Creators. Yes, both see the world in concrete factual terms. But sensory information is a turn-on for the Creators. Information is a signal from the world, a stimulating experience, something heightening the senses, encouraging action, telling you "Yes, yes, you're alive!" Do something! Respond! This is an opportunity! Grab it or lose it.

The information that Creators are actively searching for in their environment is much more than just a collection of dull facts and figures to be stored away in a file after they are collected and passively reviewed. You Creators don't collect facts just because you think the data might prove to be useful sometime, which is what a Guardian might do.

Take a moment to imagine the volumes and volumes of human experiences that have been triggered in your life by an endless stream of sensory information that's constantly being generated all around you in your everyday world, at home, at work, and on social occasions:

- *Sounds:* Singing, jazz, a roaring jet, motorcycles
- *Sight:* Cable news, an art museum, a loved one's eyes

- *Taste:* Hot fudge sundaes, pasta, cocktails, espresso
- *Touch:* Woodcarving, sex, weightlifting, snowballs
- *Motion:* Skydiving, dancing, hiking, Tai Chi, sailing
- *Smell:* Perfume, pipe smoke, gardening, ocean spray

Each piece of new information can evoke a sensory experience for Creators, depending on their unique talents and craft, on the information, and on the passing moment. Knowing all this about themselves, Creators seems to have a built-in radar system that is instinctively searching their world for new information that will create new sensations to make them feel alive.

ACTIVELY SEARCHING FOR NEW THRILLS, CHILLS, SPILLS

So for you Creators, information is not "out there." You immediately internalize it, drink it in, absorb it in the mind, body, and spirit. For you, every piece of new information can be an upper, a turn-on, an *aphrodisiac,* another peak experience of being alive! And that excites you, setting you on another search for more information, not because it has any inherent value, but for what it does to you—and for you and within you. It comes from "out there" and makes you feel alive "in here."

Quite the opposite for Guardians, for whom Sensory information works more like a *tranquilizer,* calming them down. Sensory information makes Guardians feel more relaxed, more comfortable with life because new information tells them they're anchored on a more secure footing. Information helps them know just a little more about the mysterious world they are trying to master and control. And that calms them.

Perceiver: Don't Fence Me in; Turn Me Loose, Let Me Wander!

The second half of the Creator's personality formula—they are *Perceivers* as well as a *Sensors*—really sets them apart from their distant relatives, the Guardians. Like those old Wild West cowboys on horseback, singing as they rode off into the frontier, "Don't fence me in; turn me loose, let me wander!"

The Creators and the Guardians are as different as night and day, like Felix and Oscar, the mismatched divorced men sharing an apartment in Neil Simon's Broadway play, *The Odd Couple.* Fastidious Felix, the Guardian, lives a very organized life and wants everything neat and tidy. Oscar, the happy-go-lucky Creator, on the other hand, takes life as it comes, enjoying the moment, and he can't be bothered with a structured life. Extremes, yes, but you get the point.

Waiting for the Best Alternative at the Last Possible Moment

Remember, Perceivers need to hang loose in a very flexible world, one that gives them the freedom to enjoy the moment. They can't stand being locked into a set, rigid schedule, tight hierarchical organizations, and a structured life. They're always coming up with new alternatives, new solutions in response to new information–and often having a tough time making up their minds, delaying their decisions until the last minute.

Above all else, there's one thing you Creators sense deep in your hearts (actually, it's a mixture of gut feel, life experiences, and a still small voice talking to you): No matter how hard Guardians (or others) try to predict future events, organize life, and control the world around them, it won't work; it's a rapidly moving target.

Expect the Unexpected—Then Go Get It!

Ask Creators and they'll tell you that all you can do is live for today, notice what's immediately around you right now, and respond to events in a dynamic playing field–like a quarterback in the stadium, a batter at the plate, a point guard on the court.

You can't know what's coming up next, so it's best to stay alert and hang cool. When things explode, join in the action, meet the challenge, enjoy the adrenaline rush–welcoming that feeling of being alive. Treat life as a game, play it to the best of your abilities.

Different Kind of Planning: Training for Peak Experiences

Long-range planning means something different to Creators than to the typical Guardian who works in numbers, charts, data, reports, and future plans. The best of the Creator athletes, superstars like Tiger Woods, Lance Armstrong, and Michael Jordan, spend many hours over many years planning and training for that moment of competition–the PGA Tournament, the Tour de France, the NBA championship. Similarly with Special Ops training for combat.

The bottom line is that Freelance Creators actually welcome the unknown, the unexpected, the surprise elements in life that become turn-ons and make you feel alive. You Creators will even spend your entire life searching for more of these peak experiences. You're a risk taker, because taking risks puts you in situations that will challenge and energize you.

That's right, unlike the Guardians—who work hard to keep the established social order pretty much as it is—Creators actually invite, encourage, and go after change. They love the new and the different. In that sense, they are revolutionaries.

Coming Alive in Crises: Excelling under Pressure

Creators are great in crises: You folks become take-charge leaders—quickly assessing the problem, making decisions, allocating resources, mobilizing and inspiring a team, springing into action, focusing on specific solutions. Every step along the path you are alert to changing situations as new information pours in rapidly, spotting dangers and opportunities, reworking your entire game plan, if necessary. You are a master at this, and it's pure magic watching you at the peak of your game.

Competitive athletes, firefighters, pilots, and paramedics are just a few of the obvious examples of the Creator personality. A wide variety of other careers attract this personality: promoters, stockbrokers, CIA agents, news reporters, filmmakers, veterinarians, choreographers, foresters, fashion designers, crime scene investigators, entertainers, and troubleshooters of all kinds.

Each has a unique collection of skills, talents, tools, and abilities that grow out of a unique Creator temperament that loves being where the action is because it makes you feel alive.

Do Whatever's Necessary—Just Get the Job Done

Occasionally Creators will frustrate people around them with their unpredictability and spur-of-the moment spontaneity. Well folks, too bad, that's just what they are. The Perceiver in them has no interest in abstract concepts about the future, no pie-in-the-sky thinking, no cosmic theories about the universe.

Their goal is simple: Get the job done. Now. Period. Forget yesterday, forget tomorrow, all you have is today, right now. There's a job to be done. Get to it, before it's too late.

As a result of their natural reaction to solve immediate problems,

Creators often jump into action before thinking things through. In the process, they may miss some obvious connections between what's going on and the bigger picture. Yes, they'll break the established rules to get the job done, often failing to secure necessary approvals. Either way, they invite trouble. For the most part, however, their ability to handle crises under pressure makes them an incredible asset in business.

Convert Personality Quirks into Career Pluses

You Creators are so much into the moment that you often lose interest in yesterday's hot buttons and move on to the next new thing–easy come, easy go. As a result, you may lack the necessary follow-through on a job because you get bored with all the mundane tasks that unfortunately need to be done. This attitude can be unnerving to Guardians and to anyone else (employers, partners, subordinates) who needs day-to-day consistency.

On the other hand, Creators waste as little of their precious time as possible rehashing the past. This can be a huge advantage during a life-and-death emergency, when it's absolutely essential that you focus all your attention and energy on solving the crisis right in front of you.

Moreover, you Creators are more likely to see, evaluate, and grab new opportunities while the Guardians are wondering whether they should allocate money to study the situation. Just remember, whatever other people may say are your shortcomings, they are probably also your greatest strengths if you develop them properly.

Solid Rewards—Intangible and Tangible, Too

The perfect career? You could be an entrepreneur, the millionaire next door, a jazz musician, pro athlete, film director, television actor, or maybe even work for Corporate America, but you need lots of freedom, action, and a wide variety of tasks that use your talents to the max, plus opportunities for immediate intangible and tangible results.

Whatever you do, find work that capitalizes on your unique talents: You'll not only enjoy the immediate personal rewards you need from a job, you'll have a chance for better compensation. Remember, you have something the world desperately needs–creativity, leadership, and courage under fire.

* * * * * * * *

I don't care who likes it or buys it.
Because if you use that criteria,
Mozart would have never written *Don Giovanni,*
Charlie Parker would never have played anything
but swing music.
There comes a point at which
you have to stand up and say,
this is what I have to do.

Branford Marsalis,
Jazz saxophonist

CHAPTER

SYSTEMS MASTERMINDS: INTUITIVE-THINKERS (NT)

Great leaders move us.
They ignite our passions and inspire the best in us. When we try
to explain why they are so effective,
we speak of strategy, vision, or powerful ideas.
But the reality is much more primal:
Great leadership works through emotions.
No matter what leaders set out to do—
whether it's creating strategy
or mobilizing teams to action—
their success depends on *how* they do it.
Even if they get everything else just right,
if leaders fail in this
primal task of driving emotions
in the right direction,
nothing they do will work
as well as it could or should.

Daniel Goleman et al.,
Primal Leadership

SYSTEMS MASTERMINDS

- Commanders in chief (ENTJ)
- Master Innovators (ENTP)
- Chief Strategists (INTJ)
- Visionary Thinkers (INTP)

While the Guardians are dedicated to keeping the established order together and stable—whether the establishment they're serving is a company, a family, a baseball team, a civic group, a college, a church or any other organization—the Masterminds have a very different goal. They are the grand innovators, the new system builders, the strategic planners, the world's change agents.

The World's Change Agents

Rationals, that's what Keirsey and Plato call them. True, they are rational, logical, strategic thinkers. But they are much more. In today's incredibly vast and complex world of overlapping and interconnected systems, networks, and enterprises—encompassing commercial, industrial, economic, social, entertainment, political, scientific, military, and global—the phrase *Systems Masterminds* best identifies this unique personality: The system—whichever one they are in—is simply an *extension* of their mind.

Unlike the Guardian, Masterminds are not focused on security and safety. Quite the opposite, they work well within the system, but they are not really interested in maintaining the establishment on a status quo course that respects history and traditions.

Masterminds are focused on the future, on growth, expansion, transformation, increased productivity and efficiency, new directions for tomorrow. In the extreme, they, like the architect in Ayn Rand's *Atlas Shrugged,* will challenge and even destroy the existing system to make way for their new vision.

They are adventurers of the first order, and their personal mission statement might well be the one directing the spaceship *Enterprise* in *Star Trek*—to "boldly go where no one has gone before," and, God willing, they will drive themselves to get there in this lifetime. Wherever "there" is for each of them individually, they know at some level that they are a breed apart in search of excellence.

Leaders in Search of a Destiny, Changing Their World

Masterminds are natural-born leaders, obsessed with making the world a better place to live. Whether they're heads of major corporations, inventors, scientists, architects, economists, judges, cardiologists, or investment bankers—*whatever* their life's mission—they have a powerful inner drive to achieve "something" and leave their mark on the world.

Masterminds are not content with simply being good at what they do; they *need to excel,* to be the top gun, captain of the ship, the director, boss, or chairperson—the mastermind in command of the system. In that position, they also become master of their own fate. In fact, they are so driven to be in charge of their own fate that they tend to operate very independently, even within an organization, often seeming detached and unapproachable.

When they have an assignment, they're swinging for a home run, every time, and more often than not they will end up in the winner's circle. Let's take a closer look at this unique breed, a mixture of Intuitive and Thinker.

The Intuitive: Fitting All the Pieces into the Bigger Picture

When it comes to how they see the world and collect information about it, the Mastermind's brain works as an Intuitive, intellectualizing everything and everybody all the time. Forget Sergeant Friday, because it is *not* "just the facts ma'am" for Masterminds. They are *not* looking for specific raw facts in the same way that Guardians and Creators do, both of whom are Sensors.

Masterminds are looking at the bigger picture. They have a vision of the whole system, today and tomorrow. What is it? How does it work? Why is it happening? Where is it headed? When will it change? How? What does it mean? Facts, data, and information have no meaning by themselves. They must fit into preconceived ideas, theories, concepts, and hypotheses. Masterminds love the mental challenge of figuring out alternative scenarios and making them happen.

Their brains work overtime, operating like 24/7 computers, constantly piecing together complex mental puzzles, searching everywhere for trends, patterns, and interrelationships within the system they're responsible for. They need to figure out how everything fits into some abstract concept of the system they're working on. Where's its future? What can I do to change and improve the system?

MEMORY BANKS AND SYSTEM PROCESSORS CONSTANTLY SPINNING

The mind of the Mastermind is truly working nonstop on some system of special interest to that individual. For example, it could be the human genome system, online educational systems, architectural systems for space stations and polar icecaps, agricultural and political systems in underdeveloped countries, weather prediction systems, the criminal justice system, terrorist tracking systems, foreign banking systems, strategic planning systems for businesses, or maybe even a simple virus/spam-free e-mail system.

Masterminds have theories and solutions for systems everywhere they go. Even in the privacy of their homes and at local social gatherings, the brains of some large-corporation executives just keep clicking away: ideas for the county master plan, reorienting the local school curriculum, fundraising for the church, family vacation plans. It's in their blood and in their genes. They can't help themselves—they make the world go round.

GOING SOMEWHERE OVER THE RAINBOW—FOR A POT OF GOLD

They are more interested in where they're going than in what's happening today. Today is just the starting point for the bright future in their masterminds. They are always looking over the horizon, with visions of a new world, new possibilities, new opportunities, new plans.

Moreover, they're not just looking somewhere over the rainbow, speculating for the sake of speculating about some raw data, even information. They need to convert all that into knowledge and wisdom to empower themselves and the world. They are driven by a powerful need to make their dreams come true and change the world, whether as a bold business leader, charismatic politician, inspiring college professor, or creative inventor.

Their brains love solving problems, working things out, virtually anything, for the sheer pleasure of pulling the pieces together and making something happen. They need to achieve, succeed, accomplish, and their system of collecting information supports that inner drive.

INNOVATION AND STRATEGIC PLANNING: CREATING NEW REALITIES

It starts early: as a kid, working on a science project, the fund-raiser for the class trip, organizing a school political rally, questioning the theory of relativity. Whatever the system, whether local or global, you can bet there's a Mastermind already digging into it, searching for ways to improve the system. They really can't help it. That's just the way their minds operate—going, going, going all the time!

Their minds never stop. And they're not collecting facts, data, and numbers because they want to update a statistical file or write the weekly sales report. Masterminds' computer-like brains are preloaded with theories, concepts, schemes, and ideas that constantly haunt them, pressuring them to take the information, the system, and the theory and make it a reality.

Systems and data integration are natural for Masterminds. When their brains see new data, they automatically assimilate it, downloading the information into their memory banks under an existing system or creating a new memory file under the heading of a new system. Most likely, they are recording the information under multiple systems, encoding everything for easy access and control within the grand computer system of their minds.

The mind of an Intuitive is unquestionably different than that of a Sensor. Sensors, whether Guardians or Creators, deal with specific data in the immediate present and in relationship to past information.

In contrast, Masterminds are systems-oriented futurists less interested in data than in data integration and how it fits into the multiple theories and systems in their brains. Most important, Masterminds' need to achieve compels them to take the information, solve problems, and channel their ideas from the idea stage into the real world.

The Thinker: Cool, Calculating, and Objective

Masterminds make decisions you'd expect from a judge, in a thinking mode, objectively, impersonally, and dispassionately. They collect the facts, integrate the information into the relevant system, and weigh all factors in the bigger scheme of things, calculating alternatives objectively, like a computer, and then selecting this or that alternative—it's nothing personal.

Masterminds are dispassionate. They see the world through microscopes and telescopes, ultrasonic scans and blood screens, particle accelerators and global positioning systems, demographic and marketing statistics, computer spreadsheets and systems research, poll data and actuarial tables, missile guidance systems and corporate earnings guidance.

FOCUSED ON WHAT'S RIGHT FOR THE COMMON GOOD

At one time or another, we've all seen supercool, superrational Masterminds make decisions. You'd think they have ice in their veins, acting totally objectively and impartially, with little or no show of emotion, practically staring right through you, perhaps even saying something like, "Now don't take this personally, but . . ."

Remember, the decisions of a Thinker really aren't personal. Unlike the Feeling types, who personalize everything when they make decisions (worrying about how a decision will affect them personally and everyone else, too), Masterminds look at people as a group, in the abstract. Not as individuals, but impersonally, without feelings and emotions.

Ultimately, their decisions are based on doing what's right for the overall system—*the corporation, the legal system, the community, the church, the good of humankind, or some other objective standard*—rather than for specific individuals. Yet, paradoxically, the Mastermind also has an uncanny ability to read the emotional energy of people, individually and in groups, the power to arouse them at a gut-feeling level, and the stature to inspire them into action when necessary.

BALANCING YOUR FEELINGS WITH MY BOTTOM LINE

The Mastermind sees the world as an objective network system. People are subsystems, to be evaluated by their contribution to the overall productivity, efficiency, and growth of the whole system. To Masterminds, these subsystems are evaluated and rewarded or punished based on how much their skills and competency contribute to the goals of the system— so many widgets per hour, sales per month, increased earnings per year. Subsystems are to be measured objectively, as machines or androids, not as humans with feelings.

Their objective, impersonal way of dealing with everything in the world has obvious drawbacks on the road to achieving their dreams of making a mark in the world. They can become so rigid in their systems thinking and strategic planning, so lost in the bigger picture, and so obsessed about succeeding that they ignore the more immediate problems of everyday life, *their own and that of others,* and in the long run undermine the very goals they're trying to accomplish.

In addition, their computer-like intellectual need to improve everything in their path may be labeled as genius, but their overly intellectual approach may also become too challenging, too critical, too complex, too self-serving, and too impatient with folks of average intelligence. They know they are superior. So does everybody else. But, hey, couldn't they just be a little bit more humble about it?!

OVERCOMPENSATING: FEAR OF FAILURE BECOMES
AN OBSESSION TO ACHIEVE

This attitude also accounts for the way Masterminds treat people. Since their natural tendency is to objectify everybody and intellectualize everything, the Mastermind is likely to come across as an arrogant snob. Okay, they're intelligent. Yes, they are just being who they are, but they can lose touch with people, distancing themselves in a world of their own.

However, their failure to consider the feelings and needs of the very individuals affected by their decisions—including everybody from associates, employees, and customers to voters, neighbors, and family—can seriously alienate the very people they're trying to help and whose support they need.

Over time, most Masterminds can learn to compensate for their impersonal views of the world. Often, it's simply the frustration of endless confrontations with bosses, associates, subordinates, spouses, and children that teach them that ignoring other people's feelings isn't always the best strategy. They often learn the hard way that even if they don't really understand why people are getting so upset about this or that issue, the failure to consider people's feelings can backfire on them and prevent them from achieving their own goals. So a Mastermind will listen to other people's feelings, but in a strange impersonal way, to avoid any negative impact on their bottom line

More likely, however, repeated successes in their field of expertise will give them the self-confidence they desperately need—and thus diminish their fear of failure. The fact is, underneath their supergenius exterior, many Masterminds are driven by an intense, subconscious fear of failure, a fear they may not fully understand.

Becoming a supercompetent, successful achiever in the eyes of the world is their way of overcompensating for deep feelings of inadequacy, which they hide under a cold, aloof, intellectual exterior.

The Journey of the Hero: An Adventure in Finding Yourself

Say what you want, the contributions far outweigh the shortcomings of Masterminds. They are indeed the change agents of the world. These people are forever out there, questioning everything, challenging authorities, pushing the envelope, in a quest to make the world a better place to live, somehow, some way.

Look inside, their genes are encoded with an enormous energy telling them that they *must* leave their mark on the world in this lifetime in order to be someone and fulfill their mission. Somehow, they feel compelled to make a contribution by improving some system within the greater universe of systems.

Masterminds often lock onto their field of interest early. It becomes an all-consuming passion in a life spent on their "journey of the hero," where the end is not so much an amazing product or some grand reward, or even experiencing the joy of a job well done—*all of which are crucial to the Mastermind's journey*—but ultimately, as Joseph Campbell put it, "the goal of the hero's journey is yourself, finding yourself."

* * * * * * *

The important thing is not to stop questioning.
Curiosity has its own reason for existing.
One cannot help but be in awe
when he contemplates the mysteries of eternity,
of life, of the marvelous structure of reality.
It is enough if one tries merely to
comprehend a little of
the mystery every day.
Never lose a holy curiosity.

Albert Einstein

THE PATHFINDERS: INTUITIVE-FEELERS (NF)

And both that morning equally lay
In leaves no step had trodden black.
Oh, I kept the first for another day!
Yet knowing how way leads to way,
I doubted if I should ever come back.
I shall be telling this with a sigh
Somewhere ages and ages hence:
Two roads diverged in a wood, and I—
I took the one less traveled by,
And that has made all the difference.

Robert Frost,
The Road Not Taken

THE FOUR PATHFINDERS

- Inspiring Teachers (ENFJ)
- Champions and causes (ENFP)
- Healing Counselors (INFJ)
- Mystic Heroes (INFP)

You might suspect that Pathfinders and Masterminds have lots in common. Both are Intuitives. Both are looking out over the horizon into the future, quite different from the Guardians and the Creators, who focus more on the present and the past. Both Pathfinders and Masterminds are searching for new ways to make the world a better place. In that sense, both groups are idealists.

Making a Difference with People

Once you look past the labels, you see two remarkably different characters that channel their idealism down extremely different roads. As you've already seen, Masterminds will likely discover their life's mission in the fields of science, mathematics, law, medicine, finance, or business, for example—*careers with a heavy reliance on objectivity and impersonal and impartial decision making.*

Pathfinders, on the other hand, will more likely follow their heart and dreams into the humanities—*most likely finding a career in the liberal arts, philosophy, social work, education, and psychology, or working as counselors, diplomats, negotiators, ministers, union leaders, motivational speakers, journalists, poets, editors or novelists, or possibly missionaries, new age healers, or human resources specialists*—careers that naturally build on a spirit of caring and compassion for people, a strong need for personal contact and sharing, and a natural drive to create a world of harmony, peace, and justice for all.

A Totally Different Kind of Leader

This rare combination of Intuitive and Feeling traits makes for a rather interesting character, someone with a decidedly personal touch and a genetic need to help individuals, groups, and entire cultures—as teachers and mentors, as champions and counselors, inspiring others to rise to their highest potential as humans. In short, the Pathfinder is a leader, but with a different agenda and style of leadership than the Mastermind's.

Masterminds lead by the pure force and power of their character and authority. They are military commanders or corporate heads, uniting people, supplies, machines, and other resources into a single integrated organization with a clear mission—an organizational mission that is in fact an extension of the Mastermind's own life's mission.

However, the Pathfinder isn't your traditional boss. These types are too heavy into feelings—yours, theirs, and everybody else's. They take everything personally, even the slightest criticisms. As a result, they have trouble criticizing others and disciplining them. They find normal games played by business competitors negative and uninspiring. Moreover, they can become too darn idealistic, neglecting practical business tasks that demand objective analysis.

Pathfinders lead in a very different way—by example, by inspiring you and me and the next guy to reach for the best in us, by encouraging us, motivating us, touching us personally, on a one-to-one personal level. Regardless of their field, they are skillful communicators because they let it all hang out and are often possessed with a charismatic ability to make us feel what they feel. They have a passion for life that draws us into action with them.

In a very real sense, Pathfinders *inspire us as individuals to become our own leaders, to become self-actuated, inspired by a secret power deep within each of us,* and from that common source emerges a common commitment to work together on shared goals, each of us becoming Pathfinders in our own right.

Feelers: Personal Values Drive Their Decisions

Pathfinders are passionate individuals and are passionate about other people. They genuinely care about the struggles you're going through, your suffering, your dreams, your growth as a person, and about your family, how you relate to others. They also care about the struggles and triumphs of communities, society, entire nations, cultures, and the planet.

However, they are not emoting simply to let off steam. They not only use their emotions to communicate with you and the world around themselves, Pathfinders use their emotions to better *understand themselves and where they fit in the world.* Ultimately, they are on a quest of self-discovery.

WE HEAR THE WORDS, WE REMEMBER THE EMOTIONS

For example, remember something said by your favorite classroom teacher, coach, or minister, or perhaps the message of a motivational speaker or enthusiastic politician, or maybe the words of one of your parents, an uncle, or your therapist.

Do you remember how you felt? What impact did the words have on you? Guidance at a crucial turning point? Support during a time of trial? Some warm honest appreciation for the extra effort you put into a thankless job? Encouragement to pursue your dreams when the odds seemed impossible? The ability to make an important decision without compromising your values? You remember them. Why?

All these people had one thing in common—they were able to tap into your emotions, to touch you at a deep-feeling level to get you to change a belief or to take some action. Maybe they inspired you to take risks and reach your full potential, or perhaps they encouraged you to go in a new direction, down a road less traveled, or to be less selfish and more of service to others. They touched you emotionally, and in so doing they brought out the best in you. That's why you remember them!

THE LANGUAGE OF THE SOUL SPEAKS OF VALUES

Pathfinders have the power to reach deep into your soul and stir up your emotions—deeper than entertainers skilled at making you laugh or cry, deeper than advertisers whose goal is to make you feel good so you buy their products.

Advertisers know that the best way to induce you to buy their products is to tap into your emotions. The same is true for most solicitations for political donations and charitable contributions. They know the best way to reach your pocketbook is through your emotions.

The Pathfinder communicates on a different level, worlds apart. Emotions are a secret language that lets Pathfinders communicate one soul to another. In their highest form, emotions are the language of the soul. They communicate your values, your moral beliefs, your principles, your integrity—not just verbally and in writing, but emphatically in nonverbal behavior and actions.

YOUR RADAR SYSTEM ABSORBS FEELINGS NONSTOP

Pathfinders not only connect with people, they identify with them, bond with them, actually feeling what others feel. *They are compassionate humanitarians.* Coupled with that, Pathfinders are telepathic, able to psych out emotional energies because they understand the pulse beat of the world—including business associates, customers, clerks, people they bump into on the street, their communities, the nation, world cultures, and family and friends. They are one with everyone.

The emotional system of a Pathfinder resembles a highly sensitive radar system designed to pick up feelings radiating from anyone, anywhere in the universe, *your* universe. Remember, they are Intuitives. They do indeed have a psychic sixth sense, relying on hunches, gut instincts, and intuition more than the raw data. They are always searching for what's beneath the surface, behind the mask, within the hidden self.

Pathfinders are psychic in a very natural way. This instinct is built into their genetic code and their personality type. It happens automatically, and most of the time they can't explain how or why they know what they know, they just *know.*

Sometimes they walk around all day with their antennas up scanning people for signals, reading body language, detecting subtle changes in voice intonations, movements of the eyes in conversation, or by analyzing vocabulary, grammar, and rhetoric, always on the alert for clues about the inner feelings of everyone around them—traits that make them great negotiators, diplomats, and peacemakers.

The same goes for books, newsmagazines, television reports, and sometimes purely telepathic information from unknown sources. Pathfinders are constantly reading between the lines, looking for deeper meanings, and searching for the emotions that express the meaning of life and happiness—because ultimately, emotions are the channel that Pathfinders use to communicate with your soul, to touch your values, and to express the values deep in their own soul.

IDEALS AND HEROES CAN FALL OFF THE PEDESTAL YOU BUILT

Pathfinders are so keenly sensitive to the feelings of others largely because they themselves are highly sensitive human beings. While this is an asset, it can also work against them. For example, as long as the Pathfinder's radar system is accurately picking up and interpreting the feelings of others, then the Pathfinder's own reactions, conclusions, decisions, and behavior have a reasonable chance of being in the best interests of others.

However, if the radar system is malfunctioning, the instincts of the Pathfinders will be misleading. For example, they may be doing a lot of wishful thinking. They may have misinterpreted signals from other people. They may simply be projecting their own feelings on others—absolutely convinced they are right and unaware they're misleading themselves. When this happens, the more astute Pathfinders will learn from their mistakes over time.

Pathfinders can also have a tendency to idealize people, institutions, and beliefs, becoming fiercely loyal to their image of the perfect alternative, often denying anything to the contrary.

Total commitment to an ideal can be an asset when, for example, you're pursuing a life goal against heavy odds. But here again, know that your mind may be playing tricks on you. When your ideals and heroes suddenly fall off the pedestal you erected, you may be in trouble.

Problems, yes, but that's the unavoidable price of being idealistic. As Michaelangelo put it, "The greatest danger for most of us is not that our aim is too high and we miss it, but that it is too low and we reach it."

Intuitives: Visionaries Driven to Make a Difference

Pathfinders are visionaries, born with a sense of destiny and a need to make a difference in the world, locally or globally. Keirsey and Plato call them *idealists,* although in a real sense all personality types have ideals and personal goals. Their ideals and goals may be substantially different, but they do have them, each in their own unique way.

The four personality types in this temperament are perhaps more like the classic idealists—think of all the inspiring teachers, preachers, coaches, journalists, and motivational speakers you've run across in your lifetime. Something instinctively tells you these unique people are themselves on a path. They are passionate about life. You can feel it deep in your bones. You see it in their actions. And you know they live by their principles.

The Pathfinder's life is a journey, a search for the answers to life: What's it all about? That's the Intuitive gene encoded in Pathfinders. They are seeking not only the meaning of life in some general sense—*they are searching for the meaning of their own life*. They are on a personal search.

In fact, they have no choice: This is who they are. It's in their DNA, encoded in their personality type. It is a calling that cannot be denied. Pathfinders are destined to find their path, and they *must* go down that path with a passion that drives them from deep within their soul out into the soul of the world—they cannot avoid their destiny.

FEELINGS SHARED: ON THE PATH AND WALKING THE TALK

Paradoxically, the Pathfinders' *search for the meaning of their own life must be shared*. That is also a part of their genetic code—the need to connect and bond personally with others, sharing their passion for life.

Once again, remember how you were inspired by some teacher telling you all about his or her fascination with biology and butterflies, abnormal psychology, or social reform. What about that coach who pushed you to your personal best when you thought you had no more to give? The minister who encouraged you to stick by your principles when you were the only one? The therapist who helped you through over-whelming grief? A dying friend's message of gratitude?

Something in you connects with the love these amazing people have for life. You know that whatever these Pathfinders are telling you comes from a mysterious source. You know they believe passionately in what they are telling you. They are not just talking the talk, they are walking the walk. They are not just giving you a canned sales pitch, they live and breath what they teach and preach.

DEDICATING YOUR LIFE TO SOMETHING BIGGER THAN YOU

For many Pathfinders, the passion and the sharing have some mysterious spiritual core. At the core, the Pathfinders' passionate search for the meaning of life, plus their genetic need to share their life's mission, is somehow connected with something beyond them that can only be called *spiritual.*

That spirit has many names: The Creator, God, Nature, the Tao, Universal Energy, the Force, Holy Spirit, Higher Power, Gaia, Great Spirit, Yahweh, Jesus, Buddha, Mohammed, your conscience, or simply, the still small voice within you. Underneath the name tag is an undeniable spiritual energy driving the Pathfinders on their personal journey, a burning passion they must share with people, individually and in groups, universally and mystically.

An unmistakable magnetism draws you to them. If you are also a Pathfinder, you instinctively understand this spiritual unity that links together your search for the meaning of life, your life's mission, your integrity of purpose, and your need to help people—all united by some mysterious calling from within that commands you to be a Pathfinder.

The Pathfinder is a hero in the classic sense. As Joseph Campbell said in the *Power of Myth,* "A hero is someone who has given his or her life to something bigger than oneself." In that sense, Pathfinders are heroes whose calling means sharing their path and, in so doing, making the journey a search for something bigger: to find it in other people, yes, to find it in the Spirit, yes, *but most of all to find it deep within their own souls.*

* * * * * * *

Many of us contemplate fording the
difficult passages that we meet,
or consider taking the less-traveled path,
but we do not dare
because we have no idea what is on the other side.
Some of us wrestle all our lives
with the possible but never do it.
The difference is, pathfinders do it.

Gail Sheehy,
Pathfinders

14

GUARDIANS OF THE ESTABLISHMENT: SENSOR-JUDGERS (SJ)

> The Establishment is always
> invested in the old paradigm.
> So the new paradigm does not
> get adopted just because
> it is neater and works
> better than the old one.
> The old crowd wins
> the first few battles,
> and in fact the paradigm
> doesn't change until the
> old crowd dies and the
> new young crowd grows up and
> rewrites the textbooks and
> becomes the Establishment itself.
>
> Adam Smith,
> *Powers of Mind*

Want to know who's holding down the fort? Who's our anchor in the storm? Who keeps the organization running smoothly? Who is waving the flag at the Memorial Day parade? Who's a scout master? Coaching little league? Organizing a church fund-raiser? An active member of civic, professional, and historical associations? Talking up family values? Our Guardians of the Establishment, that's who.

Guardian Angels: "Like a Rock"

All across America these Guardians are "like a rock," to borrow from a popular truck commercial. Yes, they are America's Rock of Gibraltar, the

GUARDIANS OF THE ESTABLISHMENT

- Chief Executive Officer (ESTJ)
- The Diplomat (ESFJ)
- Results-Oriented Expert (ISTJ)
- The Master-Servant (ISFJ)

stabilizing force in all of our establishments, companies, and organizations across America. You might even call them Guardian Angels, because they watch over and protect us.

Consistent and trustworthy, they live by the book and follow the rules. You can count on them. Their word is their bond. If you're one of them, you are likely to place a high value on traditions, history, organization, structure, authority, and spiritual principles.

They need to belong to groups and often join clubs, associations, and societies. As members, they're reliable, disciplined, and consistent, guided by a strong sense of duty and a commitment to the group and what it stands for.

Money, Property, and Other Fundamental Values

Guardians are the rock-solid backbone of Corporate America, investing regularly in their IRAs and 401(k)s. They prefer a regular paycheck and may invest in tax-deferred college tuition programs for their kids. Their portfolios, well diversified and rebalanced regularly, are in five-star funds run by established managers with long-term track records. Guardians become millionaires the slow, conservative way.

Because of their personal preferences for security and safety, Guardians focus rather intensely on material things, like making money, owning property, and preserving the established order, more than other people. Let's look more closely and see why.

Sensors: Searching for Hard Facts about the World

Remember that when it comes to understanding the world and collecting information about the world around them, the four Guardians are first and foremost *Sensors*. They want the facts, concrete data, and hard evidence. They need to see the trees first in order to understand the forest.

Like Sergeant Friday in *Dragnet* they'll listen to speculations, theories, conjectures, hypotheses, and ideas for only so long. Any such mental gyrations make them uneasy and impatient, too up in the air. They need to feel grounded, anchored in the earth.

Whatever your job, trade, craft, or profession, if you're a Guardian and you're listening to too much of what sounds like a lot of pie-in-the-sky talk, at some point you'll shift gears in the conversation and ask specific questions of witnesses, or quietly go off and do independent research, or maybe you'll check historical records, or review past statements of witnesses—whatever is necessary to make you feel as though you have a better grasp of reality.

HEAD IN THE CLOUDS—FEET FIRMLY ON THE EARTH

Just give me the facts, ma'am. Guardians feel more grounded with numbers and statistics, whether they're collected from the Federal Reserve Board, the *U.S. Statistical Abstract,* the NBA, the American League, the Super Bowl, or from family birth records, calorie counts, or crossword puzzles. Numbers and facts ground you mentally, make you feel safe and secure in the world, whereas abstract theories leave you feeling unsettled.

In today's business and financial world, you'll spend a lot of your days doing things like reviewing the latest accounting and sales data, project status, and inventory control reports, watching financial news on CNBC, CNN, Fox, and MSNBC, checking economic data, delivery dates, and daily stock quotes.

When you talk, you'll pepper your conversations with rather traditional sayings from familiar old-fashioned sources: Ben Franklin's *Poor Richard's Almanac,* a passage from Proverbs, a famous quote you read in the biography of a historical figure you admire, or maybe *Bartlett's,* or maybe some memorable principle your favorite grandparent said to you when you two were fishing or baking bread as a kid. My grandfather used to say, "The worst mistake you can make is to make the same mistake twice."

Guardians often issue warnings about the dangers of ignoring the established order of the world, the nation, or you personally, everything from "You better get a flu shot" to "Taxes and labor costs are accelerating; we should consider relocating." This well-meaning advice is an expression of their need to hold on to a sense of personal safety and security.

Judgers: Anchored in a Structured World of Their Own Making

The second half of the Guardian personality formula—they're Judgers as well as Sensors—actually meshes quite well with their preference for collecting specific, concrete information about the world.

Remember that Judgers need to have their daily life well organized and structured. Not only are they early to bed and early to rise, more than likely they'll even review their appointment book the night before and have a to-do list ready for the next day, perhaps taped to their mirror for review the next morning while they are brushing their teeth, and they'll review it again on their morning commute.

If you're a Guardian, you have a strong need to control upcoming events as much as possible before they happen. When you can't, you feel lost and anxious. You also believe this applies to everyone else, because that's what makes companies and society in general work smoothly: laws, regulations, company policies, procedures, mission statements, organizational charts, meeting schedules, contractual agreements, and living up to your commitments. These things build trust and loyalty.

ANSWERING TO A HIGHER AUTHORITY: YOUR CONSCIENCE AND GOD

You do things by-the-book, as the saying goes. You do it because something deep within you tells you that's what holds the world together. In short, your principles go far deeper than simply obeying the law to avoid getting caught.

You obey the law of the land because it's the right thing to do according to a higher universal law. It's the moral thing. As a Guardian, you know you are being judged by a higher authority, call it your own conscience, a universal law, or a divine being. However you identify it, you feel compelled to live by the exacting standards inherent in this higher authority.

Put another way, Guardians pride themselves in being men and women with integrity and high morals, a commitment to family values, a healthy respect for authority, a sense of loyalty to friends, community, and company, and a strong allegiance in America and faith in a God. It is hardly a surprise that their outlook toward government is rather conservative, grounded in a need to preserve these values.

WORKING IN BLUE-CHIP CORPORATE AMERICA

Guardians need stability in their lives. As a result, they are often the stabilizing member of the organization, the one holding it together and preserving its values. This is not simply a way to get good salaries, raises, and promotions, this is a deeply ingrained psychological need that has a major impact on their choice of jobs and careers.

You're likely to find Guardians working in large, solid companies like General Electric, General Motors, or IBM, or maybe in a local, state, or federal government position (Keirsey notes that about half the American presidents have been Guardians), or perhaps in management at a large institution—university, trade association, charitable organization, or research think tank. Guardians gravitate to organizations with pension plans, health care, paid vacation, and other employee benefits that offer some sense of security.

Guardians can pick from a wide variety of careers within these many organizations, but generally you'll find them in responsible positions, often as team leaders, supervisors, managers, and executives—because you can count on them. They are the kind of team players you can rely on when the pressure's on.

Regardless of where they are in the organization's hierarchy, the Guardian will be consistent, dependable, and thorough in handling the tasks at hand—the perfect employee in helping any organization achieve its goals.

Leadership of the Team, Project, Division, or Entire Company

When it comes working on projects, the Guardian is often the one in charge. They've taken the time to map out everything in advance, with specific instructions, methods, supply lines, and staff resources. Plus they'll get an early start. They'll ride herd on their team to get it done right and on time. Along the way, they'll be the ones monitoring progress, prepared with contingency plans, looking for potential delays, plugging holes, and taking care of any problems that might impact the quality, performance, or completion dates.

Guardians have an inherent need to be of service to people, to the organization, to the common good, and to a higher power. This springs from an inner drive that many Guardians find early in life—values and principles expressed in places such as the Commandments and Scout's Oath: Trustworthy, loyal, helpful, friendly, courteous, kind, obedient, cheerful, thrifty, brave, clean, reverent.

TURNING SHORTCOMINGS INTO STRENGTHS

Occasionally, their best instincts can work against them. For example, remember that the Guardian, as a Sensor, is more interested in what's going on right now, in the present, and how today's events provide a link with past trends, patterns, and historical facts.

Guardians are less interested in speculating about the future and events that they can neither predict nor control with any accuracy. They have a job to do now, and the best way to get it done is to focus on the now.

They may unconsciously minimize or even avoid long-range planning altogether. As a result, they may be unprepared for future changes in the business and financial world. The best Guardians are aware of this tendency and partner with or delegate the planning function to a trusted associate—a Mastermind, for example—listening closely to their advice and weighing their recommendations seriously.

RIGHT PERSON AT THE RIGHT TIME: A HARD-NOSED DECISION MAKER

In extreme cases when Guardians are under pressure and stressed out, they may be so invested in the old ways of doing things that they can't adapt quickly enough to rapidly changing business situations. They may even resist new programs and new information altogether. In short, strict adherence to maintaining the status quo may result in missing a window of opportunity for the future.

These may be extreme reactions, but we've all encountered Guardian personalities who were too set in their ways, rigid, and dogmatic, lacking a vision of the future, and in general, a pain in the ass to work with.

On the other hand, that may be exactly what an organization needs when their survival is threatened—a hard-nosed pain-in-the-ass Guardian willing to make the tough decisions regarding extra hours, layoffs, cutting benefits, and pay reductions. Even when they're super-tough, they may be just what the doctor ordered for the organization.

* * * * * * * *

It's an age-old story:
You think you are heading for India, and you end up in the
West Indies. You run after the ball, and you fall down the rabbit hole.
You're a prehistoric fish in a dried-up sea that's just trying to flop across
the mud to a new puddle, and the next thing you know you're breathing
air!
You think you're doing one thing,
and all of the time you're busy doing another.
Many of the biggest transformations come when you think that you're just
trying to reestablish the status quo.

William Bridges,
The Way of Transition

CHAPTER 15

HYBRIDS, DUAL PERSONALITIES, AND GENETIC CODE REPROGRAMMING

The problem was that in trying to be someone else,
I neglected to concentrate on the person I could be.
That idea was too frightening to contemplate at the time. I was
happier going along
with the conventions of the time,
measuring success in terms of money and position, climbing
ladders which others placed in my way, collecting things and
contacts
rather than giving expression
to my own beliefs and personality.

Charles Handy,
The Hungry Spirit: Beyond Capitalism,
A Quest for Purpose in the Modern World

What if you take the test and it looks like you could be one of two personality types—call it an *ambiguity*—or even two different temperaments? There are several rather interesting issues you should be aware of when you're trying to figure out why this might be the case with you. First and foremost, you should embrace the ambiguity as a special gift and an opportunity to discover the real you.

Most experts in the business of typecasting, career planning, and psych testing will tell you that your personality type is much like a genetic imprint encoded in your DNA, a computer chip embedded at birth, which remains there throughout your life, operating as an internal guidance system, telling you where true north is in your particular universe, where you should be going, and the best way to get there.

We also know, however, that sudden traumatic events, such as the death of a parent, or systematic psychological conditioning, such as ongoing physical and emotional abuse, can actually alter, suppress, exaggerate, reprogram, and possibly even erase our original guidance systems. If that happens, we may drift off course, like the Prodigal Son, and may not get back without enormous challenges and struggles.

The Prodigal Son: Searching for a Half Century

Let me use my own situation to illustrate some of the issues you should be aware of when reviewing your personality profile test results. Art was my obsession prior to joining the Marines at age 17. Somewhere around age 10 I recall my mother taking me and my drawings to a neighbor who was a commercial artist and bragging about her talented son.

Later that year I was taken away from her. Decades later I became aware that the trauma of losing her put me in a state of amnesia. I lost almost all memory not only of the surrounding events, but of everything else that happened prior to age 11.

In high school I became a solid student in left-brain rational stuff like sciences and math. I was also the class artist, creating all the artwork for the newspaper, the yearbook, murals, and posters for student events. I even enrolled in art teachers' college after graduation. Then, suddenly, I switched directions and joined the Marines. I wanted to "become a man" and save the world from communism. My gut instinct told me the Marines would help me. They did.

LIFE IS JUST A BOX OF CHOCOLATES

After testing me, the Marine Corps decided to train me as an electronics technician. I didn't know what electronics was. Four years later, I enrolled in college to study electronics engineering. Before being discharged, a Marine Corps psychologist tested me again and recommended I study architecture. I had to look it up in the dictionary. Sounded interesting, so I switched majors to architecture, then went on to study city planning, then law, and later worked in those fields.

In my forties the creative urge began pulling at me again. I left a modestly successful career in investment banking for television, filmmaking, and the newspaper worlds. All were creative fields, but I had been typecast by an extensive legal and financial background, not as a creative type.

I tried my hand at writing some stage plays and film scripts. I thought of selling them and directing, but I was advised not to give up my day job, so I held tight. Nothing sold. Later, I picked up a doctorate in psychology and worked as a chemical dependency and career counselor for several years.

"I'M 58 YEARS OLD AND STILL DON'T KNOW WHAT I WANT TO DO"

Legendary management guru Peter Drucker made that comment in a 1968 *Psychology Today* interview. It haunted me for years. In spite of some modest successes, I felt lost. Life was passing me by—I was always searching for the "right" career.

The turning point, or rather "re-turning" point, happened for me at age 57, when I suddenly—*one day while I was pulling together a lifetime of resumes for another run at selling myself as a guru and public figure*—became aware that what I loved most in life was *writing,* beginning with my journals in high school.

Prior to age 57, I treated anything creative as a hobby or merely self-promotional advertising in this-or-that profession, not as a career or moneymaker in itself. Yes, I had tons of journals and letters, scripts and stories. But it had never, *never* occurred to me that I could make a living as a creative writer. I had long ago given up the idea of being a creative artist. The business world and the therapy profession had drained me.

At age 57, I finally discovered the love of my life—*creative writing*—and made a decision that I was going to "follow my bliss" and "do what I love and the money will follow." (As oversimplified as those phrases may seem, they've been my affirmations ever since.) Yes, the money lagged, but since that moment of awareness the love has never faltered. Better late than never.

DUAL PERSONALITIES: IS THE "YOU-AT-WORK" THE REAL YOU?

The first area I noticed was the big split between the Extravert-Introvert function. Keirsey, certainly one of the more respected leaders in the field, dismisses this axis as the least important of all four functions, although he writes brilliantly about the differences between the eight Extravert and the eight Introvert personality types.

Moreover, with 2 million people taking the Myers-Briggs test annually, and probably as many more taking the tests in Keirsey's and other books, you cannot afford to dismiss its importance.

Prior to age 57, my personality tests were split evenly between Extravert and Introvert. I always felt that for pure business and professional reasons I should be "out there"—marketing, leading seminars, doing promotional speaking, making presentations, and offering lectures.

So my tests would typically straddle the axis, about fifty-fifty. After age 57 it was clear that I was an Introvert, period. I didn't want to be "out there" anymore, I wanted to be "in here," writing.

A Special Gift: Personality Splits Are Important Clues

Today, I realize that any ambiguity, any indication of a split, any time you are not clearly at one end or the other—should not be ignored, because *the ambiguity is the most important part of your genetic personality code, the piece of the puzzle that must be resolved before you can move on with your life's mission.*

For example, if your code is neither clearly Extravert nor Introvert, Thinker nor Feeler, you are being given a very special gift, a strong signal that you're off track. You are probably in a career that's not right for your personality type. You may be living a life that's not right for the real you, and the discord between what you're doing and what you *should* be doing will sabotage your opportunities for success and happiness in life.

If you do have a split personality—*two different personality types due to a split between one of the functions*—I strongly recommend that you spend a little time with a therapist, career counselor, or success coach.

Generally speaking, I'd recommend a counselor or coach, simply because therapists tend to look to the past for *problems* rather than the future and action-oriented *solutions*. Find out why you're stuck in the career you're in and target the one best suited for the real you.

Whatever you do, when you take one of the personality tests, take off your work hat and write it from the vantage point of the real you. After all, that's the whole point of this search, isn't it?

NO-MAN'S-LAND: TRAPPED BETWEEN DENIAL AND WISHFUL THINKING

Another possible reason you should pay particular attention to a split between two personality types in your test is that you may be having a whole lot of trouble accepting who you really are. You may be doing a lot of wishful thinking and fantasizing about being something else. In *Do What You Are,* the Tiegers say that the "wish to be different" is the "most common reason" for a split.

For example, let's say you're a partner in your family's law firm or manufacturing business, and you're also athletic. For some odd reason, you'd always wanted to be a science fiction writer, but your lawyer father said that you couldn't make the kind of money as a writer that you'd make in a solid profession like the law. Besides, you know how much your dad loves it and you've always wanted to please him.

Years later, when you took a personality test, maybe you were fantasizing about escaping the frustration and pressure, yet also worried about saying anything to your dad because he needed you and was proud you were following in his footsteps.

You daydream about some exciting adventures: being a stock car driver, an Outward Bound cycling instructor, or even traveling with the circus for a year—*an escape route or exit strategy.*

If you take the test when you're confused and in an escapist mind-set, your profile may lead you in a tangent rather than confirming that something like writing fiction is where you should be. Not necessarily a bad move, because at least the escape, even if temporary, sets you free to go on searching for the real you. The point is, transition is bound to result in confusing test results.

MAKE SURE YOU'RE GOING SOMEWHERE, NOT JUST ESCAPING

One word of advice, don't be in too big a hurry. In addition to a little counseling, read William Bridges's book, *Transitions,* on winding your way through a lifestyle change. Before I left Wall Street for Hollywood, I listened to a therapist and other mentors telling me for three years, "Make sure you're going somewhere, not running away from something." After going, it took another couple years to settle down.

If you're simply running away from something, you'll make great time going somewhere—but probably in the wrong direction! That may not be all bad if it gets you out of where you are. At least you broke the inertia, and you'll be in the *neutral zone,* as Bridges calls it, forced to find out what you really, really want. This happened to me when I left Wall Street, went to Hollywood, and hit some setbacks that forced me to go deeper!

CROSSING GENDERS: WHY CAN'T A WOMAN BE LIKE A MAN?

Gender stereotyping can also influence the profile you *think* you should have in order to succeed in business, both directly, for women, and indirectly, for men, who are Feeling types or Intuitives.

Thinkers tend to dominate in the business world. As we've already mentioned, male Thinkers (objective and impersonal) outnumber female Thinking types by two or three to one. And the reverse is true for Feeling types (subjective, personal, and values-oriented), where women dominate. Knowing this, women often take on a Thinker's behavior, even in their personality tests, *in order to fit in.* Eventually this role playing is bound to create internal conflict and sabotage performance.

FOUR EXAMPLES OF SUCCESSFUL HYBRIDS

Extravert and Introvert
Dwight David Eisenhower

Eisenhower is an example of an Introvert pulled into the world of Extraverts by history. For 25 years after his graduation from the West Point Military Academy he was best known as a *Master Strategist* (INTJ), working behind the scenes organizing military strategies. When America went to war in 1940, that was exactly what was needed in the *Commander in Chief* (ENTJ) of the Allied forces. Ike spent two years planning D-Day and the defeat of the Nazis, then went on to become president of the United States. Yet he always remained a very private man.

Sensor and Intuitive
Bono of U2

The world of *Entertainers* (ESFP) has always been loaded with celebrities who are also powerful *Champions* (ENFP) of various causes. Bono of the rock group U2 used his performances to promote various political and humanitarian agendas, including a trip to Africa with the U.S. Secretary of the Treasury. Actor Richard Gere supported the Dalai Lama and the International Campaign for Tibet. Television and film star Michael J. Fox sat before a congressional committee fighting for more money to research Parkinson's disease.

Thinking and Feeling
Carl G. Jung

Scholars who have studied Jung and his work on personality typologies generally see Jung as a *Visionary* (INTP), largely because of his total focus on developing a scientific approach to psychology. Yet anyone familiar with Jung in his private life, especially through his autobiography *Memories, Dreams, Reflections,* will clearly see a *Mystic Hero* (INFP) behind the visionary mask, and *both* are the real man.

Judger and Perceiver
Donald Trump

The business world is loaded with leaders who attempt to move back and forth between the role of the *Entrepreneur* (ESTP) and the

CEO (ESTJ). Many, like Donald Trump and Richard Branson, carry the flamboyant and dramatic styles of the entrepreneur into the executive suite. Others start out as small entrepreneurs and evolve into rather solid CEOs of large enterprises, such as Charles Schwab, Jack Bogle, and Warren Buffett.

Other combinations can show a whole new side of you!

FAKE IT TILL YOU MAKE IT? YOU'RE STILL A FAKE!

We also know that Sensors outnumber Intuitives, and that Sensors tend to dominate in business. As a result, Intuitives (male or female) may try to fake it in order to survive and get ahead with "the boys," minimizing their intuitive abilities in favor of hard facts. In addition, a woman Pathfinder (NF) would likely feel like a fish out of water when trying to act as a Guardian (SJ) in order to fit into the business.

Similarly, male Pathfinders (NF) can have a rough time fitting into a rational, objective, and impersonal business. They may be more accepted than female Pathfinders if they play the game according to the rules of the establishment, but the fact remains that both male and female Pathfinders are compromising the integrity of their personality as long as they play the game by the rules of the establishment *rather than by their own rules.*

This took me a while to figure out. Around age 40 I was working at the Wall Street investment bank of Morgan Stanley for a few years before I figured out that I didn't belong there. In my spare time I wrote film scripts and a musical comedy, took acting and dance lessons, and directed an award-winning short film. Finally, I couldn't take the conflict any longer. I didn't belong on Wall Street and left for Hollywood.

Posttraumatic Reprogramming of the Personality

Is your personality type permanently encoded in your DNA? Or can it be reprogrammed and possibly even erased from our original guidance system? While this may sound like the makings of a science fiction novel or spy thriller, maybe a CIA brainwashing plot or human cloning experiment, it's actually something many people wrestle with for much of their lives. I did.

My mother disappeared when I was 10. I went into shock and blanked out. I had amnesia about much of my life before the trauma, also severe anxieties, which I hid well. One of the few things I do remember is that the creative arts were important to me before that turning point and for some time afterward.

The trauma also kicked my rational thinking mind into high gear. Math and sciences became a strong suit in high school. As a result, the Marines decided to train me as an electronics technician. Later, I received degrees in architecture, city planning, and law, and I worked in every one of those fields, including investment banking.

Today the split is obvious: My personality tests consistently identified me as a Pathfinder (NF). Yet virtually all my posttrauma education and job experiences were in Mastermind (NT) careers, from age eleven until my fifties, when I completed my doctorate in psychology. Work in that field ultimately led me into a career as a writer.

PLEASE UNDERSTAND ME—OOPS, I'M TALKING TO MYSELF

Reading David Keirsey's *Please Understand Me II* helped put an end to a seemingly endless life search through more than 10 careers. In Keirsey's type structure, I'm a Pathfinder (NF) temperament (he uses Plato's *Idealist* term), with a Mystic Hero (INFP) personality type (Keirsey's *Healer*).

Keirsey's description of the healer (mystic heroes) hit close to home: "Healers seek unity within themselves, and between themselves and others, because of a feeling of alienation which often comes from an unhappy childhood. . . . Healers come to see themselves as Ugly Ducklings . . . believing they are bad. . . . They wonder, some of them for the rest of their lives, whether they are OK. They are OK, just different—swans reared in a family of ducks."

Bad? Ugly? For the rest of their lives? The description hit close to home: I was an altar boy in high school and wanted to become a priest. I went into a seminary for a short while in my mid-twenties. In the Marines and on till my forties I had an extreme fear of burning in hell. I even wrote a horror film script and a musical comedy about Faust and Mephistopheles.

In my fifties I had an opportunity to join a monastic order of Christian monks. But somewhere along the way, a therapist helped me realize that I didn't have a true calling to be a priest and help people. All I had was a blinding fear of dying as a sinner and going to hell for all eternity, and I apparently thought that as a priest I would somehow be protected by the church.

DO TRAUMATIC EXPERIENCES REPROGRAM THE PERSONALITY?

Today, my experiences, personally and professionally, make me realize that Keirsey's observations about Healers (Mystic Heroes) don't apply just to Healers and to me, but they have a much broader and more powerful meaning for society.

Whether it's the ongoing negative conditioning of an unhappy childhood or a sudden traumatic event (not just the loss of a parent, but any sustained abuse, major injuries, relocations, or other triggers of trauma), *any one of the 16 personality types may be thrown off course, split, and their genetic code altered or reprogrammed.*

Moreover, Keirsey's work helped me better understand that I actually have a second split in my personality types–I switch back and forth between two quite different sets of four Temperaments, as a Pathfinder (NF) and as a Mastermind (NT).

Both are Intuitive. However, one uses impersonal Thinking when making decisions, and the other depends on personal values and subjective Feelings. The same kind of switching can occur with a Creator, for example, if a traumatic event reprograms that person from a Sensor to an Intuitive. My wife, a psychotherapist, also had a major childhood trauma, which results in shifts between being a Performer totally into the moment and a Healer searching for answers to the mysteries of the personality.

TEMPORARY SPLITS TRIGGERED BY STRESS AND TENSION

I have noticed that this switch between Temperaments often happens under stress. When anxiety peaks, I resort to the Thinking Mastermind personality to quiet extreme emotions, and that suppresses the Pathfinder. Moreover, I've come to understand that the early childhood trauma probably made my Mastermind dominant over the Pathfinder, at least in the work arena.

Moreover, today, after 10 years of enjoying a career as a writer, my intuition tells me that as a child I probably would have tested as a Pathfinder. By the time the Marines tested me, however, my brain and my genetic code had somehow been altered or reprogrammed into a Mastermind with a surpressed Pathfinder alter ego.

As I continue growing, I see all these personality functions merging. Journalism and writing are typical Pathfinder careers. In any event, the Mastermind in me can now rationalize that the wonderful little creative child is very much alive today as a Pathfinder–a wordsmith creating artistic images with words.

Rationalization? Not really. Perhaps an intuition or a new sensory perception. The integration of our whole personality was central to Jung's work, a merger of the four major polarities—including the senses, intuitions, thinking, and feeling—a process that becomes more pronounced as we age and develop.

JUNG'S DEVELOPMENTAL STAGES PROGRESS INTO A WHOLE SELF

We know that humans change and develop over time as we transition through the stages of our lives. As young kids we experiment with the various ways of gathering information (sensing or intuition) and making decisions (thinking or feeling). At certain stages, one or the other function may naturally dominate. A 10-year-old may naturally be more into rational thinking, while a 5-year-old may actually believe Winnie the Pooh exists.

Jung's work suggests that while you're born with a specific genetic profile and a dominant function (for example, highly intuitive thinker or Mastermind), your sensing and feeling functions are still part of your personality, although subordinate and less developed.

Over a lifetime, however, as you exercise all your functions in everyday life, you develop all of them—though not all to the same degree. As we age and develop a more rounded personality, we at least have the opportunity to better balance all our functions.

Thus, in their later years, tough, ol' hard-nosed Masterminds may find themselves at times behaving like Freelance Creators, a heretofore suppressed alter ego of theirs. They might, for example, take up watercolor painting and hatha yoga. Perhaps they even find themselves more and more attracted to creative types, possibly even marrying one, which will certainly force them to balance their natural objectivity and impersonal instincts in a relationship!

Personalities Splitting from Having "One Too Many"

Addictive behavior is also guaranteed to split anybody's personality and sabotage your life's mission. I know. On top of the childhood trauma, I was a practicing alcoholic for 20 years, from the time I went into the Marine Corps at age 17 until age 37, when I bottomed out and got into recovery. The problem ran in our family for generations.

My long bout with chemical dependency may well be the primary reason for my years of wandering as the Prodigal Son. In fact, add addictive behavior of any kind to major trauma, losses, injuries, and lifestyle transitions and a split personality type may be inevitable.

My life really did not begin, or at least didn't get back on track, until I got sober more than 30 years ago. Since then I've been fortunate to have the support of others trudging the same road. Today, I believe I even understand why I had to go down this road. Like the Prodigal Son, I have a better, although belated, appreciation of the gift of life. I'm one of the lucky ones, however, because a large majority of addicts and alcoholics never make it into recovery.

SILENT SABOTEUR IN THE AMERICAN PERSONALITY

My journey has given me a unique perspective. Over the years I've had an opportunity to help others personally and professionally as a chemical dependency and career counselor. I've seen firsthand how addictions not only affect America's 30 million alcoholics and addicts, but also impact the lives of as many as 100 million people around them—loved ones, family, friends, business associates, and innocent strangers.

Add to the mix all the other normal life challenges and you can easily see that at any given point in time more than half the nation's population may be under pressures that could in some way confuse their personality types.

These experiences convince me that addictive behavior of any kind is one of the most destructive forces in our culture. Addictions so severely damage judgment and behavior that those who are in any way addicted cannot tap into the mission encoded in their genes and their personality profile.

In fact, individuals engaged in regular, heavy use of alcohol and drugs, either illicit or prescription, very probably will test in the wrong personality code. Or they will underperform. Or, more likely, both. In short, they will not be achieving their full potential in this lifetime.

It's Not the Test . . . It's You . . . and It's a Gift

Remember, any time you see ambivalence in your genetic Millionaire's Code, any indication that you may fit in more than one personality type or temperament—*there's nothing wrong with the test—it's you! You are going through a transition, and the split is a gift from the universe telling you to pay extra attention to what you are doing with your life.*

Please do not ignore the signal. It's actually a very positive sign, a gift. Regardless of what is causing the ambivalence—a traumatic event, major grieving, a developmental stage, gender differences, a lifestyle transition, an addiction—*do not dismiss it, because it is not the test, it is you!*

Accept the challenge, because an ambiguity could be the single most important part of your genetic code, the piece of the puzzle that must be resolved before you can move on with your life's work. Dig deep. Uncover what's hidden. Rediscover the real you.

* * * * * * * *

Where change begins.
Connecting with one's dreams
releases one's passions, energy, and excitement about life.
In leaders, such passion can arouse enthusiasm
in those they lead.
The key is uncovering your ideal self,
the person you would *like* to be, including
what you want in your life and work.

Daniel Goleman et al.,
Primal Leadership

PART

THE 16 MILLIONAIRE PERSONALITY CODES

THE 16 MILLIONAIRE PERSONALITIES

> It pays to be different.
> The millionaires say:
> How did we become
> wealthy in one generation?
> It has a lot to do with our
> selection of the right vocation . . .
> a minority of people in
> the general population can
> honestly say their present vocation
> allows them full use of
> their abilities and aptitudes.
> But we are different.
> We are of the millionaire mind.
> We were wise in
> selecting the ideal vocations
> given our abilities, aptitudes, and
> strong interests in
> becoming financial independent.
>
> Thomas Stanley,
> *The Millionaire Mind*

Yes, it does pay to be different—if you want to become a millionaire. But having a million bucks in the bank isn't enough. Nor is it enough if you're just working toward the goal—making good money, saving regularly, doing all the right things so that you're on track to accumulating a million bucks. You can be on track to a million bucks and *off course in your life*.

You want to financial freedom. And financial freedom—*becoming rich in fact and in spirit*—is a double-barreled formula. Yes, you're working on the tasks to help you accumulate a million bucks by retirement. But that's just part of the equation.

The more important part of the equation is your state of mind. You must be in sync with who you are—*who you really are*—what Thomas Stanley's *The Millionaire Mind* says is the key to becoming wealthy, selection of the right vocation.

Most Are Not Different—*Not* in Sync with the Code

Unfortunately, that seems to be an impossible task for most people! Why? Because only "a minority of people in the general population can honestly say their present vocation allows them full use of their abilities and aptitudes," says Thomas Stanley in *The Millionaire Mind*.

In other words, only a minority of Americans are in careers that match their personalities. Only a minority are in sync with the Millionaire's Code for their own their unique personality.

Most people are *not* different. Instead, they work hard to fit in, to be the same, to take the easy path, to do what other people want them to do. In the process, they melt into an indistinguishable gray mass of people who decide to blend in with everyone else—and never discover their true destiny.

Why does this happen to most people? Because, quite honestly, it is tough to be different—it's tough to be who you really are, to follow your unique calling!

It's a sad fact but true, most people are *not* in sync with their true personality. As a result they are underperforming, operating below their potential, like an Indy racer missing on one cylinder, and that's unfortunate.

THE TOUGHEST STEP: THE DECISION TO BE DIFFERENT, TO BE YOU

When you are out of sync with your Code, you are not only inefficient as a productive person, you are inefficient financially, earning less than you could in the right career. Worse yet, the happiness and fulfillment gauges on the dashboard of your racer register below optimum levels. You may even be running on empty, stressed out, burning out. Stanley puts it succinctly:

> As most millionaires report, stress is a direct result of devoting a lot of effort to a task that's not in line with one's abilities. It's more

difficult, more demanding mentally and physically, to work at a vocation that's unsuitable to your aptitude. It's even worse if you know you are a round peg assigned to working in square holes. Add the realization that your vocation has little or no probability of making you wealthy, and you are stressed out big-time.

In other words, the financial and emotional *costs of not being in sync* with your personality code are extremely high—much higher than the cost of striking out on your own, being different, and going down the "road less traveled."

Yet nobody has to spend a lifetime running into cul-du-sacs, blind alleys, and dead ends. You *can* be different. You *can* select the right career. But first you must know how different you are—*who you are*—and then make a conscious choice to run with the ball, giving it 100 percent.

You have to make a conscious decision to go against the crowd—*perhaps even against your parents, your family, your advisers, your mentors, possibly everybody in your community.* You have to make a conscious choice to do whatever is necessary to find out who you really are, your real personality type, and act on it.

General Format of the 16 Personality Profiles

Once you take the test and know your four-letter code—*own it*. Once you know the code, you're pointed in the right direction. Read the personality profile that best fits you. Each of the 16 profiles follows a similar format and includes the following basic sections:

- *Overview of personality.* Here are some of the key features that make this personality unique. What makes these individuals tick? What motivates them? Included are biographical sketches of celebrities and historical personalities who fit the profile.
- *Your Millionaire's Code.* Next, each profile has specific descriptions of each of the four letters in this unique personality code—Extravert or Introvert, Sensor or Intuitive, Thinking or Feeling, Judging or Perceiving.
- *Alternative career possibilities.* This section provides a list of opportunities that work for this personality type. Remember, however, that the name tag, the title, and the job description are unimportant. The key question is, how do *you* personally fit in a specific position—are you living out your true destiny?

- *Moneymaking tasks.* Finally, each of the 16 profiles includes some general comments on how this particular personality is likely to respond to the goal of wealth building.

Armed with your personal profile, you can choose the career that best fits *you,* not just your abilities and aptitudes. Not just a career that'll make the most money or satisfy your family. But a career that fills you personally with excitement and passion every day, a career that makes you want to get up in the morning thrilled to go to work, a career that says, "This is why I was born!"

To Be Really Different, Do What You Love, period

Warren Buffett, speaking to a group of students at the University of Nebraska, had this to say about the *only difference* between himself and the students:

> If there is any *difference* between you and me it may simply be that I get up every day and have a chance to do what I love to do, every day. If you learn anything from me, this is the best advice I can give you.

And that is indeed the best advice Buffett (or anyone) could give you: Pick a job, a career, a vocation that makes you get up every day with the opportunity to do what *you* love—*whatever that is*—where you feel as full of joy as Buffett: "Money is a by-product of something I like to do very much. Every day when I get to the office, so to speak, I do a little tap dance."

Get in Sync with the Code: Go for it!

Each of us is totally different, as unique as a snowflake, with totally different fingerprints, with totally unique DNA. Each of us is unlike every other human being in the world, with a vast array of unlimited opportunities ahead of us.

Once you know your code, each of the 16 personality types becomes a unique doorway to many specific new job opportunities for each individual. Knowing your secret code, knowing which of the 16 personalities is the real you, points you in right direction. Don't compromise. Go for it. Go in that direction with all your heart and soul. Fulfill your destiny. Grow rich in spirit and in fact.

* * * * * * * *

You are the only you that will ever exists in the entire history of the world. You are unique in the way you navigate life. Every individual has his or her own personality, attitude, and way of being present day to day. Every individual has his or her own personal way of being. Every person has their own personal best persona for generating results.

Your task is to discover and define your formula. . . .

If it works for you, based on results, then that's the test. . . .

Whatever it is, find your formula and live it with pride.

Phillip McGraw,
Life Strategies

FREELANCE CREATORS

FREELANCE CREATORS: SENSOR-PERCEIVERS (S-P)

- Entrepreneurs and Promoters (ESTP)
- Entertainers and Performers (ESFP)
- Master Craftsmen (ISTP)
- Directors and Composers (ISFP)

CHAPTER 17

ENTREPRENEURS AND PROMOTERS (ESTP)

DONALD TRUMP, RICHARD BRANSON, ROBERT KIYOSAKI

> I don't do it for money,
> I've got enough, much more than I'll ever need.
> I do it to do it.
> Deals are my art form.
> Other people paint beautifully
> on canvas and write wonderful poetry.
> I like making deals,
> preferably big deals.
> That's how I get my kicks.
>
> Donald Trump,
> *The Art of the Deal*

> My attention span is short. . . .
> Instead of being content when everything is going fine,
> I start
> getting impatient and irritable.
> So I look for more and more deals to do.
>
> Donald Trump,
> *Surviving at the Top*

Elvis was the King! Springsteen–the Boss! Sinatra–the Chairman of the Board! Jackie Gleason and Ali–the Greatest!

But in New York City (and probably the rest of the known world, if he has anything to do with it), it's Donald Trump–the king of opulent skyscrapers, the flamboyant boss of casinos, the chairman of the board of the Big Apple, the world's greatest ego—who is simply known as "The Donald," a testament to his grandiose and royal lifestyle.

Donald Trump leveraged his father's real estate business and went on to create a billion-dollar empire, complete with his own castle, the grandiose Trump Tower. He's had his own airline, the Trump Shuttle, a professional sports team in the 1980s, and gambling casinos loaded with exciting show-biz acts and beautiful women.

Yes, he's been overextended, close to bankruptcy, even written off in the early 1990s. But Trump trumped the critics. The comeback kid not only rode the bull market to recovery, he was toying with a run for the American presidency by the end of the decade—a consummate gesture of grandiosity.

I Want What I Want When I Want It, and I Want All of It

Donald Trump epitomizes the ESTP personality. They are like hyperactive kids in toyland. Every day's a party; they gotta try everything, have fun, play, celebrate, own everything, and they never want it to end. Yes, it starts early.

They are action-oriented risk takers who enjoy living a fast-paced lifestyle. They live for the moment, focusing on immediate results, and are impatient with complex theories, long explanations, and long-term planning. They have great people skills and are extremely loyal to their peers. They are friendly and flexible, and they'll bend the rules when the rules get in the way of realizing their personal goals and plans.

In a way, all four of the Freelance Creators are natural entrepreneurs. They prefer working for themselves, creating their own world. The ESTP is an entrepreneur's entrepreneur, a promoter's promoter.

As entrepreneur Robert Kiyosaki says in his *Rich Dad, Poor Dad* series, "The problem with having a job is that it gets in the way of getting rich." These Promoter personalities must be their own person. They need to create and leave their mark on the world. And, like the kid demanding a lot of attention, they'll make sure the world knows they are around, because they are great at the self-promotion game!

Millionaire's Code for Entrepreneurs
Extravert, Sensor, Thinker, Perceiver (ESTP)

Turn up the klieg lights. Start the band. Bring on showgirls. The promoter is about to take command of the center ring, the stage, the podium, the auditorium, the arena. And why not? They're *Extraverts*. Life is a popularity contest, and they can't stop until they win all the chips on the table. People energize them. They come alive in front of an audience. They love people, and they love being in the action, the spotlight, the center of attention.

Actually, *they* are the stage, supremely confident and trying hard to gain your confidence! They are magnetic, charismatic, majestic. Wherever they are, they are "on," working the room, waving at fans, shaking hands end-lessly, complimenting the hostess, soliciting votes, name-dropping, kissing babies, charming ladies and gents alike, amusing everyone with the latest jokes, witty stories, whatever fits the occasion, mesmerizing you with details about their latest trip—and staring intently as they explain why their latest project is a surefire winner.

Years ago, William Zeckendorf's daughter invited me to dinner. Her father was taking about 20 of us to Manhattan's China Town. Zeckendorf was The Donald of an earlier generation. The invitation was totally impromptu. We were ushered into limos and cabs. Like most promoters, he knew the "in" spots, the best restaurants, the waiters. Downtown, he moved with the military precision of a general and grace of a drum major, leading the entourage to his favorite restaurant. Later, he handed out money to people to buy souvenirs. Nothing was too good for those around them. Even with family and friends, he was a showman in com-mand of the stage—the world around him.

Nothing's Too Good for My Friends— and Me, Too!

These Promoters and Entrepreneurs are also *Sensors,* totally aware of the world around them—*right now, this minute.* They see and hear things oth-ers may miss. Specifics, the facts from the five senses, concrete informa-tion. They love to feel the finer things of life, a custom suit, a silk gown.

They have a keen sense of smell (extravagant fragrances, flowers, Cuban cigars) and a taste for elegant dinners and fine wines. And their internal radar automatically targets people who have the money, power, and prestige to support their favorite projects and new business opportu-nities.

People Are an Investment: What Do I Get in Return?

Thinkers, as you will recall, make decisions objectively. Oh, feelings are important in a self-centered way: They enjoy the praise, cheers, and adula-tion of starry-eyed supporters, fans, and friends showering them with warm feelings. All of that helps them know they're in control and important.

And, of course, the feelings of others come into play when they are trying to get you to agree to a project.

In the final analysis, however, relationships are an investment, and they expect a return. Underneath all the charm, the romance, and the laughter is a cold, calculating, Machiavellian mind that wants something, and these individuals often bend the rules, manipulate your feelings, and tell a few white lies to make sure they get what they want.

Create a Crisis, Rescue the Maiden, You're a hero!

The Millionaire's Code for Promoters and Entrepreneurs also includes the *Perceiver* function. They may come prepared with knockout legal briefs, spellbinding sales pitches, convincing negotiating strategies, and grand master plans, but what distinguishes them is the ability to think spontaneously on their feet and to stay flexible, keeping their options open and adapting quickly as new facts arise.

They are consummate risk takers who love living on the edge. Surprises actually turn them on, challenging them to peak performance, where they can prove, under pressure, that they really are a winner.

They often have plans for the future and projects that can take a long time to complete—for example, a large shopping mall—but what energizes them most is an unplanned moment that catches them by surprise in the present. Suddenly they can play to their strengths and be the hero in a crisis or emergency, coming in at the last minute with several ingenious solutions and the courage to get into action and bull their way across the goal line—that's what turns them on and makes them feel alive.

Forget Swinging for Singles— They're Home-Run Hitters!

In *Eight $teps to $even Figures,* Charles Carlson's fourth action step is, "Swing for singles . . . you'll strike out fewer times and hit some home runs in the process."

Sorry, but that's not the Promoter's way, not the path of the entrepreneur. They're risk takers and rule breakers. Yes, they lack the patience, discipline, and long-range perspective to start saving early, putting aside money each month so it can compound to a million bucks over 40 years or so. But it's more than that.

They believe in themselves. They are superconfident of their ideas, projects, and businesses. They know they can earn a higher return by investing in themselves, in "Me, Inc." Like Babe Ruth and Barry Bonds, they want to hit a home run. Swinging for singles is just not very exciting.

Guardians may be content with singles—doing the same job for 40 years, working for the same company, building a nest egg in 401(k)s and IRAs. But Entrepreneurs are risk takers whose gut tells them to put everything on the line. Celine Dion's promoter-husband saw the singer's extraordinary talent when she was just a 14-year-old kid and took out a second mortgage on his home to promote her career.

Although it's against every principle of sound personal finance, excessive credit card debt is often the only credit available to entrepreneurs. One producer I worked with was so broke when he finished shooting his low-budget action film that he was able to borrow only enough money for a one-way ticket from New York to Hollywood to screen the film for the studios. But he believed so much in what he had "in the can" that it was worth the gamble. He was on the Coast just a few days before making a deal. A limo took him to the airport and the studio flew him home first-class—with a $10 million advance!

Making Money and Careers:
The "Right Stuff" for a Promoter

There are Promoters and Entrepreneurs in many areas. Remember, we're dealing with a personality type, not a rigid job description for an impersonal corporation. There are a lot of places you probably won't find them, or if you do, they won't be happy campers. For example, routine work with numbers, like accounting, would drive them crazy. Any kind of counseling that involves intense personal feelings is out of the question.

And a career holed up in a lab as a research scientist would be a waste of talent for someone with the natural abilities of a promoter. . . . Well, wait a minute, maybe not! The astronomer Carl Sagan comes to mind.

Remember Sagan's incredibly thought-provoking books, *Cosmos, Comet, Broca's Brain,* and *Pale Blue Dot: A Vision of the Human Future in Space,* to mention a few. Or his *Nova* series on astronomy for PBS. Or his adventure novel turned into the movie, *Contact,* with Jodie Foster as a skeptical scientist exploring the meaning of human existence through contact with extraterrestrial life. Sagan was a promoter—*promoting science.*

Before you eliminate possibilities, remember this brilliant scientist and philosopher. Any field can be a launching pad for the promoter. John Walsh, producer of *America's Most Wanted,* was a hotel manager who became one of America's most powerful crime fighters after his young son was brutally murdered—a Promoter for justice.

Home-Run Hitters Play Ball in Many Fields

There are many career paths taken by men and women driven by the entrepreneurial spirit. And as might be expected, they often wind up in high-profile positions that become darlings of the press and media, which in turn gives them many opportunities to promote their projects, their clients, their causes—*and themselves:*

- *Deal makers of all kinds*
- *Defense lawyers*
- *Motivational speakers*
- *Fashion leaders*
- *Building contractors*
- *Wholesale distributors*
- *Coaches and fitness trainers*
- *Stockbrokers*
- *Personal financial planners*
- *Small business owners*

Although tragic events or the slow passage of time may be necessary before the real you emerges after perhaps stumbling earlier in life, the energy of an entrepreneur is often quite visible at an early age.

DYSLEXIC TEENAGER BECOMES BILLIONAIRE PROMOTER

Richard Branson, the flamboyant billionaire founder of the Virgin empire (music, airlines, cola, you name it, his Virgin brand includes 150 enterprises) was an embarrassed dyslexic kid who did poorly on standard IQ tests and had trouble with spelling—yet not only did he overcome his so-called handicap, his first entrepreneurial venture was with words!

At age 17, while at boarding school, Branson published an innovative newspaper, *Student.* Innovative because it was for students and linked together students from many schools. It was a huge commercial success. He successfully solicited corporate advertisers and filled the newspaper with articles written by rock music stars, intellectuals, movie celebrities, and ministers of the British Parliament. The headmaster of his boarding school wrote: "Congratulations, Branson. I predict that you will either go to prison or become a millionaire." Not bad for a dyslexic teenager.

This kind of success story goes against everything preached by the conservative "diversify and minimize your risks" Wall Street community and all those "save a hundred bucks a month for 40 years and you'll retire a millionaire" financial planners.

There's an incredible lesson here: *You gotta be who you gotta be, the real you!* In spite of his so-called handicap, dyslexia, or maybe because of it, Branson was able to tap into the incredible energy locked in his genetic code, become a billionaire, and have a helluva lotta fun doing it (he still is!).

Branson's grandmother wrote, "You've got one go in life, so make the most of it!" And he has, in grand style. Her words go right to the heart of his conviction that you've got to make it on your own—exactly what you'd expect from one the world's most exciting Promoters and Entrepreneurs.

THE ENTREPRENEUR'S SECRET: THE POWER OF LEVERAGE

Yes, Entrepreneurs and Promoters are a breed apart. They don't think like the rest of the world. But then, that's the beauty of personality typing—we are all a breed apart! In the eyes of most conservative folks, these adventurous souls spend too much, borrow too much, and take too many risks. If the rest of us did that, we'd likely die poor. But they aren't like others. It's in their blood, and they're making the most of the one life they have, every day.

Robert Kiyosaki is another successful Entrepreneur and gifted self-promoter through his *Rich Dad, Poor Dad* book series. In *Retire Young, Retire Rich,* he says, "The reason less than 5 percent of all Americans are rich is because only 5 percent know how to use the power of leverage." The rest are afraid of the risks of leverage. "Leverage simply means the ability to do more with less," like borrowing a million bucks to build a small retail business or apartment complex.

The Entrepreneur sees the average American as being stuck in a mindset of working 40 hours a week for a modest salary. For 40 years. Saving modest amounts. Investing in mutual funds for a modest 10 percent return. If you're lucky, Wall Street tells them, the money will compound to $1 million after decades of hard labor.

If this is the case, you're *not* thinking like the rich, warns Kiyosaki: "People who work hard have limited leverage. If you're working hard physically and not getting ahead financially, then you're probably somebody else's leverage." You're an employee making "them" rich. Or an active investor making your broker rich.

Worse yet, says Kiyosaki, even if your money is in long-term retirement accounts like IRAs and 401(k)s, "then others are using your money as their leverage." They'll retire young and rich. But not you. Or they won't retire, they'll just keep having fun getting richer and richer—leveraging on your hard labor for decades.

A Million Bucks Isn't "Rich" to an Entrepreneur

Let's go deeper into the mind of the Entrepreneur. They believe the vast majority of Americans are helping *someone else get rich,* working their butts off, praying they can at least retire someday and live modestly, if they're lucky. The Entrepreneur can't live that way.

A million bucks may seem modestly comfortable, but it isn't "rich" by the standards of Entrepreneurs like Kiyosaki. They know that most investors aren't rich, and most won't retire young.

What makes you rich? It's not just the money, says Kiyosaki, it's a state of mind. It's not even retiring financially secure with a million bucks. First you must "find the leverage that works best for you," the kind of leverage "you can use to acquire and create assets to allow you to get ahead financially faster."

That's the secret goal of the Entrepreneur—to create, acquire, and *own assets* using leverage—not to work for a salary. It also means that Entrepreneurs aren't thinking about IRAs and 401(k)s, company pension plans, and mutual funds, because they aren't working for "the man!" As Kiyosaki's rich dad put it, "The problem with having a job is that it gets in the way of getting rich." You've got to make it on your own!

TWO STAGES: FIRST, RETIRE EARLY, THEN GET REALLY RICH

The entrepreneur's strategy worked in two stages for Kiyosaki: First, he had enough assets to become financially independent in his late forties. With passive assets generating about $100,000 a year, he retired young. But he wasn't rich at this point, merely free.

Second stage: "You retire young in order to get rich," by leveraging yourself. "*Forbes* magazine defines rich as $1 million or more a year in income," says Kiyosaki. "We were not yet rich when we retired. . . . After retiring, our plan was to spend time investing and building businesses." Today, he says he fits the *Forbes* definition.

That's the way the entrepreneur thinks: First you retire young and financially free. Then you have time to get rich. Obviously, this is not a strategy for employees of Corporate America. There's no investing in long-term retirement plans. And it's not about mutual funds, which, by the way, Kiyosaki dismisses—no leverage.

Instead, Kiyosaki's *Rich Dad, Poor Dad* books teach people how to create assets, mainly businesses and real estate. In *Retire Young, Retire Rich,* he focuses on his philosophy of leveraging three things: Your mind, your ideas, and your actions—to create "assets that work hard so you don't have to."

ENTREPRENEUR'S ROAD MAP: HIGH RISKS, LONG BETS, BIG PAYOFFS

Should you follow Kiyosaki's strategies? Not unless your millionaire's code is ESTP—then maybe you should quit your job, become an entrepreneur, and start creating businesses, developing real estate, or however you choose to create "assets that work hard so you don't have to."

The fact is, most people aren't psychologically cut out to live this way. They won't, or can't, do what it takes to become rich. In fact, they are quite content working for a corporation or the government. Most of these people have a different life path. They probably won't even read Kiyosaki's books.

And the chances are, when it comes to all the conventional rules of planning, saving, investing, and spending money, you can be sure that the Entrepreneur will ignore all of them—or will rely on a slew of tax accountants and attorneys to help minimize their impact.

No wonder Thomas Stanley, one of the authors of *The Millionaire Next Door,* told *Newsweek:* "I don't think the government loves these people." Why? Because they pay only 2 percent in taxes, compared to 12 percent paid by the average American, he said.

The "secret is to put money somewhere that it will grow without your having to pay taxes on it immediately. It could be in real estate. It could be in the stock market. Or it could be in your own business." That's the same point Kiyosaki was making.

Entrepreneurs and Promoters understand all this instinctively. The other personality types may envy them, but successful Entrepreneurs will always travel their own road—and enjoy the journey their own unique way.

* * * * * * * *

It is not the critic who counts, not the man who points out how the strong
man stumbled, or where the doer of deeds could have done better.
The credit belongs to the man who is actually in the arena; whose face is
marred by the dust and sweat and blood; who strives valiantly; who errs
and comes short again and again; who knows the great enthusiasms, the
great devotions and spends himself in a worthy course;
who, at the best, knows in the end the triumph of high achievement, and
who, at worst, if he fails, at least fails while daring greatly; so that his
place shall never be with those cold and timid souls who know neither
victory or defeat.

Teddy Roosevelt

CHAPTER 18

ENTERTAINERS AND PERFORMERS (ESFP)

FRED ASTAIRE, TOM HANKS, BRUCE SPRINGSTEEN

> I'm not a
> planning-type of guy.
> You can't count on
> nothing in this life.
> I never have expectations
> when I get
> involved in things.
> That way,
> I never have
> disappointments.
>
> Bruce Springsteen,
> *Time* magazine

Who can ever forget Fred Astaire dancing in the dark with Ginger Rogers—or dancing with the beautiful Cyd Charisse in Vincente Minelli's 1951 MGM musical comedy, *The Band Wagon*, singing "That's Entertainment."

And *that* is the perfect theme song of this engaging personality type. *They are Entertainers!* They love to make us laugh and make us cry, gasp and swoon, cheer and fear. They have to. It's in their genes—*they're Entertainers!*

Lights, camera, action! Klieg lights! The show must go on. Tony Bennett singing with his friends, Ray Charles, Sheryl Crow, Billy Joel, Stevie Wonder, Bonnie Raitt, and B. B. King! Celine, Gloria, and Mariah together on stage. The Three Tenors. The Dixie Chicks. *That's entertainment.*

How about comedy routines by Chris Rock, Robin Williams, and Whoopi Goldberg. Lucy, Carol, and Jerry Seinfeld? Billy Crystal wheeled into the Oscars as Hannibal Lecter. *That's entertainment!*

Do you remember Jimmy Stewart in *It's a Wonderful Life?* Or Jim Carrey in *How the Grinch Stole Christmas?* Clint in *Dirty Harry?* James Bond? Captain Kirk? Darth Vader? Harry Potter? Entertainers become the characters.

We see them everywhere: Andy Rooney on *60 Minutes!* Oprah. Regis. Bruce. Cher. Prince. Tina. Rush. Dr. Laura. Julia Childs. Jay Leno. Ebert and Roeper. Christy Brinkley. Chuck Norris, martial artist. Vegas showmen Siegfried and Roy and those wonderful rare white tigers. David Copperfield's magically vanishing elephants. Cirque du Soleil acrobats. Steve, the Crocodile Hunter. Hulk Hogan and Smack Down. Evel Knievel, the daredevil motorcyclist. *Now that's entertainment!*

Let Me Entertain You "with the Song in My Heart"

For every person in the limelight there are thousands of creative talents offstage, in the wings—understudies waiting for the big break, just doing what comes naturally, making people laugh, cry and sigh, ooh and aah. The world is blessed with many less visible but nonetheless gifted entertainers who entertain us: Actors in community theaters, nightclub trios and cabaret singers, street jugglers and guitar players, maybe even a best friend.

Of course, you can't forget those "almost normal" jobs that often attract fabulously entertaining personalities. Maybe a schoolteacher who made history fun. A motivational speaker at a recent corporate seminar. A museum tour guide telling you about some odd quirk of a seventeenth-century baroness. The salesclerk whose theatrical style influenced you to buy something you didn't need. The chef with colorful culinary capers. A real estate agent with endless charm. The maître d' with flair. People who love entertaining people.

They are Entertainers. Deep in their hearts, encoded on their souls, every one of them has a story, a joke, an impersonation, a pep talk, or a song. The lyrics are the same for every one of them: "Let me entertain you!"

SHY PEOPLE NEEDING LOTS OF ATTENTION AND APPLAUSE

Actors, shy? Tom Hanks was painfully shy as a kid! That's right, the poster boy for the ESFP entertainer, performer, presenter personality type had few friends as a kid after his parents broke up. His dad was a chef who had to move often for jobs, so he and his two older brothers rarely stayed in one place long enough to make friends, although, as with many other Entertainers, the signs were there. Hanks was the class clown, and, left to his own devices, he cultivated an active imagination.

His nervous energies found expression in student productions. But it wasn't until later, in college, while watching a performance of Eugene O'Neill's *The Iceman Cometh,* that he knew he was a Performer at heart and had to become a working actor—in a business where more than 90 percent make less than $5,000 a year.

From his first real part, in Shakespeare's *The Taming of The Shrew* in 1977, until 1993 when he did *Sleepless in Seattle,* he struggled, a common story: Endless auditions, a slasher film, *He Knows You're Alone,* guest spots on *Taxi, The Love Boat, Family Ties,* and *Happy Days,* a short-run television series *Bosom Buddies,* small parts in B movies like *The Money Pit* and *Bachelor Party.*

There were also solid showcase films, like *Splash* with Darryl Hannah in 1984, and *Big* in 1988, where he played a lovable kid trapped in a man's body, followed by bombs like *Bonfire of the Vanities* and *Joe versus the Volcano* that could have killed many an actor's career. But he was in sync with his code—there was no alternative for him. He couldn't *not* entertain!

Hanks hit his stride as an entertainer after 1993: Along with *Sleepless,* he won an Academy Award the same year for *Philadelphia,* brilliantly portraying a gay attorney in search of justice and dignity while dying of AIDS. Then he received a second Oscar for his role in *Forrest Gump,* playing an Alabama simpleton who becomes a war hero. Since then, he's had one memorable role after another in a wide variety of films: *Apollo 13, You've Got Mail, The Green Mile, Castaway, Road to Perdition,* topped by a prestigious AFI Lifetime Achievement Award.

Millionaire's Code for Entertainers
Extravert, Sensor, Feeling,
Perceiver (ESFP)

Entertainers need an audience to show off their creativity. They are the ultimate *Extraverts,* coming alive onstage when they can plug into the energy of their fans. Entertainers and Performers magically transform themselves right before the audience's eyes. In an odd psychological sense, the real identity of the Extravert comes alive only when that magical connection with the audience brings it to life, as with the shy Tom Hanks.

You almost feel that there's something missing in their personality, a source of energy Entertainers need to plug into, that can only be supplied "out there," by fans, spectators, or an admiring crowd and that began with adoring parents, family, and friends. Later, these needs were supplied by school or college drama, a demanding drama coach, maybe some commercials, guest stops, and appearances as extras, stand-ins, community theater actors. For them, even rejection is better than having no audience.

Note that while Entertainers (ESFP) and their siblings, Entrepreneurs (ESTP), are both Extraverts, they need people for quite different reasons. Yes, Entrepreneurs also get their energy from being around people and talking a lot, but there is a decidedly selfish motive in how they use people to achieve their personal goals, such as investors for a project. On the other hand, Entertainers genuinely want people to get something for themselves—an emotional experience of joy, laughter, tears, or pleasure. Yes, you can say the Entertainer is selfish because the audience's energy turns them on, but there is a symbiotic relationship, a balance, a dance, a love affair between Performer and fans.

Live for the Laughs today, N-O-W— No Other Way

Entertainers are *Sensors*—exciting, high-energy, here-and-now people who love to live spontaneously. There's no "let's think about," no speculating, no long-range planning, no "tomorrow's another day." Today's the day!

They have little interest in theories, research, and statistics, relying instead on their gut instincts and innate common sense. They see it, feel it, hear it, touch it, smell it—and bingo, the heat triggers an explosion! Time to react. Go for it. Have fun. Get excited, laugh, dream, sing, kiss, fall in love. Life is today, now, in the moment, grab it before it vanishes in the mist and things settle back into dullness.

Actually, real Entertainers are never content waiting for opportunities to come floating casually by. They aggressively chase them, create them. As Anthony Quinn says in *Zorba the Greek:* "To be alive is to undo your belt and look for trouble." Whether Entertainers are waiting on tables to pay the bills between gigs or waiting for the envelope to be opened at the Golden Globe, Oscar, or Emmy ceremonies, they are highly charged personalities, taking in new information and expecting an exciting surprise right around the next corner, any minute.

Entertainers are forever chasing rainbows, searching for new experiences, new ways of coming alive, constantly making their own opportunities and breaks—through auditions, scenes, tryouts, screenings, improvisations, impromptu performances, romances—you name it, they're hustling it. Even as they thrive on new experiences for themselves, they also have a strong need to help people. By entertaining others and helping them enjoy life, they're also having fun and enjoying their own lives to the max.

Some Enchanted Evening, You May See a Stranger . . .

While the Entrepreneur (ESTP) is cold, calculating, and objective, an Entertainer's (ESFP) decisions are based totally on *Feelings*. Performers and Entertainers make decisions and get into action based on their emotions—they trust their immediate gut instincts about situations and people. For them, life is in session, to be experienced to the max, today, right now!

Somebody else's cold, hard facts may be pushed aside because the Performer feels the right thing to do means going a different way, like rock millionaire Bono of U2 traveling to Africa with U.S. Secretary of the Treasury Paul O'Neill, pushing for more aid. Or Entertainers may act on impulse, flippantly convincing themselves that "the devil made me do it, I couldn't help myself."

The fact is, Entertainers *can't* help themselves when it comes to people. In a real sense, their identity is tied to the reactions of others. Their self-confidence and sense of self-worth rise and fall on whether they receive a standing ovation or boos from an audience. Not just elation or depression, but existence or nonexistence. They are romantics, falling in love at the drop of a hat or in a instant—on an enchanted evening when they see a stranger across a crowded room.

Their love of people has no bounds, and they love showing it. Not just audiences. Family, friends, lovers, other pros in showbiz. We've seen it in many ways: The $10 million diamond Richard Burton gave Liz Taylor. The fully loaded BMW a rock star gives to his gopher assistant just because he likes the kid. Heartthrob Ben Affleck's expensive gifts to music diva Jennifer Lopez early in their dating. And Frank Sinatra was well known for his behind-the-scenes gifts to fellow Performers in need. Entertainers feel deeply for people.

Live for Today: Tomorrow Will Take Care of Itself

Yes, it seems romantic. Life on the road. The band's touring bus. The circus traveling from town to town. Short runs at this and that community theater. Breaking down and setting up for huge rock concerts in one arena after another. Not knowing what's ahead, which film project might draw the attention of some whimsical studio chief—and even then, not knowing whether this project will be the big one that'll finally make you a star (forget retirement, that's too far away, you gotta hit it big first).

This is no way for solid-citizen Guardian personalities to live, but this nomadic life fits the Entertainer. The *Perceiver* element encoded in the personality of Entertainers tells them to keep their options open, to hold off making commitments until the last minute.

They hate schedules, structure, organization. It's easy to understand why so many great Performers avoid the structure and phony formalities of Hollywood and prefer, like Robert Redford, to roam around on a big ranch in Wyoming or, like Clint Eastwood, to live in the quaint town of Carmel, California.

While working with Morgan Stanley in New York, I took acting lessons at Strasberg Institute and directed a short film in a TV Academy workshop. Though limited, these experiences gave me a sense of how important improvising is in an actor's training. It helps you get into a character and out of yourself. It helps you get in touch with your emotional core and tap into your life experiences. Most of all, improvisation teaches you to think on your feet, in the moment. For great Entertainers, that seems to come naturally, like a two-hour Robin Williams monologue or Jay Leno's routine on the *Tonight Show*. Others need to hone the skill.

WAITING FOR THE CREATIVE SPARK—MEANWHILE, LET'S PARTY

The *Perceiver* traits in the Millionaire's Code also make Entertainers natural procrastinators. They are waiting for the right moment, new information, a creative spark that ignites their energy. Or for a better offer to come along. Or they're so much into the moment, they just don't have time for the mundane things of life like planning for retirement (besides, they'll never exit the scene).

They wind up putting off decisions till the last minute, or they let agents or spouses make the decisions. This suits them, because all you have is right now! Live life to the fullest. When the chips are down and you *have* to make a decision, you will. Meanwhile, the Entertainer is like a kid having fun, without a care in the world, enjoying the ride, the fast cars, the pranks, coffeehouses, affairs, vacations, trips, lunches—whatever grabs their attention at the moment.

The Entertainer's way of life won't work for most people, but it sure does for Entertainers. After all, it's in their genetic code, their blood, their nature. It's where their creative genius comes from. While the rest of us may shake our heads, thinking they're kids who never grew up, or we may secretly envy their "live for today, and tomorrow will take care of itself" lifestyle, the great Entertainers trust this process. They know that their creative inspirations come from the energy of the moment.

IT'S NEVER TOO LATE TO CATCH A RISING STAR

Entertainers and Performers may have the genetic code, yet never make it to Broadway, the Silver Screen, or the television set. Although child actors like Drew Barrymore and Haley Joel Osmond are well known, some Performers take other paths before discovering their true calling.

Chuck Norris, a world champion martial artist, later became an entrepreneur businessman with a successful chain of martial arts studios. When he was in his mid-30s, actor Steve McQueen (a student of Chuck's at the time) asked him why he didn't become an actor? Norris expressed interest but doubted he'd make it.

In *The Secret Power Within,* Norris notes, McQueen responded, "Remember that philosophy of yours that you always stressed to students: Set goals, visualize the results of those goals, and then be determined to succeed by overcoming any obstacles in the way. You've been preaching this to me for two years, and now you're saying there's something you can't do?"

Since then, Norris has had an exciting career, with more than 25 films to his credit—for example, *Delta Force* and *Missing in Action*—in addition to his Black Belt championships and the long-running television series, *Walker, Texas Ranger.* Norris is proof that every fighter who steps in the ring is an Entertainer at heart.

Careers for Stars Off-Broadway and on Main Street

As in virtually every profession, every business, and every personality type, there are many career paths. Many Entertainers and Performers find their destiny away from Broadway, Hollywood, and concert arenas.

Even if these types are working in the mail room, running errands, and copying endless documents, they're probably dramatically whistling, telling jokes and stories, humming songs. Hollywood and New York City are filled with waiters and waitresses paying their dues while between gigs or taking bit parts and adding a little bit more to their bio.

However, many Entertainers and Performers enjoyed the spotlight in high school plays, read a few stories about the constant struggle and high

risks of making it in showbiz—Broadway, Hollywood, the record industry—and decided it wasn't quite what God had in store for them in this
lifetime. Their unique genetic code guided them down a different path.

Whatever their paths, one thing's for certain: There's a song in the
hearts of these people that says, "Let me entertain you!" Whatever career
these special, gifted people pick, they must entertain people. These folks
want to enjoy the experience of living life to the max. Life should be
exciting. Think about the fabulous opportunities to entertain in so many
professions, businesses, and careers.

ENTERTAINERS, PERFORMERS, AND MILLIONAIRES NEXT DOOR

For example, there was a senior partner at Morgan Stanley, the investment banking firm I worked for years ago, whose responsibilities covered
public relations, schmoozing clients, and handling the press. He had the
kind of personality that always had the right joke at hand to break the ice
when conflicts heated, and he knew when and how to defuse any situation.

There are so many careers for Entertainers and Performers far off the
beaten paths to Broadway and Hollywood, careers that give them an
opportunity to help people, express their creative talents, and have fun
doing it. Here are some examples:

- *Primary-school teachers*
- *Sales agents of all kinds*
- *Flower shop owners*
- *Travel agents and tour guides*
- *Special events' planners (weddings, birthdays, etc.)*
- *Restaurant hosts and hostesses*
- *Hairstylists*
- *Receptionists in business establishments*
- *Real estate brokers*
- *Corporate trainers*
- *Airline flight attendants*
- *Advertising account managers*
- *Motivational speakers*
- *Sports announcers and coaches*

My friend, Calvin Holt, started as a professional dancer in New York
City. When he quit dancing, instead of staying in showbiz and becoming
a dance teacher, he opened the popular Serendipity restaurant in Manhattan. Later, he had a small private group of us in his Soho loft to enjoy

his dance meditation group, but his greatest pleasure was hosting his restaurant. You could feel the energy rise when he appeared. He was onstage. The lights came on. He entertained patrons and waiters alike, laughing, joking, telling stories—and they loved it.

WAITING FOR A BIG BREAK: UNDERSTUDIES IN THE WINGS

Many others are happy and satisfied staying in showbiz in less prominent roles: doing commercials, voice-overs, regional radio and television, working behind the camera on film and television crews or behind the scenes in theater. Look closely at the credits of the next big-screen movie you see. For every Entertainer on-screen, there may be 50 or more costume, set, and property designers, stuntpeople, sound and camera operators, and more. If you can't get star billing, at least you can be in and around the excitement of the entertainment business. After all, they do give Oscars, Emmys, and Tonys to the people in the wings, too.

Once an Entertainer, always an Entertainer. It's in the blood, and it better be honored, because it'll never really go away. The Entertainer personality comes out no matter what career they pick. They need to perform. Calvin Holt found that living life to the fullest meant entertaining patrons in his restaurant.

After 17 Long Years, an Overnight Sensation!

How do Entertainer types become millionaires? Almost by accident. Entrepreneurial and Promoter personalities may join the entertainment business to get rich and enjoy a rather glamorous lifestyle, but that's not the main goal in life of Performer and Entertainer personalities.

Entertainers and Performers are driven by something far deeper and infinitely more powerful than the lure of money. Why else would they buck the great odds against becoming a working actor, let alone a star? Yet many an actor will tell you they love it so much they'd work for nothing, just so they can perform, and many practically do work for nothing.

Some make it as kids, like Michael Jackson. But most struggle for a long time. Harrison Ford was a carpenter for years before Lucas cast him in *Star Wars.* When my friend, Dan Travanti, won the role of Captain Furillo in *Hill Street Blues,* he laughed about how he had finally become "an overnight success, after 17 long years." Yes, Travanti, Hanks, and thousands of other extremely creative performers have a powerful inner need to entertain people—and they prove it by paying their dues for many, many years.

FAME AND FORTUNE? OR JUST A CHANCE TO BE WORKING?

Obviously, the fact that a large majority of Screen Actors Guild members don't even make enough money in the business to qualify for insurance benefits proves how committed they are to their life's mission.

Most television contracts are for seven years, although most series rarely last that long. Most end the first season, or after the first few episodes. Many never get past a pilot. Most film contracts are for as long as a film takes, maybe a week's work, maybe a few months' shooting. Broadway is littered with short runs. Music deals are hit-and-miss.

Bruce Springsteen was living in a small apartment on Manhattan's East Side, taking home $350 a week, when America's new Rock Sensation—the "Kid From New Jersey"—first hit it big with his album, *Born to Run,* in 1975. As with most entertainers, money didn't mean much more after the big break than before: *Music* was the motivation. Money gave him more freedom, but creating music was the reason *he* was "born to run," why all Performers are born.

Wannabe Superstars and Overnight Multimillionaires

Savings and investing? Entertainers and Performers are in a cyclical, feast-or-famine, project-oriented business, much like Entrepreneurs and Promoters. Different motivations, yet equally unpredictable. Often, long quiet periods are followed by big chunks of cash for 80-hour weeks for months on end. Planning is almost impossible in this highly uncertain environment, and it's often deferred.

> *Before the big break.* Living on the edge means tight spending budgets while Entertainers are paying their dues. There are few 401(k) plans. There's little money left for much more than an IRA, and that's likely to be competing with essentials such as food, gas, and acting classes. However, waiting 17 years before a big hit to start saving can be dangerous. If it never happens, the Entertainer is then forced to run a handicap race later in life.

> *After the big break.* Entertainers and Performers would have it no other way. When it comes to money, they do have one thing in common with Entrepreneurs (ESTP)—they're swinging for the fences, trying to hit home runs, and trust me, *they are not going to change,* not the next Tom Hanks. In fact, rejection and failure spur them on to try harder than ever, convinced that it's only a matter of time before their uniquely creative talent is discovered.

Before the money starts really flowing, *and after,* most Entertainers could use a rock-solid experienced financial adviser they trust absolutely to handle their money, control expenses, encourage savings, and, at minimum, invest in an IRA. *Making money is not their prime focus in life, performing is.*

Often, a good manager can serve as a money mentor for Entertainers, or better yet, a professional financial planner to advise them on investments and tax matters. For example, they might choose a wholly owned loan-out corporation to take in all their contractual income (which often arrives unevenly, in chunks), pay the Entertainer a salary, and retain the rest in the corporation to take care of taxes, retirement savings, and investments. This helps to even out erratic bursts of income.

If you have the creative genes of an Entertainer, you'll have it no other way. As Springsteen once put it, "This music is forever for me. It's the stage thing, that rush moment that you live for. It never lasts, but that's what you live for." Of course, future royalties also come in handy if you're a rock star with a hit record, or a television star with a series in reruns, or a film action hero negotiating a deal for the sequel to one of last year's blockbusters.

* * * * * * * *

That's the way I have always lived,
for the laughs—today.
N-O-W.
No **O**ther **W**ay.

Mickey Rooney

MASTER CRAFTSMEN (ISTP)

CLINT EASTWOOD, TOM CRUISE, MICHAEL JORDAN

> The champion's true edge exists solely in the mind and over
> the years I have observed three attitudinal characteristics which
> are common to
> every superstar I have ever known. . . .
> First is the champion's profound sense of dissatisfaction with
> their own accomplishments.
> They use any success, any victory,
> as a spur to greater ambition. . . .
> Second is an ability to peak their performance,
> to get themselves up for
> major tournaments and events. . . .
> Finally it is their ability to put their opponent away. This is
> referred to as "the killer instinct." . . .
> In the champion's mind he is never ahead.
>
> Mark McCormack,
> *What They Don't Teach You
> at Harvard Business School*

Americans love heroes. These rugged individuals love action, pushing themselves to their limits, taking great risks, often in the face of great danger. Why? Because it's the right thing to do, that's why. More important, because it proves they are alive.

Moreover, it proves they are alive and operating to the best of their abilities to the *only* person that really counts—the one in the mirror. It's an inner yardstick. Master Craftsmen are the only ones who can measure their success or failure; no outside can do that. Only them.

They're always pushing the envelope, upping the ante for yet another personal best, another peak experience; they know can always do better, and they never stop trying.

Adventurers Reliving the Spirit of the American Frontier

You'll see the spirit of the Master Craftsman in many areas of American life: as athletes, especially in extreme sports like skydiving and base jumping, as members of the military's Special Forces commands, as fighter pilots, rodeo cowboys, and race car drivers. Closer to home, you'll see this spirit in police officers, firefighters, surgeons, steelworkers, machinery operators and construction tradespeople.

Even if it's not expressed in their chosen career, it is in their attitude, an attitude described by Keirsey: "The carpenter gets to work a little late because the surf is up or the fish are biting; the surgeon rides his motorcycle to the hospital; the athlete, actor or musician races cars or learns to fly."

They hate routine and love living on the edge, breaking the rules, bristling at having to live by society's rules or the rules of any authorities, which can try the patience of an employer. The only rules they consider sacred are their own rules: To thine own self be true.

Careers: Master Craftsmen and Their Power Tools

The Master Craftsman is like Clint Eastwood, the "man with no name," the gunslinger with few words and a quick draw in the spaghetti Westerns. Behind the strong, silent facade, however, is enormous power, where actions speak louder than words, quite the opposite of the Entertainers and Performer (ESFP), whose power comes from words.

In fact, one of the single most distinguishing characteristics of Master Craftsmen is the unique bond they forge between themselves and their source of source of power, usually some special tool, instrument, or piece of equipment that helps them leverage and magnify their personal power. As they develop this union with the tools of their particular trade, they become masters of these power tools in many careers:

- *Aircraft and boats:* Pilots, sailors, astronauts
- *Vehicles:* Race car drivers, heavy equipment operators

- *Tools and equipment:* Surgeons, sculptors, jewelers
- *Machinery:* Tradespeople, custom designers, manufacturers
- *Weapons:* Military, police, detectives, hunters
- *Athletes:* Individual and team sports, martial artists

The baseball bat. Golf club. Scalpel. Knives. Chisels. Hammers. Motorcycles. Sniper rifles. Fighter jets. Aircraft carriers. The power of police officers is intimately linked to their weapons. Every single one of these "tools" is a source of power that expands and leverages the power of the Master Craftsmen, even including athletes' bodies and teammates as extensions of their individual power.

At one level, the Master Craftsman is a kid having fun with his or her toys. At a much deeper level, there is a mythic or mystical connection bonding the craft and the craftsman, a modern reincarnation of ancient traditions—as in the East, where the sword was the soul of the Samurai warrior, and in the West, where the sword was the power and protector in the quest for the Holy Grail. In this way, the craft and the Craftsman become one with the universal Craftsman in a sacred mission. Such is the Way of the Master Craftsman.

Prove That You Are Alive: Be All You Can Be!

Master Craftsmen have become cultural icons, part of our history, symbols of our nation's heritage of freedom—larger-than-life pioneers and adventurers. America's action heroes regularly dramatize this spirit: John Wayne in *The Searchers,* Clint Eastwood in *Dirty Harry* and *The Good, the Bad & the Ugly,* Sylvester Stallone in *Rambo,* and Chuck Norris in *Missing in Action,* a hero going behind enemy lines at great risk to rescue prisoners of war.

These guys live for the action, and they really love having it delivered in surprise packages. That's how they know they are alive, by responding successfully to the unexpected. The military knows how to tap into this American spirit. New young blood is recruited with the challenge to "Be an Army of One" and to "Be All You Can Be!"

By their own choice, they are tested to their limits and beyond. For example, at the Navy Seals training camp, the entrance sign warns, "The only easy day was yesterday." So you damn well better "be all that you can be."

One of Harrison Ford's classic lines comes when the adventurous Indiana Jones is lost in the jungle and about to be overrun by a deadly tribe. He comes up with a hastily devised escape plan that includes a truck. When he's questioned about where he's going to find a nonexistent truck in the middle of nowhere, he simply says, "I don't know, I'm making it up as I go along." And he will. At some level these Master Craftsmen have absolutely no doubt in their ability to overcome impossible odds whenever challenges hit them.

INVINCIBLE MAVERICKS, CONFIDENT THEY WILL DO THE IMPOSSIBLE

Master Craftsmen are the ultimate nonconformists. It's burned into their genetic code. It irritates the hell out of them to go along with the crowd, with any authorities, or with the establishment. They are obsessed with the desire to prove they are doing things their way. They hate being told *how* to do things and *when* to do them. They have to be all that they can be. Even when they appear to be tolerating some organization and authority, by God they're still going to do things a little differently, just to prove they are unique and in control.

Watch Tom Cruise in *Top Gun*. You see a fighter pilot who has the perfect call sign for these Master Craftsmen: "Maverick!" And everything about this guy fits the profile of this engaging personality type, right from opening scenes: Heavy rain. Maverick returns to the pitching deck of the *Kitty Hawk* aircraft carrier in his 40-ton F-14 Tomcat fighter after encountering a MiG-21 fighter. This sky jockey really is the ultimate risk-taking maverick. The Russian plane makes a four-G inverted dive to evade this irritating American.

Maverick one-ups his opponent, outmaneuvering him, rolling over, canopy to canopy, within two meters of the MiG-21's cockpit. The enemies lock eyes for a few harrowing seconds as they cruise in this dangerous pattern at a supersonic 900 knots. The surprised Russian waves tentatively. Suddenly, Maverick gives the Russians the finger, while his flight engineer takes a Polaroid shot of the MiG pilots as a souvenir. The MiG breaks off and runs for cover.

Running out of fuel. Maverick's about to land on the carrier deck when he hears that another pilot is in a crisis, losing it, about to eject. *Vertigo*. Maverick takes matters into his own hands, waves himself off into the dark and rain. In another risky maneuver, he guides the other pilot down. Shaken, he resigns and gives up an appointment to the Navy's Top Gun Flight School, paving the way for Maverick to attend.

BORN TO BE TOP GUN: A HERO, SAVING THE DAY

Next scene, Maverick's getting reamed out by the captain: "You're a hell of a flyer. Maybe too good," screams his frustrated captain, "you just can't seem to follow orders." But now he has an opportunity to teach Maverick a lesson.

The skipper sends Maverick to Top Gun School, where the Navy trains the "best of the best" fighter pilots. "I'm gonna send you up against the best. They are better than you. Maybe they'll knock that shine off your eagle and you'll see, finally, where discipline and teamwork fit it."

Of course, not all Master Craftsmen fly F-14 Tomcats. But something in their genetic code tells them they are born to be "Top Guns," to excel in their career, profession, trade, or business, whatever it is. They have the right attitude. The thirst for the action and excitement. The ability to stay cool under pressure. To stay calm and centered in a sudden crisis. They master their particular craft. They need new challenges. They desire to take risks and prove they are the best. And yes, they'll have fun doing it if they can.

Millionaire's Code for Master Craftsmen
Introvert, Sensor, Thinker, Perceiver (ISTP)

Master Craftsmen are very much *Introverts,* they live in a world of mythic proportions within themselves, one that is private and seldom shared, because their dramas play out whether they are awake or asleep. They derive their life force from within rather than from the external world: "Great art is an outward expression of an inner life in the artist," says painter Edward Hopper. Real people are extras in a drama played in the minds of Master Craftsmen.

Jungian analysts probing our dream world tell us that in our inner creations we are like directors of a film in progress—we pick the script, and each of the characters is part of us, some dominant, others in the shadows. As directors, everything is under our control as the drama unfolds.

The drama becomes even more powerful when Master Craftsmen are awake, for in the real world there are challenges and opportunities to master their craft, master the world, and most of all, master themselves. In fact, each day becomes yet another new call in their search for excellence, an opportunity to live out the mythic quest described by Joseph Campbell:

> The hero's journey always begins with the call. One way or another, a guide must come to say, "Look, you're in Sleepy Land. Wake. Come on a trip. There is a whole aspect of your consciousness, your being, that's not enough of you there." And so it starts.
>
> The herald or announcer of the adventure . . . is often dark, loathly, or terrifying, judged evil by the world; yet if one could follow, the way would be opened enough through the walls of day into the dark where the jewels glow.
>
> The call is to leave a certain social situation, move into your

loneliness and find the jewel, the center that's impossible to find when you're socially engaged. You are thrown off-center, and when you feel off-center, it's time to go.

Actions that are so crucial in the life of Master Craftsmen are a very real part of their internal mythic journey of the hero. Otherwise, life would be rather dull, boring, and mundane. Maybe they spend months in the garage restoring a 1967 Mustang. Or a few hours out on the open road on the Harley or swinging the golf club. Maybe it's the thrill of working all day on earth-moving construction equipment. Or using the tools of a jeweler, dentist, or carpenter. Perhaps working as a chiropractor or traveling the long, lonely road of training as a marathon runner. The mythic journey comes alive in *the action.*

They are the typically strong, silent people who "walk softly and carry a big stick." There truly is something mythic going on when they go off alone to hunt and fish, something akin to the slaying of the dragon or rescuing MIAs from a prison deep in the jungle.

Yes, they really do enjoy being one with nature—the exercise, the quiet action, the power, and the feel of their "weapon." And yes, it may be just a time to have some peace and quiet and privacy and think. But the truth is, there's much more going on in the interior mind of Master Craftsmen on their hero's adventure through life. They not only enjoy their own company, they prefer it, and they are at peace with their lives as Introverts.

Sensors: Living Your Wildest Dreams Now, in Real Time!

The journey of the Master Craftsman is an immediate experience, here and now, in the present moment. These people are *Sensors,* totally immersed in the present: "Art is neither past nor future. All I have ever made was made for the present," said Picasso. "A painting is not the result of working toward a goal, it is a stroke of luck, an experience." Indeed, the experience takes over: "I can't do anything but paint, the paintings just come to me," said Jackson Pollock, "when I am painting I am not aware of what I am doing, the painting has a life of its own."

While they are Introverts, carrying their world around in their heads, they are also Sensors, with an overpowering need to experience their aliveness by discovering that their inner world is real through touching, seeing, tasting, smelling, and hearing. They couldn't care less about the mythic adventures of the past or making up future ones—*they are the myth in action,* now, today, living it in wide-screen CinemaScope with surround-sound.

MICHAEL JORDAN: ZEN MASTER MEDITATING IN THE GAME

Anyone who has ever watched Michael Jordan of the Chicago Bulls in action has seen the ultimate Master Craftsman at one with the experience of the moment. Here is one of basketball's greatest players, a craftsman of mythic proportions, flying through the air, dominating, moving gracefully, with the other nine players reacting as if they were no more than a projection of his very private inner world and an extension of his incredibly athletic body—and yet, all the time, you sense that his only real competition was Michael Jordan.

As great as he was, that wasn't enough for him. He was always pushing himself, not just to excel or beat the pants off the competition, but to far exceed the high standard he set for himself alone, to achieve a new personal best, to experience another peak performance. Jordan's coach, Phil Jackson, captured this spirit in *Sacred Hoops:*

> The first time we practiced meditation, Michael Jordan thought I was joking. Midway through the session, he cocked one eye open and took a glance around the room to see if any of his teammates were actually doing it. To his surprise, many of them were.
>
> Michael always maintained he didn't need any of "that Zen stuff" because he already had a positive outlook on life. Who am I to argue? In the process of becoming a great athlete, Michael had attained a quality of mind few Zen students ever achieve. His ability to stay relaxed and intensely focused in the midst of chaos is unsurpassed.
>
> He loves being in the center of the storm. While everyone else is spinning madly out of control, he moves effortlessly across the floor, enveloped in a great stillness.

The Sensing function perfectly fits the character of the Master Craftsman. These people gather information about their world from the five senses, immediately, in real time. Jordan gets it for 48 minutes on the basketball court. A jet pilot gets it from the immediacy of his aircraft in motion. A sailor from the wind and waves. A surgeon from a scalpel and the body's vital signs. A firefighter from the noise and heat. A Special Forces officer from the dangers lurking everywhere in the still of the night.

MORE THAN JUST WINNING—YOU COME TO LOVE THE BATTLE

Watch them closely, and you'll often see how much they love living on the edge, flirting with danger, standing in harm's way, risking life and limb, time and again. Why? In *The Mental Game, Winning at Pressure Tennis,* sports psychologist James Loehr, puts it this way:

The final stage of mental toughness is reflected in the challenge response. You actually find yourself investing more positive intensity, more of yourself as the situation gets tougher. You find that problems you face in competition are not threatening but stimulating. You've gone well beyond simply loving to win. You have clearly come to *love the battle.* As a result of this emotional response, you have become an excellent problem solver. When everyone else is heading for the trenches as the problems start mounting, you smile inside because you know you got the emotional edge.

Unlike their opposites—*Intuitives,* who are prone to speculation about the immediate future—*Sensors* love the battle so much and are so totally into the immediate experineces of the moment that they aren't thinking about the future.

Thinking: A Higher Calling to the Right Thing, Right Now

While Feeling types make decisions subjectively, often dismissing hard evi dence, putting more weight on how their decisions will affect other people, *Thinkers* make their decisions objectively, logically, rationally—they want to do the right thing. They are impartial, motivated by the principles and values of justice, morality, legality, and what's good for society, country, and the world. For them, the greater good, the Commandments, and universal law take precedent over personal desires, whether theirs or those of others.

It should be apparent that the Master Craftsmen's quest to do the right thing, is at a deep level, more than just being impartial and objective in making decisions—at its core it is a strong spiritual quality. By far one of the most powerful examples of this quality is in the Special Forces Prayer, written during the early stages of the Vietnam War by Special Forces chaplain John Stevey:

> Almighty God, Who art the Author of liberty
> and the Champion of the oppressed, hear our prayer.
>
> We, the men of Special Forces, acknowledge
> our dependence upon Thee in the preservation of human freedom.
>
> Go with us as we seek to defend the defenseless and to free the enslaved.
>
> May we ever remember that our nation, whose motto
> is "In God We Trust", expects that we shall acquit

ourselves with honor, that we may never bring shame
upon our faith, our families, or our fellow men.

Grant us wisdom from Thy mind, courage from Thine
heart, strength from Thine arm, and protection by Thine hand.

It is for Thee that we do battle, and to Thee belongs the victor's
crown.

For Thine is the kingdom, and the power and the glory, forever.
Amen

The Special Forces Prayer characterizes the way in which the Thinking
function works in the Master Craftsmen's genetic code. Their thinking is
not pure logic. Theirs is not a story told by entertainers about mythic
knights going off to save damsels in distress, killing dreaded fire-eating
dragons. It is not a film with Sylvester Stallone rescuing prisoners or war.
This is the real myth, live action, real time. Often for them, "uncommon valor
is a common virtue" as they risk the ultimate sacrifice to honor their duty
to God, country, and self.

They are the real thing. Trained killers, yes, but theirs is a higher calling to do something noble, defending our freedom. Not a selfish under-
taking for wealth and vainglory. These men are compelled forward on a
quest that can only be described as their personal "Journey of the Hero,"
a fulfillment of their unique, individual destinies during this lifetime, what
is written in their genetic code.

In its simplicity and spirituality, the Special Forces Prayer is an echo
of the Thinking function in all Master Craftsmen. These Craftsmen have
a strong inner commitment to do the right thing—while at the same time,
perfecting their craft, whether it be shooting hoops, performing triple-
bypass surgery, carving a new wood chair, racing stock cars, or parachut-
ing behind enemy lines.

These Craftsmen do this because in doing it they serve a Higher Pur-
pose, which means placing the higher good above any individual needs.
They are Master Craftsmen in their special fields of expertise, serving the
Master Craftsman who guides everyone.

Perceiver: Free Spirits Committed to a Higher Law

Master Craftsmen are *Perceivers* to the max, free spirits who just don't like
to be told how to do their job or perform their craft, which can make
them very testy in organizations run by their opposite types, nitpicking
judgers who just annoy the hell out of Craftsmen.

Master Craftsmen are self-taught experts in their fields, and they don't want some bean counter or manual-toting uptight manager telling them what to do. They'll listen to another craftsman they respect. But otherwise, authority figures would be wise to give them considerable independence on the job. Tell them what the goal is, then stand back and let them figure out the best alternatives, do the job their way, and just focus on the results.

These Craftsmen are also masters at reacting quickly to the unexpected twists and turns in a game plan. That gives them the perfect opportunity to exercise the uncanny ability to come up with several brilliant alternatives, then pick the best one and save the day. Paradoxically, they also have the ability to wait patiently in their private world for the right moment to spring into action—sometimes waiting too long or appearing too relaxed or too cavalier in the midst of their bosses and coworkers.

ZEN AND THE NEW ART OF MOTORCYCLE MAINTENANCE

Their relaxed, superconfident attitude can irritate people who prefer to work in more structured environments with tight schedules. But the Craftsmen's processes work for them and need to be honored, at least by themselves if not others. Their genetic code takes them into a mental state well described by Robert M. Pirsig in *Zen and the Art of Motorcycle Maintenance:*

> The thing to do when working on a motorcycle, as in any other task, is to cultivate the peace of mind that does not separate one's self from one's surroundings. When that is done successfully, then everything else follows naturally. Peace of mind produces right values, right values produce right thoughts. Right thoughts produce right actions and right actions produce work which is a material reflection for others to see what's at the center of it all.

Perceivers are lone wolves because they need to get into this mystical bond with their craft, whatever it is, on a conscious, material level, and at the same time, at a deeper level, tap into the spiritual power of the Master Craftsman within. They are on a unique, personal quest, much like samurai warriors, whose code of conduct tells them to live "expecting nothing, prepared for anything."

Master Craftsman: Rugged, Powerful Moneymaking Machines

Master Craftsmen have a powerful competitive spirit, what Mark McCormack called the "killer instinct" of a champion in *What They Don't Teach*

You at Harvard Business School. However, "in the champion's mind he is never ahead."

Yet their obsessive perfectionism and competitive spirit gives them an edge in the business of making money. Society needs their spirit of rugged individualism and their unique ability to leverage the instruments of their craft—and, therefore, society tends to reward them rather well. In short, if they know who they are and are in sync with their genetic code, doing what fits their personality type, they're likely to be financially successful.

In fact, they can be moneymaking machines, even though they do what they do mainly because they just love doing it and even though they believe their work speaks for itself—whether artwork, batting averages, cabinetry, orbital flights, solved crimes, or successful transplants. Their skills and work product are in demand, and the world beats a path to their door. Fortunately, making money tends to come naturally to Master Craftsmen as a by-product of doing what they love.

By nature, these Craftsmen prefer working freelance on projects. Yet, because their skills and talents are in demand, many also wind up working for institutions and companies with retirement benefit programs, such as hospitals, municipal police, the military, and trade and professional unions. Either way, they tend to be responsible in handling financial affairs and show a strong tendency of doing all the right things in saving, budgeting, and investing to wind up as millionaires.

Because they are far more interested in their craft than in the processes of personal finance, my advice for Master Craftsmen is to hire a professional financial adviser to help manage their financial affairs and to start saving early and investing regularly. You can become a millionaire doing what you love.

* * * * * * * *

When a man reaches this stage of "spiritual" development,
he is a Zen artist of life. He does not need, like the painter, a canvas,
brushes, and paints; nor does he require, like the archer, the bow and
arrow and target, and other paraphernalia.
He has limbs, body, head, and other parts.
His Zen-life expresses itself by means of all these
"tools" which are important to its manifestation.
His hands and feet are the brushes and the whole universe
is the canvas on which he depicts his life.

D. T. Suzuki,
Zen in the Art of Archery

DIRECTORS AND COMPOSERS (ISFP)

ANDREW LLOYD WEBBER, RAY BRADBURY, STEPHEN SPIELBERG

> There's a rebel lying deep in my soul.
> Anytime anybody tells me the trend is such and such,
> I go the opposite direction.
> I hate the idea of trends. I hate imitation;
> I have a reverence for individuality.
> I got where I am by coming off the wall.
> I've always considered myself too individualistic to be either right-wing or left-wing. . . .
> You have to trust your instincts.
> There's a moment when an actor has it,
> and he knows it.
> Behind the camera you can feel the moment
> even more clearly.
> And once you've got it,
> once you feel it,
> you can't second-guess yourself.
>
> Clint Eastwood

"All the world's a stage, and all the men and women merely players. They have their exits and their entrances." Shakespeare wrote these lines in his romantic comedy *As You Like It,* referring to the seven stages of life all humans pass through from birth to death. Shakespeare, always the master at understanding the inner workings of the human mind, was also telling us something very revealing about the soul and heart of this unique personality type—the *Director and Composer.*

For the director and composers, all the world is indeed a stage—*and it is located in their minds.* Moreover, all the actors and actresses, characters, plots, dialogue, music, digital effects, staging, and special effects are also *in the mind of the director, the composer, the creator of the work.* It's all in there!

With a Song in Your Heart and an Orchestra in Your Head

It doesn't matter whether the creation is a concerto, an opera, a ballad, a rock song, a jazz ensemble, a film, a novel, or virtually any other creation of the director, composer, choreographer, novelist, or others of this type—not only are the stage and characters living in the minds of these people, their minds are filled with intense emotions that are driving the music and the story, the characters, the plot, and the action.

Musical composers tell me that they actually have a "live" band or quartet or full orchestra in their minds, creating and revising the score, adding and deleting instruments, replaying the entire work over and over, perfecting it.

Yes, they can also work at the piano. But the composing and the music don't stop when a collaborative working session stops—the process continues to *live in their minds.* And not necessarily offstage.

The musicians, the instruments, the voices, and the feelings live on, often waking them at night with new lyrics, melodies, stanzas, scores, and compositions. As guitarist Jimi Hendrix put it, "My own thing is in my head, I hear sounds and if I don't get them together, nobody else will."

Choreographers have similar musical experiences, loaded with feelings, plus they have the added power of singers and actors and dancers in motion on the stage—often in live rehearsals, and always in their minds, creating and re-creating sequences anew.

THE PHANTOM IS IN THE MIND OF THE COMPOSER

You clearly sense this in Andrew Lloyd Webber's *Phantom of the Opera.* Consciously or unconsciously Webber was projecting *himself* so dramatically *through* the voice, the heart, and the emotions of the tormented Phantom in a duet with his protégé Christine, played by Sarah Brightman, who in real life was, at the time, Webber's wife.

This powerful duet between the Phantom and Christine slowly builds to a crescendo. She tells us the Phantom is coming to her in dreams, singing, commanding her. The music pulsates with a haunting beat inside her mind. He is in there, taking control. Their voices are becoming one. He has power over her dreams, her mind, her life. His face is a nightmare, becoming her dark side. He is taking over her soul. She is his mask, his persona, his facade—*we hear his voice coming through her.*

Directly or indirectly, all Composers are saying: "Listen to me, I am the creator, the audience hears my words and my music. My emotions are flowing through the actors and actresses." And the *Phantom of the Opera* is a dramatic example of the creative egos of all Composers, glorious, with no apologies—*because every word is a creation of their minds!*

"THE WORK" CONSTANTLY RERUNNING IN YOUR HEAD

Film directors have similar experiences. Content to let the Entertainers and Performers (ESFP) be exposed on film, they prefer operating behind the scenes and off-camera. I worked with Michael Phillips, who earlier produced *Close Encounters of the Third Kind, Taxi Driver,* and *The Sting.*

Over lunch, Michael often told me of his experiences: When Steven Spielberg pitched *Close Encounters* to Columbia's executives it was just a simple concept, "UFOs and Watergate." From there, his mind developed the story into a script, later storyboarding each of the camera shots and dialogue, casting, choosing locations, setting scenes, planning camera angles, shooting, then postproduction editing of the film after it's in the can.

The creative process of Directors is not just a series of technical actions "out there" when they're working together with the writers, actors, and crew—the creative process is always going on in the Directors' minds, day and night, at meals, alone, with family, when they're sleeping. It is a living thing that literally takes over your mind. I had a taste of it when I made a short film and later a video documentary—it is constantly alive, playing and replaying in your head.

CHARACTERS PLOT TO CONTROL THE CREATOR'S MIND

The same processes go on in the novelist's mind. Experienced fiction writers will tell you how they begin with an idea, a plot, some characters—possibly even worked out conceptually right up to the final climax. But when they start the actual work, strange and unexpected things begin happening in their minds as the creative process flows—the characters can literally take over the story and new ones demand entry, even as others disappear.

They quickly become more than mere players making their exits and entrances, as Shakespeare might say. You feel for them, the good, the bad, and the ugly, because they are living inside the creative mind. All the characters, the entire story, every single emotion, no matter from which of the characters, arise from a deep creative center in the soul of the director, the composer, the novelist, the choreographer, the creator of the work.

Millionaire's Code for Composers and Directors
Introvert, Sensor, Feeling, Perceiver (ISFP)

While entertainers need to be onstage in front of an audience, Composers and Directors are *Introverts,* preferring to be offstage, in the wings, watching their creations unfold slowly, as if their eyes are projectors in a theater, sending the images and voices and sounds and emotions out from their minds through the actors and onto the stage or film.

We all know of some great actors who successfully walked around behind the camera and became what the industry calls "hyphenates," merging their talents as actor-writer-director-producer. In fact, several actors have won Oscars as directors: Clint Eastwood for the *Unforgiven,* Mel Gibson for *Braveheart,* and Kevin Costner for *Dances With Wolves.*

But for every one of these hyphenates, there are hundreds of Directors and Composers who prefer working behind the camera, offstage, in the wings, all the time. Why? Because the film, the musical, the play, the story, the action, the creative work is actually going on in their minds all the time—from concept to opening night.

Their reality is within. Their "real world" is not "out there," it is in their heads. They let their creative works speak for themselves, often without revealing much, if anything, about the mysterious inner workings of the mind it came from.

That's the way of Introverts. They carry the world around with them in the heads, projecting their reality outward. There's something mystically spiritual about the way their minds work naturally—it's as if some Master Creator is working in and through the minds of Composers and Directors to create something within them, then re-create, duplicate, and finally let unfold this new creation out there in the real world. In a real sense, they are at one with this Master Creator.

For Sensors, It Is the Journey, Not the Destination

The Composer and Director personalities are *Sensors,* with a strong preference for hard, tangible evidence, for details, facts, hard information. Yet there's an air of mystery about all this to other people, because in spite of the reality of all this information constantly living in the mind of a composer, novelist, director, playwright, choreographer, or others of this type, it is not visible to other people—they don't get it; others just can't understand these strange beings.

Alfred Hitchcock had his films worked out in detail well in advance—the dialogue, rehearsals, sets, camera angles, and lighting. He used to say it wasn't even necessary for him to be there during the shooting and that one take was all that was necessary. Other directors are less rigid before shooting and use many takes, purposely allowing actors to create in the moment, and then have lots of film alternatives for editing into their masterpiece. Both are Sensors.

Sensors live in the moment, right now, today, experiencing every fact, every detail, every nuance of emotions with their inner reality flowing through their minds in "real time" as live action, and eventually their creations come alive in operas, musical comedies, motion pictures, concert tours, books, fashion shows, art exhibits, and other creative productions.

Yet the end product is not what counts for these people—it is the creative process that counts, the journey, the trip, the here and now experience. For Composers and Directors, all the sounds, sights, smells, tastes, and touches are immediate experiences, vividly real. Life is in session all the time in their minds. There are no boundaries between their minds and the outer world. For them, the two are one and the same experience.

Feelings: The Creation Explodes from Passions Deep Within

What do the Composers and Directors want most from their audience? Feelings! Emotional reaction . . . cheers and smiles, tears and laughter, oohs and aahs, ughs and groans and gasps, panting and sighs . . . then some applause, perhaps even a standing ovation. Yes, all that would be nice when the creation is finished.

But that's still not what they really want. What Composers and Directors and the rest of these creative personalities want are the feelings that come *while creating the creation,* whatever it is—film, dance, song, books, whatever. It is a personal experience, an inner experience, flooding your mind with emotion that says you are alive, you are creative, *you are creating!* The prodigious author, Ray Bradbury, captured this feeling in his *Zen in the Art of Writing:*

> The Joy of Writing: Zest. Gusto. How rarely one hears these words used. How rarely do we see people living, or for that matter, creating by them. Yet if I were asked to name the most important items in a writer's make-up, the things that shape his material and rush him along the road to where he wants to go, I could only warn him to look to his zest, see to his gusto.

After listing his favorite writers, plus other creative geniuses in poetry, painting, and music, he continues:

> Think of all these names and you think of big or little, but nonetheless important, zests, appetites, hungers. Think of Shakespeare and Melville and you think of thunder, lightening, wind. They all knew the *joy of creating* . . . these are the children of the gods. They know the *fun in the work*. No matter if creation came hard here and there along the way, or what illness and tragedies touched their most private lives. The important things are those passed down to us from their hands and minds and these are filled to bursting with animal vigor and intellectual vitality.

Then Bradbury speaks of the joy he saw in El Greco's elongated paintings, of the fun in Tintoretto's paintings, and eternal creative feelings generated by great jazz music and sculpture:

> The best jazz says, "Gonna live forever; don't believe in death."
> The best sculpture, like the head of Nefertiti, says again and again, "The Beautiful One was here, is here, and will be here, forever."
>   What does all this have to do with writing the short story in our times? Only this: If you are writing without zest, without gusto, without fun, you are only half a writer. It means you are so busy keeping one eye on the commercial market, or one ear peeled for the avant-garde coterie, that you are not being yourself, You don't even know who you are. *For the first thing a writer should be is— excited. He should be a thing of fevers and enthusiasm.*

Passion. *Feelings.* Fevers and enthusiasm. Love and hate. Zest and gusto. The creative processes of the director and composer, the choreographer and the fashion designer, the poet and writer have this in common: feelings and passion.

Their creative works are not dry news reporting, no boring technical manuals and academic texts, no hard factual documentaries—this stuff is burning with emotions and feelings, a smoldering fire consuming the soul of these creative personalities every day.

Dylan Thomas spoke with this very passion on the death of his father: "Do not go gentle into that good night. Old age should burn and rave at close of day; Rage, rage against the dying of light." Yet not just old age, but *all* ages, for was he not also creating and living his own eulogy every day?

In the final analysis, artists, writers, creators are compelled by their inner genetic code to "burn and rage against the dying light." In that sense, Dylan Thomas was speaking for all creative personalities—their passion burns every moment in the light of day, racing to bring forth a new creation, racing in advance of the dying light.

Perceivers Who *Must* Create Something Uniquely Theirs

Most normal businesses are populated by Judgers. They thrive in tightly structured organizations—with to-do lists for each day, weekly appointment books, progress schedules, yearly plans, and long-term life goals.

But all that organizational stuff makes *Perceivers* feel uptight, because they are convinced it will limit their creative juices. Their world is a world of infinite, unfolding new possibilities, not finite structures with well-defined alternatives and limited solutions. Creativity is so much more.

We now know that these Perceivers are on a creative journey that can never be defined, let alone structured and planned. In *A Joseph Campbell Companion,* mythologist Joseph Campbell perfectly captured this creative spirit:

> In the story of Sir Galahad, the knights agree to go on a quest, but thinking it would be a disgrace to go forth in a group, each entered the forest, at one point or another, where they saw it to be thickest, all in those places where they found no way or path. *Where there is a path, it's someone else's path.* Each knight enters the forest at the most mysterious point and follows his own intuition. What each brings forth is *what never before was on land or sea: The fulfillment of his unique potentialities, which are different from anybody else's.*

Creative types need flexibility. They need to be free to react spontaneously when the inspiration hits them rather than on some rigid timetable. The spark can explode anytime, day or night, unpredictably. When it does, they need to run with it as long as necessary, whether in the middle of the night, sitting at lunch with friends, or vacationing with family.

Even when a project deadline is looming, they will often delay, procrastinate, and prolong starting until the last possible moment, *constantly searching for the perfect answer.* Then, with time running out and under pressure, they will come alive in a fiery race to the finish, and, in a flurry of creative activity, they'll deliver an incredibly inspired creation.

That's just the way the minds of Composers and Directors work. If you ask, they'll tell you that "it" (the creative spirit) is the master, it is in control of them; they are not in control of the spirit; rather, it comes and goes whenever it chooses.

Career Paths: Creative Geniuses in So Many Worlds

The world needs more of these creative minds. Nobody really understands the inner workings of these geniuses, perhaps least of all themselves.

One of America's great director-writer-actors, Woody Allen, has been in therapy for decades, and we laugh at his shortcomings: "I'm astounded by people who want to 'know' the universe when it's hard enough to find your way around Chinatown." Yet for all his self-deprecating humor, we actually do get to know the world better through his eyes.

As Freelance Creators, Composers, and Directors come in all sizes, with many working quietly in the heartland of America rather than on the international stages, megabuck records, top 10 radio lists, worldwide concert tours, blockbusters reviewed on *Ebert & Roeper,* or boffo Broadway hits.

Many, perhaps as a characteristic of their introverted nature, actually prefer living and creating in privacy and obscurity, offstage, in the wings, away from the spotlight—often right there in your hometown in the heartland of America, maybe just down the street, with their kids going to school with yours:

- *Novelists*
- *Playwrights*
- *Photographers*
- *Interior designers*
- *Advertising designers*
- *Dance choreographers*
- *Drama coaches*
- *Fine arts teachers*
- *Painters, sculptors*
- *Fashion designers*
- *Graphics illustrators*

Their genius may be hidden until it finds the path of its destiny. They are often the troubled ones, even the kids voted least likely to succeed. George Lucas was an aimless teenager and a terrible student. Yet today he is one of the most innovative and successful directors, creating one of the world's most powerful and influential multimedia technology empires.

Look around your neighborhood, your town, your office. These people are the creative and original ones, big and small, with well-developed senses and a keen appreciation for beauty, aesthetics, and the arts. Sensitive, gentle, kind, and peaceful, they tend to avoid conflict. They are usually loyal, faithful, and flexible in business and personal relationships, with little interest in leading or controlling people outside their beloved corner of the creative world. Are you one?!

GIMME THAT NIGHT FEVER—MAKE THIS MOMENT LAST FOREVER!

All of them do what they do because they enjoy the immediate experience and joy of creating something. Most of all, they do it because they have absolutely no choice—it's in their blood, part of their genetic code. They need to create to prove they are alive, to themselves!

In spite of their earthy spiritual qualities, there's a little Woody Allen in all of them, as they constantly search for new ways to create yet are plagued with doubts. As Allen once said, "What if everything is an illusion and nothing exists? I definitely overpaid for my carpet. If only God would give me a clear sign! Like making a large deposit in my name in a Swiss bank." But from their doubt and their wonderment at the mysteries of the universe come the secret joy of creating; they do it no matter what, success or failure, win or lose, pleasure or pain, laughter or tears, deposits or bankruptcy.

So often, they succeed because their spirit exists in everybody, and they show it to us. *Saturday Night Fever* was a success because we all want to come alive for a while, as did John Travolta, the hardware clerk. We all want to dance and sing the magic: "Gimme that night fever, night fever, we know how to show it," creating, dancing, and "prayin' for this moment to last, livin' on the music so fine." At least hum a few bars, strutting our stuff on the way to work.

Creating Money: Getting Rich in Spirit and in Fact, Too

Yes, Andrew Lloyd Webber, Steven Spielberg, George Lucas, Clint Eastwood, Mel Gibson, Stephen King, and John Grisham are very rich. Yet making lots of money is not their goal. They need to create, with emphasis on *need*. It's as if there's a Master Creator in their brains, controlling the show, prodding them, forcing them to be creative and to manifest the show taking place within their minds.

As a result, most of these personalities—directors and composers, novelists and choreographers—tend to become rich in spirit, if not also in fact. Generally speaking, they find themselves drawn to career opportunities in the creative arts that also create comfortable lives for them, if not great monetary wealth.

LEVERAGING THE POWER OF THE CREATOR

Why? Because the value of what they do involves leveraging. What they do involves a collaboration of talents working under their direction: songs, books, photos, illustrations, plays or films paying royalties for multiple uses, or things of unusual and unique artistic quality that collectors expect to appreciate in value over time.

Although their creative siblings, Performers and Entertainers, may have more limited opportunities due to the intense competition of roles and the limited options in related fields for their talents, Directors and Composers are more likely to find opportunities to make a reasonable living at what they do before the big break happens.

However, because many of the career and business opportunities tend to be entrepreneurial in nature, they may live from project to project. Therefore, savings and retirement plans, a matter of personal initiative, are easily deferred in favor of more immediate or long overdue needs.

Since these creative types are more interested in the business of creating than the business of making money, which is more a "necessary evil," they would be well advised to seek guidance from spouses and professional financial advisers early in life—people who can manage budgets, spending, financial affairs, and savings and retirement plans, SEP/IRAs, and other tax-advantaged retirement programs. That way Composers and Directors can better focus on what they do best—*creating*—in doing what they love so the money will indeed flow naturally.

* * * * * * * *

The key to the mystery of a great artist
is that for reasons unknown,
he will give away his energies
and his life
just to make sure that
one note follows another . . .
and leaves us with the
feeling that something is right in the world.

Leonard Bernstein

SYSTEMS
MASTERMINDS

SYSTEMS MASTERMINDS: INTUITIVE-THINKING (N-T)

- Commanders in Chief (ENTJ)
- Master Innovators (ENTP)
- Chief Strategists (INTJ)
- Visionary Thinkers (INTP)

CHAPTER 21

COMMANDERS IN CHIEF (ENTJ)

WINSTON CHURCHILL, RUDY GIULIANI, JOHN F. KENNEDY

> We shall not flag or fail.
> We shall go on to the end.
> We shall fight in France,
> we shall fight on the seas and the oceans,
> we shall fight with growing confidence
> and growing strength in the air,
> we shall defend our island,
> whatever the cost may be.
> We shall fight on the beaches,
> we shall fight on the landing grounds,
> we shall fight in the fields
> and in the streets,
> we shall fight in the hills;
> we shall never surrender.
>
> Winston Churchill

Commanders in Chief, or Commanders, are one of the four Systems Mastermind personality types. Commanders are natural-born leaders, *change agents,* strategic thinkers destined by their genetic code to make the world a better place. They know this instinctively, it is in their blood, and they can't avoid the call.

Commanders are leaders of people, and the systems they command come in many forms, big and small—as president of a nation, your local mayor, a military general, a team leader, a blue-chip corporate honcho, a small business owner, a university president, or the local PTA chairman.

Leaders command in many ways, but what distinguishes these leaders? What special qualities make a leader in a particular field? You can identify their four-part Millionaire's Code from the personality test. But can you create leaders? The literature certainly suggests that possibility.

Walk into any bookstore and you'll see an overload of books on leadership. Many are how-to manuals and textbooks by theorists, teachers, and consultants. But the eye-catching popular ones focus on the leadership style of public leaders in the military, government, sports, industry, and the pages of history.

These books present dramatic and engaging personalities with an outline of what makes them successful leaders—suggesting that if you just follow their "secret" rules, you, too, will be transformed into leaders like them:

- *The Leadership Secrets of **Colin Powell***
- *What It Takes to Be #1: **Vince Lombardi** on Leadership*
- ***Ulysses S. Grant** on Leadership: Executive Lessons from the Front Lines*
- ***Robert E. Lee** on Leadership: Executive Lessons in Character, Courage, and Vision*
- ***Elizabeth I** CEO, Strategic Lessons from the Leader Who Built the Empire*
- ***Machiavelli** on Modern Leadership: Why Machiavelli's Iron Rules Are as Timely and Important Today as Five Centuries Ago*
- *The Leadership Secrets of **Attila the Hun***
- ***Jesus** CEO: Using Ancient Wisdom for Visionary Leadership*
- ***Moses** on Management: 50 Leadership Lessons from the Greatest Manager of All Time*
- ***God Is My CEO:** Following God's Principles in a Bottom Line World*

There are many, many more books on the subject, including titles like *Peanut Butter and Jelly Management,* leadership lessons for parents.

Leadership Enigma: Born, Made, or Late Bloomers?

Reading one book on leadership, or even a thousand, cannot magically transform you into a leader. Oh, you may get some hints on how to minimize your weaknesses and maximize your strengths, as Buckingham and Clifton promise with their list of 34 strength builders in *Now, Discover Your Strengths.* In final analysis, however, you are who you are, and some people are dealt a better (or rather, different) hand than others, so you work with the material encoded in your genes.

Leaders are born with certain genetic traits that distinguish them from their peers. Many take command and gain notoriety at an early age as they aggressively seek out positions of authority and power in their school years and as young adults.

Others are late bloomers: They possess the same leadership qualities as other leaders, but are less visible for years due to any number of family and social factors. Then, perhaps in a crisis, the leader rises to the occasion, taking command. As James Allen wrote in *As a Man Thinketh:* "Circumstances do not make a man, they reveal him," the real leaders are destined to change their world.

OVER-THE-HILL OUTCAST—SUDDENLY THE OBVIOUS CHOICE

For example, in 1940, Winston Churchill was an over-the-hill 66-year-old politician. British leaders had dismissed him as an old warmonger while they appeased Germany, including the now infamous Munich Pact with Hitler. However, while he is often considered a romantic and emotional personality, the truth is that throughout the 1930s Churchill was the one rock-solid voice of reason warning against the Nazi threat.

Churchill came from a distinguished British military dynasty dating back to 1702, which should have given him an edge in life. But he had a childhood speech impediment, didn't get in the right prep school, and felt inadequate, agonizing over speeches his entire life.

His family heritage really didn't help much. His father, a political failure, considered his son a disappointment, even calling the young Churchill a "show-off" who lacked "cleverness, knowledge and any capacity for settled work." His life might have ended like his father's, except World War II changed everything–the aging outsider became prime minister and against great odds led his country to victory.

THE MAYOR, THE MARTIAL ARTIST, AND THE WINDOW WASHER

In the days following the terrorist attacks in New York on September 11, 2001, Mayor Rudy Giuliani's leadership inspired Americans everywhere. "For a few weeks after September 11, I read about him," Giuliani said, turning to the spirit of Churchill. "The idea wasn't so much to copy him. It was just to get confidence that we could get through it, just as England got through the bombing in World War II."

There were many other leaders who shared honors with Giuliani, such as Todd Beamer, the martial artist whose "Let's roll" command initiated the takeover of the flight that crashed in Pennsylvania. Another who took command, less noticeable, perhaps, but no less a leader, was Jan Demczur.

Six men were descending on an elevator when the terrorist jet hit Tower One, "mostly executives and a window washer, carrying his bucket and a squeegee on a pole. . . . Who led the way out? The window washer,

Jan Demczur," wrote psychologist Daniel Goleman, coauthor of *Primal Leadership, Realizing the Power of Emotional Intelligence.*

The window washer directed the men as they used his pole to pry open the door—only to discover a blank wall with the number 50. It was an express elevator with no opening. He remained in command as they took turns using the pole to dig through three layers of drywall to freedom. A hero, yes, and definitely a leader.

NOT ALWAYS THE SMARTEST, THE TOUGHEST, OR THE OFFICIAL BOSS

"Leadership is *not* about who's smarter or tougher," says Goleman in *Parade* magazine. At that moment in time, Demczur, the window washer, exhibited the several traits of leaders—"self-confidence, initiative, optimism and team-work"—and he instinctively took command.

Goleman also mentions that the quality of leadership is often evident in "small, everyday acts." For example, "business leaders who achieve the best results get people to laugh three times more often than do the mediocre leaders."

Laughter is but one of the little things that count a lot with the successful leaders. Goleman notes how artfully a flight attendant handled a planeful of frustrated passengers already delayed and missing the Super Bowl kickoff. The plane was taxiing to the gate when it suddenly stopped several hundred yards away. Passengers stood, reaching for bags, a no-no when a plane's still moving. In a singsong voice, as though talking to a lovable but mischievous four-year-old, the flight attendant admonished, "You're *staaaanding. . . .*" The passengers laughed and sat down . . . that's real leadership.

FOUR GREAT LEADERS AND WHAT MAKES THEM THAT WAY

Although the qualities of leadership can be elusive and perhaps even suppressed in many people, Goleman uses four strong individuals as examples of some of the primary leadership characteristics:

- *Motivator.* Yankee manager Joe Torres is a great motivator, bringing out the best in his players, and pulling them together as a team.
- *Empathic.* Unique leaders like Oprah Winfrey have to relate, listen to, and communicate with millions.
- *Integrity.* The moral leadership of the Dalai Lama is based on an unwavering position of humility, nonviolence, and tolerance.
- *Diplomatic.* Leaders like Colin Powell have the unique ability to connect with people, helping them resolve differences.

There are other traits, such as setting measurable goals, handling stress, and focusing on the future. These skills can be developed, says Goleman, which is encouraging, since many natural-born leaders may never have the opportunity to fulfill their genetic potential.

These leadership traits are rarely found in the same proportions in every leader; however, one combination among the 16 millionaire's personalities tends to identify the four key characteristics of the natural-born leader as a powerful catalyst for change–the Commander in Chief.

Millionaire's Code for Commanders in Chief: Extravert, Intuitive, Thinker, Judger (ENTJ)

Commanders are *Extraverts* and leaders of people, whether they are in corporations, schools, parishes, unions, whether they are investors, voters, audiences, armies, or nations. They connect with the people, reaching out, walking among them, listening, talking, touching them in their hearts. Leaders know how to get people to take action toward a common goal.

Something deep within the Commander knows instinctively how to relate, inspire, motivate, drive, encourage, persuade, cajole, manipulate, demand, direct, and, generally, bring out the best in people–as individuals and as a group. Leaders come to life when they are working with people, whether one-to-one on the phone, in small gatherings, in huge arenas, or with national audiences. They are the ultimate Extraverts.

We call it *charisma*–the mystical bond forming between a leader and the people being led, an indefinable magnetism that energizes, unites, and draws people to common goals and purposes behind their leader. At the same time, the leader is also energized–the leader is magically drawn to the people and literally forced by them to march out ahead of them.

Leaders are compelled to fulfill their personal destinies by *serving* the people being led. We know this happened to Churchill, an outsider who, at that defining moment in history, suddenly became the obvious choice as Britain's wartime prime minister, a crisis that transformed him into the Commander in Chief.

WE ARE MASTERS OF OUR FATE, CAPTAINS OF OUR SOULS

Churchill rose to the occasion. In the dark days of 1940 and 1941, after France fell to Germany, Britain stood alone, without allies, outgunned, sustaining nightly bombing attacks on London, and anticipating a German invasion at any time. Churchill rallied his countrymen in 1941 with speeches to students and politicians:

Today we may say aloud before an awe-struck world: We are still masters of our fate. We are still captain of our souls. . . . Never give in—never, never, never, never, in nothing great or small, large or petty, never give in except to convictions of honour and good sense. Never yield to force; never yield to the apparently overwhelming might of the enemy.

The British people welcomed a leader who could command them to do the impossible, give them cause to unite behind his leadership. Later, when victory came on V-E Day 1945, an exuberant nation heard him congratulate them for their heroic efforts during five long years:

God bless you all. This is your victory! . . . My dear friends, this is your hour. This is not victory of a party or of any class. It's a victory of the great British nation as a whole . . . we came back after long months from the jaws of death, out of the mouth of hell.

The ancient saying, "When the student is ready, the teacher will appear," easily applies here—for when the people were ready, the leader did appear. Leaders like Churchill emerge as the right person at the right time, able to rally people behind a common cause. They are Extraverts of the best kind, commanding people with their charismatic leadership.

What we see here is a magical blend of the Commander's personal need to achieve coupled with the broader needs of the people and their goals. They bond together in a dynamic exchange of energy: The Extravert leader is energized by his followers . . . they become an extension of the leader's grand vision . . . the people are energized by the leader's charisma . . . and together they are locked in a synergistic relationship where the leader becomes one with the group, feeling its pulse, defining its dreams, harnessing its energy, leveraging its power—and becoming the voice that articulates its message.

The Intuitive: Creating a Better Future for the World

The Commander is also an *Intuitive*. Unlike the Sensor, the Intuitive's mind is systems-oriented, with a broad vision of the future, whether in politics, the military, industrial enterprises, educational, medical, or scientific institutions.

In simple terms, Sensors gather information about their world by focusing more on the trees, so to speak, while Intuitives focus on the forest, the bigger picture. Sensors collect more immediate, hard data about the present, mostly facts you can see, hear, touch, taste, smell. They confirm and test against past data. They are focused on today, now.

In contrast, Intuitives look for patterns and trends, theories about this or that system, focusing on future scenarios and outcomes. Typically, there are huge gaps in the facts they consider important. Indeed, Intuitives have a natural distrust of raw facts, because they know there's more than meets the eye. Statistics can be manipulated to support any argument and generally tend to confirm the conventional wisdom rather than tread the lonely path into unknown futures.

That doesn't really bother them much, because they know there's little information about the uncertain future of whichever system they're commanding. In fact, the unknown energizes them. They love making the unknown known. It's a challenge that excites them and an opportunity to prove how good they are—and they do have an extraordinary need to succeed in life. So they must enter the unknown!

Commanders love speculating about information in their mental computers, speculating about unknown futures, strategizing alternatives, developing plans of action. Out there among all their future scenarios, facts about the present are useful only as hints of tomorrow, either supporting or conflicting with the Commander's vision of the world as a complex system.

LISTEN TO EVERYONE, BUT TRUST ONLY YOUR INNER VOICE

Moreover, Intuitive Commanders operate with total conviction that their vision of the future is the best and probably the only path to take. As a result, they trust their own gut instincts and intuitions about the best way to proceed into the future. Where there is any doubt or conflict, *they trust their own inner voice* first and foremost, because they know it is the one source they can rely on. That makes the Commander a true pioneer, explorer, and visionary leader of people.

Intuitive Commanders are born with a mind preprogrammed to achieve, and they quickly discover that they can accomplish their personal ambitions best by making the world a better place. They learn that they can do this by leveraging the power of the people. Some, like Franklin Delano Roosevelt in a speech before Congress in 1941, lead with a grand vision of the entire world:

> We look forward to a world founded upon four essential human freedoms. The first is freedom of speech and expression . . . everywhere in the world. The second is freedom of every person to worship God in his own way . . . everywhere in the world. The third is freedom from want . . . everywhere in the world. The fourth is freedom from fear . . . anywhere in the world.

Perhaps even more important for leadership, Commanders may often have but few followers, may work with a handicap, and their ideas may be totally rejected by the masses, as we saw with Churchill. Yet, though he was a lone voice for many years, he never wavered. All leaders know this, know that they must stand by their principles regardless of the opposition and often at great personal risk. When Churchill said, "Never give in, never, never" in the dark days, he was speaking to himself as well as the British people.

For example, President Teddy Roosevelt, more outspoken and less tactful about the need of leaders to stay true to their own principles and vision of the future (even when they are in conflict with the vast majority of their public), was known for brash comments such as, "I don't know what the people think, I only know what they should think." In a sense, the Commander is the conscience of the people, defining what they *should* think collectively.

Thinkers: Commanding Decisions Based on Logic and Reason

Commanders like Churchill and Roosevelt are Extraverts, people persons whose energy comes from people served. In fact, Daniel Goleman says that a leader's "abilities fall within the domain of emotional intelligence—an adeptness at managing ourselves and our interactions with others." Emotional intelligence is what makes real leaders, their charisma, their unique connection with people.

Yet when it comes to actually making decisions, Commanders are *Thinkers,* making decisions based on objective criteria, in contrast to Feeling types, who make decisions based on criteria that are more subjective, relative, personal, and emotional. Commanders make decisions using reasoning, logic, science, and strategic thinking.

Yes, they do trust their instincts, but that's different from sudden impulsive reactions. They are proactive after weighing all the information and considering all alternatives, because at some point the unknowns may outweigh the knowns, and yet a rational choice must be made before action can be taken.

SUBJECTIVE AND OBJECTIVE: BAY OF PIGS AND CUBAN MISSILE CRISIS

The difference is clearly evident in the presidency of John F. Kennedy and his handling of the Bay of Pigs invasion in April 1961 and the Cuban Missile Crisis in October 1962. The Bay of Pigs disaster came very soon after Kennedy's election. The new president wanted to make his mark with a bold move, freeing the people of Cuba from Castro and communism. Unfortunately, his intelligence was bad, the strategy was flawed, and the military forces were ill equipped. Within hours, the invasion began falling apart. Kennedy said to White House correspondent Hugh Sidey:

> There were 50 or so of us, presumably the most experienced and smartest people we could get, to plan such an operation. . . . How could we have been so stupid? When we saw the wide range of the failures we asked ourselves why it had not been apparent to somebody from the start. I guess you get walled off from reality when you want something to succeed too much.

Why? Because the decision was subjective, based on emotions rather than rational judgment. Like most Commanders, Kennedy had a high regard for men of superior intelligence and knowledge, 50 of the best and brightest minds, he said. But all those brilliant minds went astray, misguided by an initial decision grounded in emotions. He was humiliated.

SHIFTING FROM THE HEART TO THE HEAD, FEELING TO THINKING

Kennedy did not want another military conflict in 1962, but his hand was being forced, this time by Russia. U.S. spy planes spotted Russian missile sites under construction in Cuba. One plane was shot down and the pilot killed. The arms buildup was accelerating. More Soviet ships loaded with missiles were on the way. Kennedy ordered a blockade.

For 13 tense days the two superpowers were eyeball to eyeball, close to starting a nuclear war. Advisers discussed options: invasion, air strikes, naval blockade, diplomacy. Information flew back and forth between intelligence, military, and diplomatic sources, always incomplete, always demanding judgment to fill in the blanks.

Kennedy met with the Russian ambassador and communicated directly with Khrushchev in Moscow. Emotions ran high as the brinkmanship continued and the United States demanded withdrawal. This time the president was making decisions rationally. It worked.

In making decisions, a Commander's mind functions as a judge—dispassionate, objective, and impartial, driven to do the right thing, wanting to do what's right for everyone in the long run. Is it fair? Is it just? What's best for the country or the community? The highest good? The universal law? Commanders must be cool heads in the midst of a storm, the final arbiter, the one responsible for deciding on a course of action.

At their best, they are guided by universal laws that transcend any personality type. They are not making relative judgments based on what's right or wrong on a personal basis. Moreover, they will use reason and research, logic and precedent, every resource necessary to lead them to the best possible decision—whatever it takes to do the right thing, because they are judged by a higher law that applies to them, too.

Judger: Result-Oriented Organizational Genius

Commanders are obsessed about making a mark in life—about success, achievement, accomplishment. Their Millionaire's Code virtually guarantees it for them. They are Extraverts, gifted leaders of people. They are Intuitive, with a commanding vision of the future. They are Thinkers, with the ability to act logically and objectively, serving the highest good of the people. Finally, they are *Judgers,* organizational geniuses that make things happen according to their master plans and strategies.

Judgers are the exact opposite of Perceivers, those easygoing individuals who feel restricted by things like organizations, schedules, and deadlines. Commanders embrace the role of Judgers—they have a mission to accomplish in life, and being Judgers gets them where they're going and keeps the people they're leading focused on the target.

Commanders are highly disciplined Judgers, who take charge of their destiny. They often go to bed at night with detailed to-do lists for the next day. They're up early, reading papers, exercising, eating healthy foods. They're at work early. Everything possible is worked out in advance—research schedules, alternative scenarios, strategic solutions, mission statement, goals, targets, monitoring progress, testing, deadlines, and backup plans.

They spend their days working and dealing with people, gathering new information, progress updates, changes, reassignments, and evaluations while reinforcing the mission, the master plan, and their strategies and checking tasks. You can find these Commanders on the front lines in wartime, working as managers in manufacturing plants across America, as business executives in every field, as school principals and college deans, as hospital administrators and building contractors.

Career Paths: Making Money and Making a Difference

Commanders are in positions of leadership, which invariably means working with budgets in the millions, even billions, managing expenses, salaries, income, sales—how the money flows in and out supports the goals of the organization. This applies whether they're in nonprofit organizations, government, small businesses or big corporations.

Money often becomes the one visible sign of success for many Commanders—their salary, the size of the budgets, growth in sales figures, profit margins, new products introduced, the company's increasing stock price, as well as the personal advantages such as a nice home in the right location, the kids attending a good school, a strong social network.

As a result, many Commanders work in business, industry, and finance because they not only have a knack for making money, they actually enjoy making money—not just for the sake of making money, but because what they are doing also tells them they are on track, fulfilling their destiny and accomplishing their mission in life.

THE MILLIONAIRE NEXT DOOR AND OTHERS MAKING A DIFFERENCE

Yes, there are many such moneymaking opportunities for Commanders in the large money-center banks, multinational giants, major investment companies, and blue-chip manufacturers. Witness Warren Buffett and Bill Gates. We also see examples of successful leaders whose lives transcend making money—Winston Churchill, Joe Torres, Oprah Winfrey, Colin Powell, and the Dalai Lama.

The truth is, most Commanders find opportunities closer to home, in local communities where they may occasionally get their names in the local newspaper, a church bulletin, or PTA flier. Thomas Stanley and William Danko tell us in *The Millionaire Next Door* that the local success stories are almost never mentioned in *Forbes, Fortune,* and the other national business magazines. Yet most of the opportunities for Commanders are close to home in your local community. There they often succeed quietly, making money and making a difference as change agents leading people:

- *Bank managers,* financing community development projects
- *Home builders,* providing new homes and tradesmen with jobs
- *Mayors,* working to get a new master plan approved
- *Small business owners* expanding into larger facilities
- *Radio station managers,* using programs to help a community
- *Fund-raisers* for new community fine arts' theaters
- *Community development directors,* bringing in new industry
- *Hospital administrators* expanding community health care
- *YMCA directors* and other local sports program organizers
- *School principals,* energizing students, teachers, and parents

The opportunities are enormous, both to make money and make a difference. Once they understand their ENTJ genetic code and their need to achieve by leading people, opportunities emerge all around them.

The fact is, most Commanders don't wind up in bright lights and history books. Some have big egos, but most are centered in themselves, confident of who they are, and satisfied with their place in the scheme of things. That's enough for them. They know they are on track fulfilling their destiny.

For example, according to Stanley and Danko, not only doesn't the millionaire next door get mentioned in the national business and financial press, but *they don't care*—they'd rather get a mention in some obscure trade journal like *Scrap Metal Recycler,* because that's the niche making them rich and famous (in their small corner of the world, of course). That's what provides for their families and prepares them for retirement. And that's what makes them feel they are in fact fulfilling their destiny, making a little bit of difference in their small world.

Making Money Is Easy and So Is Making a Difference: Just Do It

Let's cut to the bottom line—making money really is easy for Commanders, and it becomes even easier the less they worry about making money and the more confidence they gain knowing that their talents are in high demand. Moreover, they seem to instinctively and naturally know how to save, invest, and budget money, whether for themselves, their families, or their megabuck organizations.

Of all the personality types, Commanders may have the strongest understanding of the bottom line and how to get there—whether in business, government, health care, research, education, or the military. Commanders are obsessed about leading people to a successful bottom line.

Think about it. They have all the right stuff—charisma, leadership, confidence, judgment, strategic planning, and drive. They are born leaders. And born moneymaking machines. Making money isn't difficult for them.

And neither is making a difference. Why? Because Commanders are born to make a difference. They are the ultimate change agents. Their genetic code tells them they must achieve something and make a difference leading people or they will always feel unfulfilled in life, if they become nothing but a moneymaking machine. Yes, money is important, but it is not the true goal of a Commander, merely a tool. They must lead. They must make a difference. They must leave the world a better place than they found it.

* * * * * * * *

I want employees to ask themselves whether
they are willing to have any contemplated act
appear on the front page of their local paper the next
day, be read by their spouses, children, and friends. . . .
If they follow this test, they will
not fear my other message to them:
Lose money for my firm and I will be understanding;
lose a shred of reputation for the firm,
and I will be ruthless.

Warren Buffett

MASTER INNOVATORS (ENTP)

THOMAS EDISON, BENJAMIN FRANKLIN, THOMAS JEFFERSON

> Jack Mingo's book,
> *How the Cadillac Got Its Fins,*
> is entertaining.
> And it contains a very sobering message.
> That is, really neat stuff
> seldom comes from "the suits"
> (especially if those suits
> are charcoal or black).
> To do something out-of-step requires . . .
> an out-of-step person. . . .
> It's the cracked ones that
> let the light into the world . . .
> the winning edge is that
> fire in their eyes!
>
> Tom Peters,
> *The Circle of Innovation*

B y far, one of the more fascinating personalities of the four Systems Masterminds—*let's rephrase that*—one of the most fascinating of all 16 personality types is the Master Innovator. They are the world's ultimate change agents, and they accomplish their mission in a very practical way.

These unconventional, upbeat oddballs have brains that are going a mile a minute, constantly cooking up new ideas about anything and everything and everybody! They're like kids in a candy store—they love inventing ingenious new gadgets, tools, mechanisms, processes, and a thousand big and little ways to improve their world and make it a better place to live in. They love talking to everybody and anybody about all the exciting stuff they discover—friends, coworkers, and strangers—anybody who'll listen!

There's never a dull moment when Innovators are around. They're dynamic, high-octane standouts who love trying new things. To them, everything in life is an exciting adventure, all day long, anything to break up the monotony of a routine day, including manipulating the rules of the organization and even challenging authorities—anything to protect their independence and their creativity niche. When the daily routine gets dull and boring, you can count on the Innovator to spice things up with a prank, some wild story, maybe a joke, another new idea, and a new way to make life a bit more efficient and more fun.

Innovators Touch It, See It—Then Start Reinventing It!

Perhaps the best-known Innovator is Thomas Edison, holder of more than 1,000 patents for his inventions: "I never pick up an item without thinking of how I might improve it." Most notable among Edison's inventions are the lightbulb, motion picture camera, telegraph and phonograph, an electrical vote recorder, and a universal stock ticker. All practical, all for human use, all for the common good: "I never perfected an invention that I did not think about in terms of the service it might give to others."

You're also likely to find Innovators doing more than just inventing "things." They improve technologies, too: for computers (microprocessors), cameras (digital), automobiles (global positioning), aircraft (stealth cloaking), weaponry (night vision and medical equipment (artificial hearts). They also invent new and more efficient *processes* for individuals and organizations in such areas as construction management, demographic research, investment analysis, social sciences, and politics.

Moreover, many Innovators are "closet inventors" who hold down normal jobs while tinkering away on new ideas in their garages and dens on weekends and evenings, like actors waiting on tables until the big break. Innovators can't help themselves; it's in their blood. Like Edison, they're idea generators, and ideas are always pouring out of their heads. Part of their genetic code tells them to serve humanity with their genius.

REVOLUTIONARY LEADERS: EDUCATORS, ARCHITECTS, PUBLISHERS

America has a rich heritage of Innovators such as Thomas Jefferson. History books highlight his role in the American Revolution, as author of the Declaration of Independence, and later as governor of the Commonwealth of Virginia, founder of the University of Virginia, and the third U.S. president. When I attended "Mr. Jefferson's University," I imagined him commuting 125 miles to his job as president in Washington—*on horseback.*

Like all the best Masterminds, Jefferson had a thirst for knowledge and an insatiable curiosity for new ideas. He was an inventor as well as a draftsman, surveyor, horticulturist, astronomer, musician, historian, and attorney. As secretary of state he invented an encryption machine.

Jefferson was the architect for both the university and his nearby home, Monticello, which today is the only house in the United States on the United Nations' prestigious World Heritage List of sites that must be protected at all costs. He designed many practical inventions for his home and plantation, such as an efficient plow, automatic doors, swivel chair, refrigeration, pedometer, and copy machine, that made Monticello seem centuries ahead of its time.

IDEA-GENERATING MACHINES THAT JUST KEEP ON GOING!

Ben Franklin, a contemporary of Jefferson, was also an Innovator—and a Renaissance man, to boot. Although his formal schooling ended early, he taught himself algebra, geometry, navigation, logic, history, science, and five languages, and later he became a successful printer. He signed the Declaration of Independence and eventually served as the new nation's ambassador and first postmaster general.

In his lifetime Franklin invented many now-familiar things—bifocals, the lightning rod, electric storage batteries, a safe stove, the first ventilation system, the harmonica, swim fins (he was a good swimmer who became even better with these), the rocking chair, a medical catheter, an odometer (for his carriage), the circulating library, daylight saving time, streetlamps, and the first municipal departments for fire fighting, lighting, and street cleaning. He was the father of modern dentistry, the first political cartoonist, and the first publisher to use illustrations and commercial advertising.

Like all Innovators, inventors, Renaissance men, and jacks-of-all-trades, Franklin was an optimist who genuinely wanted to help make the world a better place, and one way was by inventing new and improved ways to make things work. He never profited from his inventions, they were for the people.

INNOVATION AND CREATIVITY: A KICK IN THE SEAT OF THE PANTS

Innovators make what they do seem so simple: "To invent, you need a good imagination and a pile of junk," said Edison. The average person may need to work at this a bit. Probably one of the best summaries of what goes on in an Innovator's mind is *A Kick in the Seat of the Pants*. Author Roger von Oech is president of Creative Think, a consulting firm that works with businesses to stimulate innovation and creativity. The four processes are:

1. *Explorer.* You're searching for and collecting information from which you can make up new ideas. ⌐NOT ALL
2. *Artist.* Now your imaginative, ⟨playful artist⟩ takes all the bits of information that the explorer has "collected and transforms them into original new ideas," lots of new ideas without yet judging which is best.
3. *Judge.* Next, the judge evaluates what the artist created and decides "what to do with it: implement it, modify it, or discard it."
4. *Warrior.* Finally the doer takes the ideas the judge approved and puts them into action.

Roger von Oech says that "normal" humans would be wise to break down their processes of innovation and creativity into these four steps, *without skipping or overlapping them.* Otherwise, he says, there is a tendency to become lazy, judge the first idea as the best one, and make it *the* new solution. The problem is that by doing this, you are likely to miss out on other, better ideas that the Explorer and Artist might have developed.

While so-called normal people and organizations are better off if they methodically use this four-step process, *Innovators wrap all four steps into one big idea-generating machine* that's racing in overdrive all the time—that's their four-letter genetic code working. Remember, as Edison said: "I never pick up an item without thinking of how I might improve it." Imagine a brain that can't see, touch, or pick up *anything* without thinking about reinventing and improving it—or inventing a better one. Now *that's* an Innovator!

Millionaire's code for Master Innovators
Extravert, Intuitive, Thinker, Perceiver (ENTP)

Extraverts love being with people, and Innovators are among the best at it. Not only do they get ideas from every item they pick up, they get new ideas from talking to people—"Yeah, wow, I love whatcha said, buddy, does that ever give me a great idea. Gee thanks. Now, what do you think about . . ." and they're off and running again.

Extraverts are often accused of talking first, before they even know what they're going to say, in contrast to Introverts who are more comfortable working things out before exposing themselves by discussing the matter.

Well, it is true that Extraverts do think out loud, or rather, work things out by talking to people. But when it comes to Innovators, the truth is that their minds are *always* working something out at hyperspeed, and they *need* the exchange of ideas that comes from dialoguing with individuals and groups, from friend and foe, whether positive feedback or sharp challenges. They need lots of dialogue, both to generate new ideas and as sounding boards to help develop current ones already buzzing around in their heads.

When they start up a conversation with a coworker, a friend, or even a stranger in a coffeeshop or deli, in a very real sense, Innovators are actually continuing a conversation they already have going on inside their heads; they just need to add another participant to the "meeting," so to speak. It's a natural process for them, and there's often something rather charming about their way of engaging people as they pull people from the outer world into the ingenious workings of their inner world.

What? It's true, sometimes they seem as though they're engaging in idle chatter, talking just for the sake of talking. Or they appear to be nonsensical Rube Goldberg contraptions that are humorous. Other times they discuss what seem to be grand, cosmic schemes based on sophisticated theorems.

The Intuitive: Change Agents with a Vision of the Future

While they are engaging with people as Extraverts, drawing energy from the world around them, something else is going on at a much deeper level between Innovators and the people they're interacting with—a nonverbal communication, perhaps in a parallel universe, at the level of the "personal unconscious" and the "collective unconscious," as Carl Jung calls this realm of connections and interactions between people. This is their *Intuitive* nature at work.

Remember that the Innovator personality is one of the four Systems Masterminds. They are change agents, focused on the future and destined to make the world of tomorrow a better place, leveraging their powers of mind, often by revolutionary means.

On a personal level, their mission is revealed to them through their dealings, interactions, and conversations with people—bosses and staff, spouses and children, store clerks and professors, peers, mentors, and students, *anyone.*

SCIENCE OF SUCCESS COMES FROM A HIGHER INTELLIGENCE

At a deeper level, all Masterminds, especially Innovators, are in search of the ultimate truth, knowledge, and wisdom about their world, not just a collection of superficial facts and figures—for in their lifelong search comes the secret to their mission in this lifetime.

In other words, their dialogues actually carry a deep psychological and metaphysical significance for Innovators. Nowhere has this search been more powerfully presented than in the work of Napoleon Hill, who spent a lifetime motivating businesspeople with the "Science of Success," the secrets Hill learned from billionaire Andrew Carnegie.

Hill spent his entire life developing this "science" while working with 500 leaders in finance and industry, including Thomas Edison, Henry Ford, and Alexander Graham Bell, and he inspired thousands in the next generation of leaders. Hill's works, including *Think and Grow Rich* and *Success Through a Positive Mental Attitude,* are classics that everyone in business and financial work turns to first for direction and inspiration.

Hill writes that he was personally guided in his life's mission by "unseen guides" as he called them. However, he admits in *You Can Work Your Own Miracles,* "For many years . . . I carefully avoided all references to them" for fear it might hurt his credibility in the hard-nosed business world, especially among those tough-minded captains of industry and commerce:

> Then one day in a conversation with Elmer R. Gates, a distinguished scientist and inventor, I was overwhelmed with joy when I learned that he not only had discovered the presence of unseen guides, but he had formed a working alliance with them which enabled him to perfect more inventions and procure more patents than had been granted to the great inventor, Thomas Edison.
>
> From that day forward I began to make inquiries of the hundreds of successful men who collaborated with me in the organization of the Science of Success, and discovered each of them had received guidance from unknown sources. [Alexander Graham] Bell, in particular, believed the invisible source of aid was nothing but a direct contact with Infinite Intelligence.

Hill personally discussed these unseen guides with Edison and discovered that this great inventor had some much more profound beliefs:

> Thomas A. Edison had an interesting view as to the nature and source of the invisible forces which he used so freely in his work of research in the field of invention. He believed that all thoughts released by all people at all times are picked up and become a part of the ether, where they remain forever [and] anyone may tune in. . . . Mr. Edison believed that the energy with which we think is a projected portion of the Infinite Intelligence.

INSPIRATION BLENDING THE PHYSICAL AND THE METAPHYSICAL

Napoleon Hill's experiences with inventors and other successful leaders suggest that when they are most in tune with their genetic code, they are most intimately in contact with a powerful universal intelligence. That intelligence communicates with them in many natural, everyday ways that are evidenced in the minds of people like Edison and other inventors:

- *Things.* At one level, this intelligence communicates information when, for example, an Innovator like Edison touches an item, anything at all.
- *People.* At another level it comes from conversations that Extraverted Innovators have with people around them in everyday life.
- *Guides.* At yet another level, an information exchange occurs between a tuned-in Innovator and the free-floating energy that the Infinite Intelligence projects in many ways to the Innovator—through items, through people, and directly to the Innovator's mind.

Unquestionably, there is a metaphysical quality to the *Intuitive* nature of the Innovator, quite in line with a related remark made by Albert Einstein in a different context: "The more I study physics the more I am drawn to metaphysics." The workings of the Innovator's Intuitive mind cannot be explained simply by reference to mental processes.

We do know that all Intuitives have visions of the future, unlike their opposites, Sensors, who focus on the immediate, the specific, the present, the concrete, that which can be tested through their sensory processes of touch, taste, sound, smell, and sight. All operating right now, today.

Not so with *Intuitives,* and most especially Innovators. They do indeed march to a different drummer, echoing the mission of the philosopher George Bernard Shaw: "Some men see things as they are, and say, Why? I dream of things that never were, and say, Why not?"

VISIONS OF A BRIGHTER FUTURE MAKE EVERY DAY A CHALLENGE

As change agents, they're driven to make the world a better place. In order to push, guide, and direct the world to a bright future, their computer-like brains are forever speculating about alternatives, essentially bored with the present. They are adventurers flirting with the unknown, challenged by the mysteries of life, excited by the prospects of molding the future—because deep down, Innovators have an incredible pressure to accomplish something in life.

To fulfill that dream, the Innovator has no choice but to "boldly go where no one has gone before," out there into the unknown world that can only be known in the speculations of an Intuitive mind.

The Innovator spends a lifetime as a perpetual student, always seeing things in a fresh new way, accumulating information about the existing world, operating nonstop—but collecting information only if it is useful to the mental concepts, theories, patterns, speculations, trends, ideas, and visions the Innovator's mind has of the world, *not as it is today,* but rather as he or she envisions it *should be in the future.*

This future orientation is a classic trait of the Intuitive mind in all Innovators. As Jefferson put it, "I like the dreams of the future better than the history of the past." *The future is, in every sense, encoded in the Innovator's genetic structure, and paradoxically, and that's what makes them so excited about the present!*

Thinking: Going Outside the Box and Doing the Right Thing

How do you make a decision, objectively or subjectively? Thinkers and Feelers are at opposite ends of the decision-making spectrum. The *Thinker* attempts to be totally unbiased and impartial, using objective criteria when making decisions. On the other hand, the *Feeling* personality tends to use subjective criteria, based on a relative emotional reaction surrounding the situation.

Ask Thinkers *how* they made a decision and they'll tell you it was "the right thing to do." It's that simple to them. We've already seen this trait in the commitment of innovators to the greater good of society—witness Edison and Franklin. *Thinkers* need to do what's fair, just, and reasonable, what's moral, and they act in accord with the law of the land, the national interest, the universal law, the commandments.

They internalize what's right in their thinking mind. It becomes the high standard they must live by, and they uniformly apply it to the world at large when they make decisions. As a result, their decisions are not based on their personal feelings; rather, they're honor-bound to do the right thing. It's locked in their genetic code.

Thinking takes on a rather unique quality, however, for unconventional Innovators. Reason and logic can be a bit too linear, sequential, and mechanistic for Innovators who are used to jumping around mentally between all the projects they're working on.

A WHACK ON THE SIDE OF THE HEAD: HARD OR SOFT THINKING?

Believe me, they do have a project-oriented entrepreneurial spirit when it comes to their innovating, creating, and inventing, because they hate routine and are likely to be extremely pragmatic as they skirt around traditional thought processes. In short, thinking is what works for Innovators. It has to in their world of the future. Edison said:

> Just because something doesn't do what you planned it to do in the first place doesn't mean it's useless. . . . Surprises and reverses should be an incentive to great accomplishment. Results? Why, man, I have gotten lots of results! If I find 10,000 ways something *won't* work, I haven't failed. I am not discouraged, because every wrong attempt discarded is just one more step forward. . . . There are no rules here, we're just trying to accomplish something.

Roger von Oech is a little more specific in defining the different kinds of thinking used in creative and innovative projects. In his book, *A Whack on the Side of the Head,* he makes an important distinction:

> *Soft thinking . . .* is metaphor, approximate, humorous, playful, and capable of dealing with contradiction . . . like a floodlight. It is more diffuse, not as intense, but covers a wider area.
> *Hard thinking . . .* tends to be more logical, precise, exact, specific, and consistent . . . is like a spotlight. It is bright, clear, and intense, but the focus is narrow.

Innovators have the unique ability and flexibility to switch back and forth between these two ways of thinking, much as they jump around between projects that may be in various stages of development and interest.

There is a time for the *soft thinking* mind-set of the *Explorer* and the *Artist,* as von Oech calls them, searching for virtually any possible creative and innovative solution. And there is a time for the *hard thinking* of the *Judge* and the *Warrior.* Innovators are among those rare personalities who seem to know instinctively which one's most appropriate and when.

Perceiver: A Powerful Magnet for Innovative Solutions

The Innovator as a *Perceiver* is probably the most adaptable and open-minded of all personalities. Conversely, the Judger is the early bird, meticulously organizing everything well in advance and insisting on discipline, deadlines, tight schedules, and specific performance measures of progress.

The Perceiver, however, has to stay open to the elements of chance and surprise—many inspirations come from the unexpected and unpredictable—from the everyday world and from stuff that spontaneously pops up from the dark corners of the mind. Edison had an amusing way of describing the inner workings of the Innovator's unique mental process:

> Because I readily absorb such ideas from every source, frequently starting where the last person left off, I am sometimes accurately described as more of a sponge than an inventor.

These people have no choice but to stay open like a sponge, adaptable to the serendipity of a volatile world and a curious mind that operates like radar, scanning the horizon to see where the last person left off and the possible next step in the progression of human life into the future.

Perceivers are both hyperactive kids and bold explorers with a vision of the future that's constantly unfolding in their minds—and they need to be the driving force on the leading edge of the adventure, out there, making the future happen with their unique creations, inventions, and innovations.

Remember, the typical business organization is loaded with more Judgers than Perceivers, and Judgers become very nervous about the apparently undisciplined and disorganized work habits of Perceivers as they jump around from project to project, idea to idea.

If you're a true-blue Innovator, accept that you need a totally flexible schedule. Work for yourself as an entrepreneur, or make darn sure you're working in an organization that knows how to live with your unique lifestyle and work habits, as well as your contributions, which will flow unevenly.

Careers: The Opportunity to Invent a New Future Every Day

Innovators aren't just working in their garages, all alone, trying to invent a better mousetrap, lightbulb, or microprocessor. This personality can also find some great opportunities in any one of several career areas that offer opportunities to avoid boring, humdrum, routine work—careers in which you can work pretty much on your own and juggle a lot of exciting new projects on the edge of tomorrow.

If you really are an Innovator, that is exactly where you're more likely to find a destiny matching your genetic code. In fact, many fields need Innovators. Here's a sample of several possible career paths:

- *Industrial product designers and developers* in an ad agency
- *Graduate university professors,* basic research, scientific field
- *Surgeons,* on the cutting edge of new medical technologies
- *Social scientists,* working in think tanks on global issues
- *Political analysts,* drafting landmark legislation
- *Investment bankers,* developing new financing instruments
- *Entrepreneurs,* working on one start-up after another through life
- *Real estate developers,* where every project is a whole new world
- *Corporate executives* in charge of special project development
- *Plaintiff's attorneys,* prosecuting cases in an untested area of the law
- *Motivational speakers,* regularly exposed to new audiences and ideas
- *Performers,* as in inventive rapid-fire mind of Robin Williams
- *Presidents,* building multi-million-dollar companies

Watch out, though, the tendency of innovators to move from project to project, idea to idea, may also manifest itself in moves from career to career, as they have difficulties picking the right career and and may become discouraged about starting over at the bottom.

True, it may have been easier to move back and forth between careers in Thomas Jefferson's day, but you only go around once. Don't worry about how your resume will look. Do what makes you happy. Explore. Experiment. If you don't like where you are, move, and fast. If you do, give it all you have while you're there. The fact is, many innovators are living examples of Napoleon Hill's "positive mental attitude"—*articulate, imaginative, creative, and inspiring*—and they do wind up in positions of leadership

Through the years, I've been in banking, law, psychology, newspapers, television, film, architecture, construction, city planning, and a few other long-forgotten fields. Treat your career—*indeed, your entire life*—as one big fascinating adventure that needs constant reinvention and new innovative elements. That's just what life is, *and that's who you are!* Moreover, that's the only way Innovators can fulfill their unique destiny.

Making Big Money on the Roller Coaster of Innovation

Innovators have the potential of making substantial sums of money from the projects they work on, especially if they are self-employed entrepreneurs. Clients, customers, businesses, and financial backers often place a high value on the unique talents of serious Innovators, as they develop a reputation for delivering what they promise.

However, the money is likely to come in uneven chunks, with quiet periods in between. Multiple projects may smooth out the flow, and later they may develop regular royalties for the sales of licenses. But in the early idea development stages, income may fluctuate. As a result, current financial needs of providing for a family and funding new projects may delay their saving for the future.

In addition, the optimism and confidence of Innovators are likely to convince them that at some point they will hit it big and be able to retire and that their best business strategy would be to invest all their extra money in their own little fledging business—including all the money they might otherwise have put into IRAs or 401(k)s.

In the long run, this is a risky retirement plan. Self-employed Innovators need professional financial guidance so that they can stay focused on their projects. Remember, it takes savings of only a couple hundred dollars a month in a diversified portfolio, starting with a fully funded IRA, to ensure your financial future. Later, when you do hit it big, review the earlier discussion of Robert Kiyosaki's *Rich Man, Poor Man.* Tuck away some savings for retirement and plow the rest into the next projects in your own business.

Innovators working in established companies are likely to have a salary and a pension or other tax-advantaged retirement program, so they can stay focused on their projects. They may, however, decide to job-hop, and, like self-employed Innovators, they will need an adviser to guide them. But don't let the financial roller coaster get you down. As Edison put it:

> Show me a thoroughly satisfied man and I will show you a failure. I believe that restlessness is discontent, and discontent is merely the first necessity of progress. . . . I always found that—when worrying—the best thing I could do was to focus attention upon something useful and work hard at it. . . . I would soon forget what was troubling me.

It may take you 10,000 failures to get where you're going, but a real Innovator would have it no other way—it's the journey, not the destination. Life is an exciting adventure for the Innovator, an experience to be lived to the max! It's not about the money.

* * * * * * *

Creativity is a experience—to my eye, a spiritual experience.
It does not matter which way you think of it:
creativity leading to spirituality
or spirituality leading to creativity.
In fact, I do not make a distinction between the two.
In the face of such experience,
the whole question of belief is rendered obsolete.
As Carl Jung answered the question of belief late in his life,
"I don't believe; I know."

Julia Cameron,
The Artist's Way

CHAPTER

CHIEF STRATEGISTS (INTJ)

DWIGHT D. EISENHOWER, VINCE LOMBARDI, CHARLES MUNGER

The final stage of mental toughness is reflected in
the challenge response.
You actually find yourself investing
more positive intensity, more of yourself as the situation gets
tougher. You find that problems you face in competition are not
threatening but stimulating. You've gone well beyond simply
loving to win.
You have clearly come to love the battle.
As a result of this emotional response,
you have become an excellent problem solver.
When everyone else is heading for the trenches as the problems
start mounting, you smile inside because you know you got the
emotional edge.

James Loehr,
The Mental Game

The four Systems Masterminds share a common characteristic: They are all change agents, men and women destined by their genetic code to change, improve, and make more efficient the world around them. They have an inner need to excel and achieve and will spend their lives creating a better world, improving whatever system they find themselves in—government, military, economic, educational, scientific, medical, you name it, they may be drawn to any of these systems—using it as a base to leverage their individual skills.

In many ways, all Systems Masterminds are a living paradox: On one hand, they rely heavily on logic and reason; on the other hand, they are revolutionaries, innovators, strategic analysts, and builders of new systems.

While Chief Strategists (INTJ) have many character traits in common with Commanders in Chief (ENTJ), Introverted Strategists have quiet reserves and prefer working behind the scenes. While Extraverted Commanders have an inordinate need to be in the spotlight, in charge of people, Strategists are more content operating in the background, working more with ideas, theories, and concepts, developing alternatives and strategic planning and letting others shine in the spotlight.

Blurred Distinctions: Strategists as Commanders in Training

History tells us, however, that the distinction between Chief Strategists and Commanders in Chief may easily be blurred and quickly breached in times of crisis and great change—when there is a pressing need for new leadership. As a result, Strategists would be wise to read closely and understand all about the Commander's code as well as their own for two reasons:

First, they may actually be late bloomers and emerge as Extraverts when they become more self-confident and secure, which happens as their strategist skills are reinforced throughout life. Second, the time may come, quite unexpectedly, when they have little choice in the matter, as the rush of history and the greater needs of people and events force on them the mantle of leadership in active command of large masses of people.

Dwight D. Eisenhower is a perfect example of a Chief Strategist who was drawn out of the privacy he preferred and into the limelight as commander of Allied forces in Europe during World War II. Yet it is in the privacy of their inner world, often in the company of great mentors, that great leaders like Eisenhower hone their skills before going public, especially for Strategists whose genetic codes reflect a personality in full command of themselves by their very nature.

RELUCTANT WARRIOR EMERGES AS BRILLIANT COMMANDER

Eisenhower entered the military somewhat by default. After working to help his brother through college, he accepted an appointment to West Point, in large part because it was tuition-free. At first he wasn't gung ho about a military career. On graduation in 1915, he accepted a commission after much soul searching.

In spite of his reluctance, he made a personal commitment to excel in every assignment. As a result, he drew the attention of his superiors as an exceptionally brilliant military strategist, organizer, and planner for 25 years in America's peacetime army.

Eisenhower served as General Douglas MacArthur's aide for five years in the late 1930s. Although he lacked experience as a combat officer, his reputation as a military strategist and campaign planner was well recognized. As a result, within a few years after the outbreak of World War II, Eisenhower was rapidly promoted from colonel to supreme Allied commander of all military forces in Europe, ultimately masterminding D-Day, the Normandy invasion.

The invasion—the "Great Crusade" as Eisenhower called it—was the culmination of his career as a strategist. The planning was in the works for almost two years, and he worried until the very last moment, working and reworking his plan: "When you are in any contest you should work as if there were—to the very last minute—a chance to lose it."

Eisenhower's preference for a more private life never left him, although he resigned as U.S. Army chief of staff in 1948 to become president of Columbia, at that time rejecting an offer to become a nominee for U.S. president. Two years later he returned to active duty to help build an effective NATO force. Finally, in 1952 he ran for the presidency and won.

Like Churchill and other great men and women throughout history, Eisenhower was thrust into a position of leadership by circumstances: the right person in the right place at the right time. Still, Eisenhower preferred a more private life, unlike Churchill, an Extravert who sought the public spotlight and, when offered the position of wartime prime minister late in life, said: "My entire life has been a preparation for this moment."

Even later, as president of the United States, when Eisenhower set about reorganizing and strengthening the presidency, he always preferred working outside the public eye and protecting his personal life. In fact, he once remarked, "I can think of nothing more boring for the American people than to have to sit in their living rooms for a whole half hour looking at my face on their television screens."

Millionaire's Code for Chief Strategists
Introvert, Intuitive, Thinker, Judger (INTJ)

The life of Eisenhower strongly exemplifies that the strategic abilities of this unique personality type are applicable in many fields, as his career moved from military commander to university president to government, where he focused on foreign affairs issues.

However, it also seems quite clear that while Strategists may prefer the more private, secluded, and academic lifestyle of *Introverts,* the inner need to accomplish something, to make their mark in life, to be agents of change, will eventually catch up with them, conflicting with their desire to protect their introspective nature, even overriding it, adding future challenges.

Furthermore, their achievements are also likely to gain them enough recognition that they will be forced into the public eye as Commanders and into positions of leadership over large groups of people.

In other words, most Strategists will, at some point in their lives— *through circumstances and accomplishments*—be faced with choices to go public or not. That is, you will be forced to ask yourselves not only whether you want the added responsibilities, but whether a more public life truly fits your personality and whether you're giving up something of yourself that may be vital to your lifestyle.

Consider the following career choices as likely to come up for reserved Strategists, either as opportunities out of the blue (headhunter calls or boss offers new job) or because they decide to go in a new direction, possibly for financial reasons, or more likely, because they feel unfulfilled in a current career:

- *University professors and researchers:* College presidents
- *Computer systems analysts/designers:* VPs and research directors
- *Psychiatrists or psychologists:* Director of mental health clinics
- *Architectural systems engineers:* Heads of marketing and sales
- *Investment advisers and brokers:* Regional district managers
- *Management consultants:* Departmental vice presidents
- *Reporters and news analysts:* Editorial news directors
- *Administrative judges:* Running for political office
- *Cardiovascular surgeons:* Chiefs of medicine at teaching hospital
- *Bank economists:* Heads of new business development
- *Research scientists:* Divisional administrative vice presidents

Look before you leap. Do you really want the exposure? Or are you enjoying your privacy more than you would like leading a team of specialists like yourself, going to meetings with experts and administrators in all other areas of your organization and getting involved in new business promotion with the general public, for example?

WHEN OPPORTUNITY KNOCKS, TRUST YOUR INNER GUIDES

If you're a true Introvert, you prefer your own company and enjoy spending time alone, which makes Strategists great students. You are energized more by your inner world than by people. This doesn't mean you're antisocial, just that you prefer the peace and quiet of your den, reading in the library, walks alone, quiet dinners, the company of a few friends and loved ones–thinking.

When you are in groups, you're more likely to listen than to talk. When you do talk, it's often from a prepared memo and more than likely rehearsed. You need the opportunity to work things out in advance before going public. You may not feel comfortable speaking extemporaneously or acting on the spur of the moment in meetings. You prefer your rich inner life to the noise from the outside world.

Career advancement opportunities may mean more money in the short run. But they can also create inner conflicts and stress for a Chief Strategist in a new position as a Commander.

Whether you make a transition to the Extravert's world isn't the main issue. Many Strategists do take the risk and go there–out of financial necessity or merely to test themselves, to see the limits of their capabilities. Whatever the choice, just make certain you keep a balance between your private and public lives, because the natural instincts of the Introvert won't just disappear. Honor them. In fact, the pressures and demands may require you to work extra hard to preserve your inner life, both at home and in work situations.

Remember, Strategists like Eisenhower are able to do it. So can you. If it doesn't work for you, better chalk it up to experience and move on rather than wallowing in a setback. There are always opportunities for gifted Strategists. Besides, as coach Vince Lombardi once said, "It's not whether you get knocked down, it's whether you get up." That's what makes you a winner.

The Intuitive: A Strategist with Vision of a Bright New Future

As you will recall, the *Intuitive* function tells us how we view the world and collect information about it. Sensors are the opposite of Intuitives. Sensors want facts, concrete information, hard data, no guesswork, sensory data they can collect and compare with past data, none of that speculation about the future allowed. "Just give me the facts," as Sergeant Friday would say.

Intuitives are quite the opposite, most obviously in their orientation toward life. Intuitives are looking to the future, and they want to make the world a better place. Their starting point is their inner mental world of ideas, theories, concepts, alternatives, interrelations, probabilities, and possibilities.

The facts are interesting, but invariably incomplete and always suspect, so Intuitives must fill in the blanks in order to test their hypotheses. They have to speculate about future scenarios, because, by its very nature, the future they are creating is an unknown.

AHEAD OF THEIR TIME: MAKING THE FUTURE HAPPEN

It's no exaggeration to say that Intuitives—most especially Strategists—are ahead of their time, often way ahead, visionaries on an exploration into the future, searching for the meaning of life and their role in it so they can make the world a better place in which to live.

They are extremely analytical and take great pride in their abilities as original thinkers, which they clearly are. As a result, they measure themselves by extremely high standards, demanding the same from others, placing a high value on the knowledge and competence of other experts of their caliber while dismissing anything or anyone not meeting their standards.

Strategists actually go beyond in this regard. Their vision of the future becomes cemented in their minds. They need to accomplish something to prove their ideas are right, and they become obsessed with making their vision a reality. Fortunately, their expertise, self-will, and confidence usually work to make it all happen!

Eisenhower, for example, had this kind of determined tunnel vision that rolled over obstacles and opposition, everything from graduating number one at the U.S. Army war college for command officers early in his career to leading the Allied forces to victory over Germany: "We succeed only as we identify in life, or in war, or in anything else, a single overriding objective, and make all other considerations bend to that one objective."

FOR THE STRATEGIST, THERE IS NO SECOND PLACE IN BATTLE

Vince Lombardi also had the same intense drive. In spirit like Eisenhower, Lombardi, former Green Bay Packers coach, is known as the "greatest football coach of all time" because he was America's best-known symbol of a single-minded determination to win:

> Winning is not a sometime thing; it's an all the time thing. You don't win once in a while; you don't do things right once in a while; you do them right all the time. Winning is a habit. Unfortunately, so is losing. There is no room for second place. There is only one place in my game, and that's first place. . . . It is and always has been an American zeal to be first in anything we do, and to win, and to win, and to win.

In fact, every Strategist has much in common with the battlefield general and the football coach. Generals develop detailed plans in advance, reviewing alternative scenarios, training their field commanders and troops. Coaches have several assistant coaches preparing the quarterbacks, linemen, backfield and ends, and special teams. Everything is focused on the battle, the game, real life.

FIERCE COMPETITORS: WINNING IS THE ONLY ALTERNATIVE

Strategists love theorizing about alternative battle plans and game strategies, but when the chips are down, winning *is* the only thing for them—they need to be *in* the game to achieve and succeed. They are action-oriented, but the action is a direct result of all the mental theorizing, preplanning, and advance training.

Once on the field, the real test is how the world sees their flexible strategies, their adaptability in the heat of battle in shifting to plan B, their preparedness in dealing with the unexpected and still winning the game or the war. Lombardi had this to say:

> Running a football team is no different than running any other kind of organization—an army, a political party or a business. The principles are the same. The object is to win—to beat the other guy. . . . It is a reality of life that men are competitive . . . any man's finest hour, the greatest fulfillment of all that he holds dear, is that moment when he has worked his heart out in a good cause and lies exhausted on the field of battle—victorious.

Strategists may be the most goal-oriented of all the personalities, often shutting out all other considerations in pursuit of the target. They have such strong self-will, confidence, and determination that once they receive the *go* signal (which they will seek) and once the objective is defined (by them), they will aggressively pursue their goals with the absolute conviction that they cannot fail, marshaling all their mental powers in order to move methodically from concept to completion—a win on the scoreboard, an enemy defeated, a victorious campaign.

THE ONLY SCORE THAT COUNTS: MAKING THE WORLD A BETTER PLACE

In the end, Strategists want not just a beautiful theory on paper, but proof positive they really are as competent in their fields as they believe they are, proof that they really are accomplishing something, and proof they are making a difference in the world.

To get positive results, you need to be in the action, winning as many games and battles as possible to prove all that. In fact, there's little room for error in the Strategist's mind. They are fierce competitors and frequent champions. But most of all, they have a burning desire to make a difference. Lombardi said it well:

> After the cheers have died down and the stadium is empty, after the headlines have been written and after you are back in the quiet of your room and the championship ring has been placed on the dresser and all the pomp and fanfare has faded, the enduring things that are left are: the dedication to excellence, the dedication to victory, and the dedication to doing with our lives the very best we can to make the world a better place in which to live.

The power of Strategists comes from their brilliance in mastering the battle plan and playbook. They may know in their hearts that they did their best and gave their all, but in the end they are well aware that they will be judged by only one thing—the result.

Thinking: Do the Right Thing, and You're a Winner

For Strategists, the *Thinking* function is not simply some mental process that takes place in the brain—computer-like rational analysis, logic, deductive and inductive reasoning, theories and hypotheses. Nor is the Strategist's Thinking function merely a way of distinguishing the Thinker's objective decision processes from the more subjective, emotional processes of a feeling-type person's decisions making.

Doing the right thing is the goal of a Thinker's decisions, most especially of the Strategist's. There can be no compromise. Strategists must live up to a higher standard. For them, decisions are a matter of character and conscience, of what's best for the common good, of living up to a universal law. As a result, the kind of personal preferences and empathy for specific individuals that may influence a Feeling personality are, in the Strategist's Thinking mind, always outweighed by the collective interests of the organization, society, and the nation.

MENTAL TOUGHNESS: COMPETITORS WHO NEVER GIVE UP, NEVER

Strategists must be impartial and objective in making decisions. They question their own willpower for failing to live up to a standard of excellence deeply ingrained in their character and soul. As a result, they invariably come across as authoritative, cold, and machinelike in dealing with people. However, Strategists see themselves quite differently—as disciplined, absolutely committed, and willing to do whatever it takes to win. Says Lombardi:

> To achieve success, whatever the job we have, we must pay a price.... Football is a great deal like life in that it teaches that work, sacrifice, perseverance, competitive drive, selflessness and respect for authority is the price that each and every one of us must pay to achieve any goal that is worthwhile.

Strategists also see a world grown soft, relying too heavily on feelings that fluctuate all over the map, weakening people and creating relative standards for society. It is not that Feeling personalities cannot make decisions, because they do. But they lack the tough-mindedness of a strategist like Vince Lombardi:

> Mental toughness is many things and rather difficult to explain. Its qualities are sacrifice and self-denial. Also, most importantly, it is combined with a perfectly disciplined will that refuses to give in. It's a state of mind—you could call it character in action.

Whether in the army, on a football team, or in a corporation, Strategists are Thinkers with this elusive mental toughness. They have the discipline to make objective decisions; they are not swayed by individual feelings; they want to do the right thing for the higher good.

Ultimately, Strategists are compelled to live up to their own standards, not to some external authority. They answer to an inner voice, their conscience, their spirit—the God they believe is guiding and driving and judging them, forcing them to live up to a higher standard than other mortals. In the process, they often arrive at positions of leadership where they are destined to bring others up to the same high standards of excellence—and win.

Judger: Aggressive Genius
Strategizing Victory

The Thinking and Judger functions work hand-in-hand for the strategists, reinforcing and overlapping one another, complementing an iron will with a determination to win. In order to do the right thing and emerge a winner, you need to make every minute count. Time is a precious commodity to the *Judger,* and time cannot be wasted. Perceivers may hold off until the last minute, leaving things to chance and a sudden flash of inspiration.

But not Judgers. They are early risers, minds in high gear, raring to go, the first to hit the books, first on the field, first at the meetings. Their work is invariably thorough, meticulously planned, and patiently executed. Why? Because they want to win the game, the battle, the prize.

There's an old saying, "If you've got an important job to be done, give it to a busy person." Well, there's a reason the choice is often a Strategist:

They *are* busy, and their appointment book proves it—meetings, calls, reports, deadlines, and other tasks to perform.

Yet in their eagerness to excel, they'll gladly take on yet another important assignment, spend the extra time, reorganize their time, tighten their schedules, and do a great job. Strategists make opportunities with their aggressive approach to their careers. Thomas Jefferson put it this way: "I'm a great believer in luck, and I find that the harder I work, the more I have of it."

Strategists: Commanders in Training

Strategists are very much Commanders in that they are Commanders in training. They are never quite sure if and when the call to lead will come. But if it does, they are doing everything possible to be well prepared for the opportunity (and secretly hoping it will come!).

Officers and athletes often choose to work with leaders like Eisenhower and Lombardi, knowing that the best Commanders will invariably *bring out the best in them,* hoping someday to be able to prove they have what it takes to become leaders themselves.

Strategists are probably more obsessed than Commanders about doing a great job. Commanders are by nature Extraverts, drawn into working with people. Although Commanders are usually great strategists, much of their energy is expended "out there," mixing with people, rather than in their heads, working out mental scenarios, game plans, alternative strategies.

On the other hand, because Strategists are Introverts by nature, in their formative years—for example, Eisenhower in his student years and later as a young peacetime officer—they are more likely to master the skills that they'll eventually need when opportunity calls them to become Commanders in Chief.

STRATEGISTS: PERPETUAL TRAINING AS FUTURE COMMANDERS

In fact, Strategists are often recognized early as Commanders in training because of their initiative, acute mental abilities, and insatiable curiosity. These characteristics are likely to result in tough assignments and promotions, because they are constantly volunteering for difficult jobs—or being tapped by senior officers who see their promise and feel confident the assignment will be done right.

In short, young Strategists are often, with or without their knowledge, being groomed, guided, pushed along, nudged out of their private worlds, and given opportunities to shine and advance by mentors—more mature and senior Commanders who recognize their unique intellectual abilities. Eisenhower spent 25 years getting ready, Lombardi 19.

Being Introverts by nature, however, Strategists may be reluctant to step out of the shadows, preferring instead to stay in the background, enjoying the mental challenges of strategic thinking without taking on the responsibilities of Commanders and all that goes along with their power and authority. A Strategist knows full well that in the real world life is unpredictable and the unexpected is always around the corner—where the Commander's role is at high risk, vulnerable to failure as well as success, where second place does exist.

Strategists as Systematic Moneymaking Machines

Of course, these traits result in supercautious Strategists developing into superconfident masters at preparing plans and contingency plans that anticipate as many scenarios as possible to best prepare for the unexpected. Continued successes inevitably help them grow in competence in their chosen field, with regular promotions and financial rewards.

In other words, the skills and talents of Strategists make them veritable moneymaking machines. They naturally gravitate to careers and positions where they end up providing services and performing tasks that are highly valued by Corporate America and Wall Street, by society, and by individuals, with higher-than-average compensation packages. Many Strategists would end up in survey lists as being the millionaire next door.

Many go into fields that are natural breeding grounds for future command positions—investment and commercial banking, business development, law, financial planning, systems analysis, medicine, economics, entrepreneurs, and the military. They have every opportunity to develop their special skills further and are often well compensated in the process.

In addition, by choice, many Strategists, like Warren Buffett's longtime investment partner Charlie Munger, prefer operating outside the public eye while sharing the power with a more visible leader.

MAKING MONEY . . . MAKING A LIFE . . . MAKING A DIFFERENCE

To keep it real simple, making money comes naturally to strategists. They have unique skills that are in high demand and typically command higher-than-normal salaries, especially in the business world. Under their supercool, machinelike exterior, they're often closet romantics.

In fact, much like Commanders, the genetic code of Strategists tells them they will not fulfill their destiny unless they make a difference in the world. They have a unique personality capable of great things—one that thrives on the mental challenges of the *Introvert.* As *Intuitives,* they're masters at long-range strategic analysis. In decision making, they are brilliant objective *Thinkers.* As *Judgers,* they have a burning desire to win at all costs. That's like being dealt four aces in poker.

Experience shows that at some point in life, as their list of accomplishments grows, Strategists decide they must give back something of what has been so freely given to them—their extraordinary talents and an ability to generate money. As Winston Churchill once put it, "We make a living by what we get, we make a life by what we give." In their hearts, Strategists know this, even though they may insist on making money first.

That is, as they hone their skills, Strategists are likely to have more than enough money to satisfy all their needs. Moreover, there is every indication that they have a natural ability for managing their financial affairs and investing for retirement, including the ability to select and work with competent financial advisers so they can focus on making money and making a difference, not just in their chosen field, but also though volunteer work and philanthropy.

* * * * * * * *

Why is it that only a minority of our population love their work? If you are
creative enough to select the ideal vocation,
you can win, win big-time.
The really brilliant millionaires are those who selected a vocation that
they love—one that has few competitors
but generates high profits.

Thomas Stanley,
The Millionaire Mind

24

VISIONARY THINKERS (INTP)

ALBERT EINSTEIN, CARL G. JUNG, STEPHEN HAWKING

> It is a special blessing to belong
> among those who can and may devote
> their best energies
> to the contemplation and exploration
> of objective and timeless things.
> How happy and grateful I am for having
> been granted this blessing,
> which bestows upon one a
> large measure of independence
> from one's personal fate and from
> the attitude of one's contemporaries.
> Yet this independence must not inure us
> to the awareness of the
> duties that constantly bind us to the
> past, present and future of
> humankind at large.
>
> Albert Einstein

Auguste Rodin captured this personality in his powerful master-piece, *The Thinker*—his sculpture of a pensive mental giant, sitting motionless, leaning forward, deep in thought, eyes staring at the floor, elbows resting on his thighs, one hand under his chin, holding his head up, his mouth silent . . . frozen in time . . . forever lost in thought. Vision-aries are often lost in thought, and most of them prefer living their whole lives that way!

The Visionary has much in common with the Innovator (ENTP), its intellectual twin among the personality types. Both have brilliant minds. The difference is that while the Innovator, an Extravert, enjoys interacting with people and is turned on by talking with anyone and everyone, the Visionary is an Introvert, exhausted by the "futility of words," as Carl Jung put it, who prefers living in his or her own head.

Visionaries' passion for life comes from their mysterious inner world, a private sanctuary far from the madding crowd. In there, they can explore the far reaches of the universe, uninhibited. In there, their batteries are recharged and their soul is fully energized. Out here, they often have difficulty articulating their grand ideas, giving them an air of mystery—and making them easily misunderstood.

Visions of the Farthest Reaches of Inner Space

Albert Einstein's grade-school teacher told his father, "It doesn't matter what he does, he will never amount to anything." Later, Einstein's vision of reality and the universe challenged the conventional wisdom of Newtonian physics, which had dominated science for almost two centuries. The public and the press made Einstein a reluctant celebrity. Here are his own words:

> I hate crowds and making speeches. I hate facing cameras and having to answer to a crossfire of questions. Why popular fancy should seize upon me, a scientist, dealing in abstract things and happy if left alone, is a manifestation of mass psychology that is beyond me.

Another well-known Visionary, psychologist Carl G. Jung, shared the same views privately in letters with friends:

> Solitude is for me a fount of healing which makes my life worth living. Talking is often a torment for me, and I need many days of silence to recover from the futility of words. . . .
>
> I am a solitary . . . because I know things, and must hint at things which other people do not know, and usually do not even want to know.

Fortunately Jung did hint at many things. In fact, he wrote volumes in the process of developing his science of psychology. He lectured frequently and traveled the world. Yet, like all Visionaries, his true home was always the inner sanctum of his inner world. There he was safe to roam the distant borders of time and space while creating a new map for the human mind.

JUNG'S SECRET WORLD: DEEP INSIDE THE RATIONAL SCIENTIST

As a child, Jung spent many hours playing games alone and residing "in the world of his imagination, in unusually rich and meaning-laden dreams, and in his religious speculations and experiences of which he spoke to no one, for he regarded them as his secret," says Dr. Amelia Jaffe, his longtime assistant, in C. G. Jung, *Word and Image.*

He carried his secret, private world with him throughout his life, spending long periods alone at the lakeside retreat he built over 40 years, where this incredibly complex man became very simple:

> I have done without electricity, and tend the fireplace and stove myself. Evenings, I light the old lamps. There is no running water, and I pump the water from the well. I chop the wood and cook the food. These simple acts make man simple; and how difficult it is to be simple.

Yet alone in this simple retreat for extended periods, he was always searching for the secrets of human mind, in history and literature, in science and medicine, in the paranormal and the occult, in alchemy and astrology, in angels and demons, in the tarot and *I Ching,* in psychic phenomena, flying saucers, dreams, yoga, and more—always searching to uncover more of the mind's deepest secrets.

Jung produced volumes. However, they were not rich with personal anecdotal experiences. His works were logical and rational. He gave the world objective research and methodically reasoned treatises that became the scientific basis for his new analytical psychology. But his personal views were filtered out. For example, Jung the scientist declared that "when I speak of God I always mean the image man has made of him," the *imago Dei,* or references to the *Self* or the *collective unconscious.*

A RIDDLE WRAPPED IN A MYSTERY INSIDE AN ENIGMA

Only after Jung's death, with the publication of his autobiography, *Memories, Dreams, Reflections,* did we get to see a profoundly spiritual human who spent his entire life guided by God:

> Nobody could rob me of the conviction that it was enjoined on me to do what God wanted. That gave me the strength to go my own way. Often I had the feeling that in all decisive matters I was no longer among men, but was alone with God. And when I was

"there," where I was no longer alone, I was outside time; I belonged to the centuries; and He who then gave answer was He who had always been, who had been before my birth. He who always is was there. These talks with the "Other" were my profoundest experiences: on one hand a bloody struggle, on the other supreme ecstasy.

Throughout his life, Jung kept this secret world totally separate from his professional life as a scientist and out of the public eye. In fact, he even left instructions that his autobiography was not to be included with his professional *Collected Works* that contained his views as a psychologist and scientist.

Einstein, on the other hand, was more public than Jung about the secrets of his inner world, often speaking in poetic imagery in his 1932 Credo:

Although I am a typical loner in daily life, my consciousness of belonging to the invisible community of those who strive for truth, beauty, and justice has preserved me from feeling isolated. The most beautiful and deepest experience a man can have is the sense of the mysterious. It is the underlying principle of religion as well as all serious endeavor in art and science. . . . To me it suffices to wonder at these secrets and to attempt humbly to grasp with my mind a mere image of the lofty structure of all that is there.

In the final analysis, given a choice, Einstein, Jung, and all other Visionaries will retreat into the wonderful sanctuary of their private inner worlds, where they can search the vast mysteries of the universe, hopefully to uncover some of its endless secrets.

Millionaire's Code for Visionary Thinkers
Introvert, Intuitive, Thinker, Perceiver (INTP)

When applied to the Visionary, the *Introvert* label somehow misses the mark. It is woefully inadequate in describing the personality. Conventional wisdom says that an introverted person is someone who is shy, reserved, preoccupied with their own thoughts, and avoids social contacts. All perhaps true, they are a bit weird—to outsiders—but that's just how "normal" people see the Visionary from the outside.

Unfortunately, that portrait is a bit negative, suggesting something may be wrong with this person—a mistake similar to the one made by Einstein's teacher. It was inaccurate in Einstein's case, and it is likely superficial in regard to every other Visionary. We need to look at Visionaries from inside their world, not from the outside with microscopes and telescopes.

When you do go inside *Introverts,* you will see their entire universe, one they cannot easily share, partly because of the "futility of words." Or because of a personal need to keep some of it secret, often because it is awesome and beyond description. Einstein would often let his inner child explain his inner world to us:

> We are in the position of a little child entering a huge library filled with books in many different languages. The child knows someone must have written those books. It does not know how. It does not understand the languages in which they are written. The child dimly suspects a mysterious order in the arrangement of the books but doesn't know what it is. That, it seems to me, is the attitude of even the most intelligent human being toward God. We see a universe marvelously arranged and obeying certain laws, but only dimly understand these laws. Our limited minds cannot grasp the mysterious force that moves the constellations.

Einstein cherished his inner world, not so much because it was the place he could "think and think for months and years," but because, as he often said, "The more I study physics the more I am drawn to metaphysics."

WITHIN US: A VAST UNIVERSE FILLED WITH UNUSUAL PEOPLE

Jung left his biggest inner secrets for posthumous publication. He did, however, give us many hints throughout his life in his professional works. Jung's most significant work was on *archetypes,* the collective unconscious within each individual.

Jung believed we are all born with a set of archetypal images and patterns embedded in our soul, or *genetic coding,* as we might call it today. (Genetics first emerged in molecular biology in 1953, late in Jung's life, and was not part of his scientific work.)

Jung identified many archetypal images and patterns, including the hero, adversary, and journey, death and rebirth, gods and demons, earth mother and wise old man, alter ego and shadow, and many others.

Everybody inherits these same universal archetypes along with our individual genes, although they take different forms for each individual. In fact, Jung said that "insofar as the archetypes act upon me, they are real and actual to me, even though I do not know what their real nature is."

VISIONARY'S ARCHETYPES: GURUS, ALTER EGOS, SECRET SHADOWS

These archetypes often communicated with Jung. Sometimes through dreams. Sometimes in reality. For example, take his mysterious guru of superior insight, Philemon: "At times he seemed to me quite real, as if he were a living personality. I went walking up and down the garden with him." Jung also communicated with his alter ego–the woman within each man (*anima*), and the man within each woman (*animus*).

> The anima has a positive aspect as well. It is she who communicates the images of the unconscious to the conscious mind, and that is what I chiefly valued her for. For decades I always turned to the anima when I felt my emotional behavior was disturbed, and that something had been constellated in the unconscious.

All Visionaries live in a vast inner world of their own making, most likely sharing some experiences similar to Jung's and Einstein's. This is something most other personalities *will never understand,* which is why Visionaries often keep much of their inner lives secret. Yet for Visionaries, all this is normal. They love their wonderful inner world.

True, viewed from the outside they may be seen as socially distant, overly shy, reserved, perhaps nerdy and a bit weird, too much into themselves. If you have the Visionary's genetic code, don't listen to "them." Trust yourself, honor who you are–perhaps even seek your inner guru, your alter ego, or one of the other fascinating characters in your private world. They are in there.

The Intuitive: Scientific "Facts" from Brilliant Theories

This second element of the four-letter genetic code is either Sensor or Intuitive as your way of collecting information about the world. In this regard, the Visionary is probably the purist of *Intuitives*. Indeed, Einstein's work in theoretical physics was clearly light-years away from that of Sensors when it comes to the collection and value of facts, data, and sensory information.

Visionaries are perhaps the personality *most* likely to ignore the facts. As Einstein once said: "Not everything that can be counted counts, and not everything that counts can be counted." Facts just don't count for much in the mysterious inner world of Visionaries: *Facts limit the future.*

Visionaries are *Intuitives* with the gift of insight and are searching for underlying meanings, connections, patterns, trends, theories, the big picture, and, above all, the future. Isolated facts are not only suspect and irrelevant, they're probably misleading.

What about Jung's disciplined scientific approach to psychology? Wasn't that more the work of a Sensor personality? In the scientific method, theories can be independently verified and tested with empirical evidence: You start by identifying a problem, collect data by experiments and observations, test your hypothesis, proving or disproving it, then modify your theory if necessary. Anyone else using the scientific approach should get the same results.

The hallmark of Sensors is not only their emphasis on sensory evidence—seeing, hearing, touching, smelling, and tasting—but also their focus on the concrete details in the present moment. They are most comfortable in the here and now and can become obsessive about collecting more hard data when the evidence is ambiguous. Moreover, Sensors tend to want current data that can be easily compared with known information from the past. Speculating about the future is not something Sensors do; they want evidence.

JUNG'S GRAND UNIFIED THEORY: THE COLLECTIVE UNCONSCIOUS

Jung knew he was breaking new ground with his new analytical psychology. He also knew that absent a scientific basis it would be little more than pseudoscientific speculations about all the other paranormal subjects Jung did study—dreams, psychic seances, myths, alchemy, the occult, ESP, UFOs, astrology, yoga, mandalas, the tarot, Zen, the *I Ching*, and more. In fact, skeptics have often accused him of lacking a true empirical basis.

Jung needed to approach his studies impersonally, and he needed an anchor in the empirical sciences. But the fact remains that his work was first and foremost grounded in a future-oriented search for a unified theory of the human psyche—and he found that scientific anchor in his theory of the collective unconscious.

Jung discovered a unified theory of psychology, something Einstein never achieved in physics. With that core theory, Jung was able to network all he studied into the images and patterns encoded in the collective unconscious and its archetypes. These patterns are encoded in everybody's genes at birth, conditioning how each of our minds perceive reality, often "speaking" for us. As Jung put it: "It is not the personal human being who is making the statement, but the archetype speaking through him." An idea difficult to prove empirically but consistent theoretically.

Even though the collective unconscious—Jung's unified theory—today remains as much a mystery as a theory, it still serves as the core scientific hypothesis for analytical psychology. But again, note, whether Jung's theories are true or scientifically provable is not relevant here. What is relevant is the fact that, right or wrong, this represents the kind of abstract thinking that goes on within the Intuitive mind of a Visionary.

The Thinker: Einstein's Simple Formula

The Thinking/Feeling polarity is the third element in everybody's genetic code. The Visionary is unquestionably a *Thinker*. This refers to the criteria you will use in making decisions.

Of course, Thinkers do have feelings, and Feelers do think. Feelers, however, rely on subjective criteria in making their decisions. In contrast, Thinkers are totally rational and logical, using objective criteria in making their decisions. They choose the right thing to do based on an objective standard rather than on the decision maker's personal feelings about the matter at hand.

Feeling types are swayed by personal considerations and emotions in making decisions. Thinkers have similar considerations but suppress their feelings, relying on higher authority to do the right thing in making their decision. They arrive at the decision by using their objective reasoning powers. In short, they are like computers when they make decisions.

Einstein lived in such an objective Thinker's world of formulas, theories, and hypotheses, though sometimes in a whimsical moment he would translate his thinking into a lighthearted formula for living: "If A equals success, then the formula is: $A = X + Y + Z$, where X is work. Y is play. Z is keep your mouth shut."

EXPERIENCE IS THE BEST, *AND ONLY,* TEACHER

Keeping your mouth shut obviously doesn't stop the Visionary from thinking, it merely drives thought deeper inside. When he was a teenager, Jung's father had a "habit of saying 'you always want to think. One ought not to think, but to believe.' " His father was a minister, as were eight of his uncles. Jung later wrote: "I would think, 'No, one must experience and know.' "

Jung's fiercely independent mind-set exasperated his father. He was constantly asking questions, challenging his father, who was not secure in his own beliefs and was a victim of his feelings. Nor could he turn to his minister uncles, whom he felt were more dogmatic and religious than truly spiritual. All of which drove Jung to search deeper into his own private world for answers.

SEARCHING FOR A UNIFIED THEORY OF GOD AND EVERYTHING ELSE

One of the truly remarkable aspects in the lives of these two visionaries (Einstein and Jung) was their common search for a unified theory of the meaning of life, in particular a search for God.

This has also been the focus of the work of another Visionary, Stephen Hawking, who is considered the greatest theoretical physicist since Einstein. In the introduction to his best-seller, *A Brief History of Time: From the Big Bang to Black Holes,* astronomer Carl Sagan had this to say:

> The word God fills these pages. Hawking embarks on a quest to answer Einstein's famous question about whether God had any choice in creating the universe. Hawking is attempting, as he explicitly states, to understand the mind of God.

Jung, as a professional and a scientist, found his unified theory in the archetypes of the collective unconscious, specifically expressed by individuals through the *imago Dei,* the image of God in our individual minds. On the other hand, Jung the man and Thinker said:

> This expression, "God's world," may sound sentimental to some ears. For me it did not have this character at all. To "God's world" belonged everything superhuman—dazzling light, the darkness of the abyss, the cold impassivity of infinite space and time, and the uncanny grotesqueness of the irrational world of chance. "God," for me, was everything.

Likewise, Einstein had a lifelong passion to understand God:

> Human beings, vegetables, or cosmic dust, we all dance to a mysterious tune intoned in the distance by an invisible player.... I want to know how God created this world. I am not interested in this or that phenomenon, in the spectrum of this or that element. I want to know His thoughts; the rest are details.

This need to understand God is critical to an understanding of the Visionary personality. We know that Visionaries are Thinkers. Their decisions are grounded in rationality, logic, and the intellect. We know their genetic code compels them to do the right thing, as measured objectively by some higher standard, such as the greater good or universal law.

ULTIMATELY, THEY ARE SEARCHING TO KNOW THE MIND OF GOD

Beyond that, it seems quite obvious that Visionaries are also on a search to uncover the basic secrets of their world—*a unified theory*—and that is coupled with a search to discover the nature of God. We see this quest to know the mind of God most clearly in Einstein, Jung, and Hawking.

Again, whether a Visionary's theory of life or concept of God is relevant is *not* the issue here. What is relevant is that this is the kind of extraordinary analytical thinking that goes on inside the brilliant minds of Visionaries—and yet for them it's perfectly normal. They have their Thinking caps on all the time, even though most normal folks may see them as as space cadets and absentminded professors.

Perceivers: Perpetual Students on the Road Less Traveled

Perceivers are free spirits, kids at heart who love to keep their options open while they go out and play in the big, wide, wonderful world. They are comfortable meandering throughout the universal playground, playing their mental games, because life really is fun.

Visionaries are a paradox in this way. All that analytical thinking about unified theories, archetypes, big bangs, and black holes might exhaust a normal person. But in the minds of Visionaries, they are having as much fun as a Michael Jordan in the NBA finals or a Donald Trump closing another hundred-million-dollar deal. To each his own.

Some famous pictures show the bushy-headed Einstein sticking out his tongue and laughing, or riding a bicycle. He had a sense of humor and could laugh at himself: "Once you can accept the universe as matter expanding into nothing that is something, wearing stripes with plaid comes easy." Einstein was a perennial child. He admits it:

> I sometimes ask myself how did it come to pass that I was the one to develop the theory of relativity? The reason, I think, is that a normal adult never stops to think about the problems of space and time. These are things which he has thought of as a child. But my intellectual development was retarded, as a result of which I began to wonder about space and time only when I had already grown up. Naturally I could go deeper into the problem than a child with normal abilities.

Hawking also had a delightful sense of humor. He opens his lecture, "The Beginning of Time," with this amusing remark:

> When I gave a lecture in Japan, I was asked not to mention the possible re-collapse of the universe, because it might affect the stock market. However, I can re-assure anyone who is nervous about

their investments that it is a bit early to sell: even if the universe does come to an end, it won't be for at least twenty billion years.

He ended the lecture, The Beginning of Time, on this note:

> The no-boundary hypothesis predicts that the universe will eventually collapse again. However, the contracting phase, will not have the opposite arrow of time, to the expanding phase. So we will keep on getting older, and we won't return to our youth. Because time is not going to go backwards, I think I better stop now.

Jung's work had a serious tone, but he also had his lighter moments, although they are not as evident as with Einstein and Hawking. When he was in college he loved dancing. Once fell madly in love with a Frenchwoman at a party. He even went to buy wedding rings for them, but lacked the money. He also enjoyed mentioning the rumor that his namesake and grandfather, the first C. G. Jung, was the illegitimate son of Goethe.

Throughout his life, Jung was a gentle man who made everyone feel at ease, a quality readily noticeable in his photographs, most especially one of his last, taken at his eighty-fifth birthday party, laughing, surrounded by 34 children, grandchildren, and great-grandchildren.

Life is an adventure for Visionaries. They are *Perceivers,* perpetual students, kids running around playing, endlessly exploring the universe, the cosmos, the nuclear world, searching for God, having a ball trying to figure out the secrets of life—not so much because they want to explain their unified theory of God and everything else to you, but because they love explaining, reworking, modifying, and reexplaining their grand theories *to themselves, over and over* as they grow from within. Yes, indeed, it is all in their heads—and they love being in there!

Careers: The Mythic Journeys of a Beautiful Mind

Are all visionaries preeminent scientists, physicists, mathematicians, and psychologists? Of course not. You'll find these wonderful people on their unique versions of the hero's journey in just about any field, as long as they are on the strange "road less traveled" of the Visionary. You just might find one of them working near you in one of these professions:

- *Architects*
- *Archeologists*
- *Artists*

- *Attorneys*
- *Economists*
- *Financial consultants*
- *Graduate school professors*
- *Journalists*
- *Historians*
- *Microbiologists*
- *Researchers*
- *Statisticians*
- *Strategic planners*
- *Systems analysts*
- *Urban planners*

These are just a few possibilities. Whatever the career, remember that the Visionary is a change agent and futurist. If you are one, you need to work independently, alone, or with a small team of highly competent experts you respect, on challenging projects, where you have an opportunity of discovering, creating, developing, and working on something exceptional and unique, of your own choosing, setting your own deadlines, using whatever tools and technologies you choose, both standard and unconventional. You need to change the world.

You could be working on a project for the design of a city, a breakthrough in medical technology, an energy-efficient building, a sculpture, a new cancer drug, an award-winning story, the missing link, or a dynamic model of the global economy—something that demands great thought and can have a significant impact on your world.

Whatever career you choose, trust that you are being *guided,* as Jung once said, "Vocation acts like a law of God from which there is no escape." All personality types are guided into their careers, often over many years of struggle, but Visionaries have a special calling to go on a unique adventure in search of a secret known only to them, a journey "from which there is no escape."

Discover How You Can Best Serve Humanity: Money Will Follow

What can we say to a Visionary about making money, saving it, and investing it? Actually not a whole lot. Money is not why Visionaries are here in this lifetime, *and they know it.* They are truly change agents who are more interested in making a difference in the world than in making money—and for that reason alone, they have a high probability of making more money than they will ever need. If they just concentrate on their work, they will eventually win the money game.

When it comes to understanding the secret of saving and investing, a Visionary like Einstein, the father of nuclear power, had that formula down pat: "There is no greater power known to man than compounding interest." That way, making money is easy. Several University of Chicago finance professors even received a Nobel prize for their work on Modern Portfolio Theory, combining compounding with diversifying to maximize returns.

The best moneymaking advice for Visionaries? Forget about the money (yes, forget it) and focus on contributing your talents where the world needs you most. Do that, and you will be rewarded beyond your wildest dreams.

* * * * * * * *

Everyone has a purpose in life,
a unique gift of special talent to give others . . .
ask yourself:
How am I best suited to serve humanity?
Answer that question and put it into practice.
Discover your divinity,
find your unique talent,
serve humanity with it, and
you can generate all the wealth you want.
When your creative expressions
match the needs of your fellow humans,
then wealth will spontaneously flow from
the unmanifest into the manifest,
from the realm of the spirit
into the world of form.

Deepak Chopra,
The Seven Spiritual Laws of Success

THE PATHFINDERS

THE PATHFINDERS: INTUITIVE-FEELING (N-F)

- Inspiring Teachers (ENFJ)
- Champions and Causes (ENFP)
- Healing Counselors (INFJ)
- Mystic Heroes (INFP)

INSPIRING TEACHERS (ENFJ)

JOSEPH CAMPBELL, GARY ZUKAV, STEPHEN COVEY

> The great events of the world are,
> at bottom,
> profoundly unimportant.
> In the last analysis,
> the essential thing is the life of the individual,
> here alone do the
> great transformations take place,
> and the whole future,
> the whole history of the world,
> ultimately springs as a
> gigantic summation from
> these hidden resources in individuals.
>
> Carl G. Jung,
> *Modern Man in Search of a Soul*

The Inspiring Teacher is one of the four Pathfinder personalities—and, of all of the personalities, the one who can have the greatest impact on our lives. As William Arthur Ward said, "The mediocre teacher tells. The good teacher explains. The superior teacher demonstrates. The great teacher inspires."

The great Teachers bring out the best in each of us—*they inspire us to reach for the stars*. That is their life's mission, their passion. Their soul lives for the opportunity to encourage, to challenge, often aggressively, to motivate, and to inspire you, me, and everyone they touch:

A great Teacher will help you learn to experience the joy of learning for its own sake, and more, the desire to remain forever a student, filled with the beginner's mind of the great Zen masters—*passionate curiosity,* Einstein called it—an insatiable childlike wonder about the world and your journey through life.

Great Teachers share with you their wisdom without making you dependent on them as a higher authority—giving you the confidence to take charge of your own life as a responsible, independent individual, knowing you are your own master, empowered by your own inner voice and in love with life.

Great Teachers will help you develop the tools of your trade; they will help you sharpen your natural skills so they can be used for the good of humanity, and more, they will instill in you a sense of values, ethics, integrity, morals, and principles, for without these all of your education is worthless.

These are the great gifts that Inspiring Teachers offer their students—a lifetime of insatiable curiosity for learning, confidence that you are indeed the captain of your fate, the master of your soul, valuable skills needed by humanity, and, above all else, a commitment to live a principled life.

They're Passionate about Their Work, about Life, about You

It's easy to see why Teachers are so crucial in the development of every other personality and why Teachers' lives are so rewarding—they not only bring out the best in their students, they help their students to discover and understand their own personality, to accept their true calling, to own who they truly are, to take control of their destiny, and to be all they can be. *Ultimately, they help their students approach life with the same passion that they themselves have.*

Throughout his entire life Joseph Campbell, a great Teacher and mythologist, encouraged his college students, the public, everyone, with one simple message—"Follow your bliss," as he put it so many times, including in his popular *Power of Myth* TV interviews with Bill Moyers.

Indeed, one brief weekend seminar with Campbell became the turning point in my life by helping me see that there was a world beyond Wall Street. More important, Campbell set an example as a Teacher with integrity about his work, and he let me feel his passion for this new world.

FOLLOW YOUR BLISS: DOORS WILL OPEN WHERE THERE ARE NONE!

Over and over, Campbell repeated the classic message you hear from every other great Teacher: "Follow your bliss . . . the heroic life is living the individual adventure . . . follow your bliss and doors will open where there were no doors before . . . follow your bliss!"

You see and hear this simple message repeated over and over throughout time by all the great Teachers, in many forms, yet all echoing the same challenge. If the student gets nothing but this core message, the Teacher's mission has been accomplished, the light goes on in the student's eyes:

- *Live with passion.*
- *Follow your dreams.*
- *Manifest your destiny.*
- *The instant millionaire.*
- *Be all that you can be.*
- *Awaken the giant within.*
- *Take the road less traveled.*
- *Go on the journey of the hero.*
- *Tap into the secret power within.*
- *Practice the seven habits of highly effective people.*
- *Do what you love, the money will follow.*
- *If you meet the Buddha on the road, kill him.*
- *Feel the fear and do it anyway.*
- *Go for it . . . just do it!*
- *Follow your bliss.*

This message of all great Teachers is very simple—yet incredibly difficult for most people to grasp, even harder to put into action. Why? Michaelangelo put it this way: "The greatest danger for most of us is not that our aim is too high and we miss it, but that it is too low and we reach it."

WHATEVER YOU CAN CONCEIVE AND BELIEVE, YOU CAN ACHIEVE

The great Teachers inspire us to set our aim higher, to stretch ourselves beyond our limits. Their example can convince us that we can reach for the stars. As Napoleon Hill says in *Think and Grow Rich,* "Whatever the mind can conceive and believe, it can achieve." *Anything.*

Teachers firmly believe this in the depths of their soul. After all, their lives are living proof it works. They are charismatic, with a special gift with words and a passion for life that inspires students, convincing them that, yes, they can reach for the stars.

The message of the great Teachers is this: *Follow your bliss.* When you are in alignment with your genetic code, when you become one with your true self, your innermost being, when you risk being all you can be, when you are living the destiny you came here to fulfill rather the one imposed on you—then you will be *rich in spirit and in fact,* wealthy in your heart and your soul and your bank accounts, and you will be happy.

Great Teachers know this because they are doing it themselves. They have awakened the giant within themselves and are following their bliss—and they must pass along their passion, for in doing that they are in tune with their genetic code. They become richer in spirit and in fact. Then the student's success is also the teacher's reward.

WHEN THE TEACHER IS READY, THE STUDENTS WILL APPEAR

You have heard the old adage, "When the student is ready, the teacher will appear." Well, the reverse is also true: "When the Teacher is ready, the students will appear," and for the great Teacher the student is *always* ready. Great Teachers are convinced that if they can open the door just one small crack, maybe the reluctant student will walk in, maybe not immediately, but the seed will be planted and another soul will be pointed in the direction of their destiny.

Great Teachers will employ every darn trick in the book to find the key to a student's passion, going way beyond the standard stuff—Socratic questioning, dialogue, lectures, storytelling, reading assignments, case studies, experiments, repetition, self-study projects, tests, papers, theses, counseling—and do whatever it takes to bring out the best in a student.

Indeed, great Teachers are tenacious, insistent, demanding, obstinate, challenging, prodding, clever, confrontational, punishing, rewarding, manipulative, complimentary—you name it, great Teachers will try it. As Winston Churchill bluntly put it, "If you have an important point to make, don't try to be subtle or clever. Use a pile driver. Hit the point once. Then come back and hit it again. Then hit it a third time—a tremendous whack!"

GREAT TEACHERS: COACHES, SERGEANTS, GRANDMAS, KIDS, STUDENTS

Teachers wear many disguises, in and out of the classroom. First, perhaps, your mother and father. Maybe a favorite uncle. Grandmother. School teachers, coaches, scout masters, and ministers. Later, college professors. Mentors. Friends. Colleagues and associates. Drill sergeants. Bosses. Media personalities. Seminar leaders. Spouses and even our children. They can all teach you something.

If you have a beginner's mind, the tables can turn, and the student becomes the Teacher. In *The Secret Power Within,* karate champion Chuck Norris tells about a lunch with one of his martial arts students, Steve McQueen. The actor had been encouraging Norris to pursue a new career in film. Norris was reluctant. McQueen was taken aback:

> Remember that philosophy of yours that you always stressed to students: Set goals, visualize the results of those goals, and then be determined to succeed by overcoming any obstacles in the way. You've been preaching this to me for two years, and now you're saying there's something you can't do?

That did it for Norris. "Turning words" he called them, enlightenment, the jolt that inspired him. Suddenly his goal became obvious, his life focused, spurring him into action. Since then, he's been in more than 20 films, including *Delta Force,* and a long-running television series, *Walker, Texas Ranger.*

Great Teachers have this gift, this knack of being there, saying the right things at the turning points—those defining moments in our lives when we change direction and embark on our real journey. If the students are ready, well, the students are ready—and they will create the Teacher.

BELIEVE NO ONE, NOT EVEN ME: EXPERIENCE IS THE ONLY TEACHER

The ultimate goal of inspiring Teachers is to create in the student a "beginner's mind," where the student becomes their own Teacher, a free spirit, independent and centered within themselves, guided by what Norris calls "the secret power within."

The Teacher and student are on equal footing when both understand what the Buddha meant when he told his disciples: "Believe nothing, no matter where you read it or who has said it, not even if I have said it, unless it agrees with your own reason and your own common sense."

In its highest state, this symbiotic relationship between Teacher and student exists on a metaphysical as well as physical level, with "nonphysical Teachers" guiding both teacher and student, as physicist and Teacher Gary Zukav says in his best-seller, *The Seat of the Soul:*

> Let go. Trust. Create. *Be who you are.* The rest is up to your nonphysical Teachers and the Universe. Take your hands off the wheel. Be able to say to the Universe, "Thy will be done." . . . The final piece of reaching for authentic power is releasing your own to a higher form of wisdom . . . give your guides and Teachers permission to come closer . . . say to the Universe: "Find me where

you know I need to be." . . . and trust that the Universe will provide, and so it shall. Let go of all. Let your higher self complete its task.

This relationship is actually much more down-to-earth and practical than the metaphysical overtones suggest. Zukav is simply saying that the great teachers know that, ultimately, it's up to the student to run with the ball–that there are mysterious forces guiding the Teacher and the students, you and me.

As Albert Einstein once put it, "We all dance to a mysterious tune intoned in the distance by an invisible player." And if we flow with those forces, if we are in tune with them, we will all achieve our goals–student, Teacher, and universe working in harmony. Know your genetic code, embrace it, and run with it.

Millionaire's Code for Inspiring Teachers: Extravert, Intuitive, Feeling, Judger (ENFJ)

The Master Teacher is definitely an *Extravert,* the first of the four elements of your generic code. As a Teacher, you draw energy from people, you love meetings and talking, chatting on the phone, lecturing at the podium, hosting workshops, running seminars, communicating, being in relationships, acting as team leader–you need people to survive and thrive.

Over time, you have developed an uncanny, natural sixth sense about people, an awareness of their *inner* feelings and thoughts that sometimes amazes them, and even you. You have an instinctive ability to read people's body language, gestures, eye movements, and tone of voice. You do it so well that you feel you are communicating with them on a soul level, without words. This is a skill that most Pathfinders possess, but most especially Teachers.

It continues at home, in social gatherings, on elevators, at meals, in the checkout line, you name it, you enjoy engaging people in conversations. Most especially, you love stimulating conversationalists who are bright, exciting, creative people who, like you, also see and feel life as a stimulating adventure.

The Teacher is an *Extravert* and a Pathfinder, a special mixture that vests in you a fascinating and critical mission. In fulfilling your destiny as a *Teacher,* you must help others identify and fulfill their destinies. As a *Pathfinder* you are helping the next generation find their paths, whatever their personality type. And as an *Extravert,* you share your passion with your students–altogether, quite a rewarding combination for you, and them.

YOU TEACH BEST WHAT YOU MUST LEARN

On the other hand, you do need time alone, even though you're not an Introvert—for researching, rehearsing, reading, travel, hobbies, fitness—as long as it's not some boring routine job. Then the walls start to close in on you. Fortunately, your beginner's mind has ingenious ways out of the trap.

Like the messiah in Richard Bach in *Illusions,* "You teach best what you most need to learn," so you are always searching for another exciting new creative project, ready to explore new territory that you feel will advance you along your path. Chances are that even with a dull subject you will figure out some new angle to spice up the presentation, probably testing it out on family or colleagues over lunch, preparing for your next opportunity with an audience of eager students.

Moreover, you have such a strong, creative imagination that you actually don't feel as though you're alone when you *are* alone. How's that? When you're working on a new project and researching a new field, your vibrant imagination actually brings people into your private world, *so you're not really alone*—a virtual audience shares your journey, often helping you rehearse for the next lecture presentation that you're researching and drafting.

Of course, given a choice you prefer the world of the Extravert, lively interaction and conversations with other bright, challenging, creative people who, like you, are also excited about sharing their journey. When you are out there among people, you are at your best, magnetic and charismatic, drawing people to you, because they respond to your energy and want to hear your message.

The Intuitive: Searching for the Meaning of Life

Teachers are also Intuitives, the second element of their genetic code dealing with the way they collect information about the world. The *Intuitive* looks at the world differently than their opposite type: Sensors are more interested in what's happening right now, in the present moment, on tangible evidence, detailed concrete data that can be confirmed by the five senses and compared with current and past information. The future will take care of itself.

Intuitives are on a search for the meaning of life. For them, raw information has little or no value except in the larger context. Intuitives want to understand the bigger picture. What is its significance? The future excites them—trends and patterns, possibilities, and alternative ways of creating solutions for a new tomorrow. They need to make a difference, to make their world a better place to live in.

Although, as Extraverts are compelled to help others, the Teacher's search for the meaning of life is actually a very, very personal and perhaps selfish venture, as well as a selfless, altruistic, humanitarian gesture—and must be embraced as such. Joseph Campbell must have been speaking for all great Teachers when he described it this way:

> People say that what we're all seeking is a meaning for life . . . what we are really seeking is an *experience of being alive,* so that our life experience on the purely physical plane will have resonances within our own innermost being and reality, so that we actually feel the *rapture of being alive.*

Teachers search for meaning in the world, regardless of their discipline—in comparative religions, abnormal psychology, historical trends, social patterns. It's actually part of their own personal way of feeling alive. In *Man's Search for Meaning,* psychologist Viktor Frankl offers this perspective:

> It did not really matter what we expected from life, but rather what life expected from us. We needed to stop asking about the meaning of life, and instead to think of ourselves as those who were being questioned by life. . . . Life ultimately means taking the responsibility to find the right answers to its problems and to fulfill the tasks which it constantly sets for each individual.

The search transcends and merges all three perspectives: Teachers are clearly on a personal quest, searching for the meaning of their own lives. Their careers, their research, the books and papers they publish, and their lectures are all part of a search for the larger meaning of life and the world.

Finally, Teachers need to share what they find on their journey—and in sharing, they can make a difference, inspiring students to search for the meaning of their own lives as they discover their own destiny for the future.

Feelings: Scoring High in Emotional Intelligence

The third element of their genetic code tells us how Teachers make decisions—more specifically, which criteria they use when making their decisions. The Teacher is a *Feeling* type, making decisions based on subjective criteria, based on values personal to the individual Teacher. The Teacher has an emotional radar that can quickly sense the needs of individuals and groups, then respond, touching them at a feeling level.

Thinkers are just the opposite, they use objective standards—the law of land, the common good, the Commandments, universal law, or some other higher authority—something other than their own personal values. They reach people by the sheer force of logic and the rational mind.

At first glance, you might conclude that being a Thinker might be a more effective Teacher. The new field of *emotional intelligence* tells us otherwise. Daniel Goleman's book, *Emotional Intelligence,* popularized the term and essentially created a whole new branch of psychology in the process. The *emotional quotient* (E-Q) is "an adeptness at managing ourselves and our interactions with others—not school smarts."

One early study on E-Q tested children when they were four years old and then checked their progress in high school—which ones needed instant gratification, which could delay. According to a *Time* magazine report, the kids with the lowest E-Qs were "more likely to be lonely, easily frustrated and stubborn. They buckled under stress and shied away from challenges."

EMOTIONAL POWER: SELF-DISCIPLINED, EMPATHIC, INSPIRING

Kids with higher E-Qs were not only "better adjusted, more popular, adventurous, confident and dependable," they averaged 210 points higher on the SATs. Goleman and other experts identify five factors that make up the emotional quotient:

1. *Self-awareness* (of your feelings, sources, strengths, weaknesses)
2. *Self-control* (managing feelings of stress, anxiety, fears, anger, etc.)
3. *Self-motivation* (channeling your emotions into positive goals)
4. *Empathy* (sensitivity to others' feelings and points of view)
5. *Diplomatic* (social, team builder, teacher, negotiator, inspiring)

Great Teachers seem to naturally have a high E-Q, with all five of these factors complementing their Feeling functions. Yet diplomacy stands out as the key factor, head and shoulders above the other four.

Having self-awareness, self-control, self-motivation, and empathy are great traits for an Introvert. But for an Extraverted Teacher, the bottom line is in how these traits actually help people: by resolving conflicts in a diplomatic way, by inspiring teamwork, by teaching leadership skills and how to live a principled life with integrity. And in the process by being a *living example* of what it means to have a high E-Q and be a person of character.

TEACHERS INSPIRE US BY TOUCHING US AT AN EMOTIONAL LEVEL

The emotional strength of great Teachers is perhaps their greatest asset. Great Teachers are great leaders, much like their sibling personality types, the Commanders (ENTJ). Goleman says that great "leaders inspire us by touching our feelings." On the other hand, many people working in schools and colleges who have the title of *Teacher* merely pass along information to students but do not inspire.

Great Teachers have a unique gift—they inspire us by touching our feelings. Great Teachers know that *if* they can touch a person's emotions they will inspire them to *bring out the best in themselves!* Touch emotions, enflame passion, and students will do the impossible, reaching far beyond their limitations to chase their wildest dreams—they will know deep within themselves that whatever the mind can conceive and believe, it *will* achieve.

In fact, great Teachers *need* to touch us emotionally; they *need* inspire us. They are on earth in this lifetime to move and inspire. That need to inspire is embedded in their genetic code. *When they tap into our feelings and inspire us, they are also inspired—they know they are fulfilling their destiny.*

Judger: Goal-Oriented, Driven, Organized, Decisive, Achiever

A Teacher is also a *Judger,* the fourth element of their genetic code. Although Teachers are sensitive to others' feelings and have high E-Qs, they also have tough taskmasters in their heads setting high performance standards and a need to achieve.

They are forever taking on new projects in their area of special interest, usually projects that demand creative solutions in as yet unexplored areas—often a few too many. For the *Judger,* however, the pressure becomes an incentive to perform, and often the incentive to step in and take charge.

Heavy workloads and performance demands (usually self-imposed) leave Teachers feeling "behind" most of the time. Their comfort level rises when they have things worked out well in advance—goals, schedules, performance standards, program outlines, people assignments, detailed plans, deadlines. As a result, they become masters of efficiency, often juggling many projects at the same time, scurrying around to get everything done on time, feeling the pressure to start things early in order to accomplish everything.

This may be a worst-case scenario, but the point is, great Teachers see themselves as men and women of character, with a strong sense of mission about their lives and a total commitment to do it and do it right.

CHARACTER ETHIC: THE HABITS OF HIGHLY EFFECTIVE PEOPLE

Much has been written about character, most recently in the work of Stephen Covey. In *Principle-Centered Leadership,* Covey focuses on the "Character Ethic," which goes beyond the psychological approach of E-Q and into the world of ethics, integrity, values, morals, and principles:

> The Character Ethic is based on the fundamental idea that there are principles that govern human effectiveness–natural laws in the human dimension that are just as real, just as unchanging and unarguably "there" as laws such as gravity are in the physical dimension.

Covey tells us that character is "primary to greatness." In *The Seven Habits of Highly Effective People,* he explains that the character ethic has been the driving force behind American success stories beginning with the work of Ben Franklin. Character, says Covey, is:

> [Character is] the foundation of success–things like integrity, humility, fidelity, temperance, courage, justice, patience, industry, simplicity, modesty, and the Golden Rule. . . . The Character Ethic taught that there are basic principles of effective living, and that people only experience true success and enduring happiness as they learn and integrate these principles into their basic character.

All great teachers have a strong conscience and are instinctively aware of this need to live with integrity and principles. It is ingrained in their genetic code.

CONSCIENCE DEMANDS THAT YOU WALK THE WAY YOU TALK!

Inspiring Teachers are keenly aware of the force of this Judging trait in defining their personality. Yes, they love the work they do. Yes, they love sharing their passion with people. But most of all, they want to be known as someone of character and integrity, someone with strong values and high moral standards.

Teachers must be principle-centered. Their conscience is judging their behavior all the time, keeping them in line. Far more important, great

Teachers know that the way they live is the main lesson they teach. Are they in fact living a life of integrity? Are they walking the way they talk? As Einstein put it, "Example isn't another way to teach, it is the only way to teach."

Careers: So Many Opportunities to Make a Difference

Inspiring Teachers are not merely employees of schools, colleges, and universities. Nor are all of them great Teachers in the sense that William Arthur Ward meant: "The mediocre teacher tells. The good teacher explains. The superior teacher demonstrates. The great teacher inspires."

This personality type, as is true for all 16 personalities, doesn't come with a single name tag. A Teacher might be working in business, psychology, politics, foreign service, or virtually any other business or profession.

Their titles are not as important as the fact that they are masters at "inspiring us by touching our feelings." Teachers love bringing out the best in people. Here are some samples of the kinds of careers that might attract them, opportunities that enable them to capitalize on their strengths and make a difference in the world:

- *Motivational trainers*
- *High school teachers*
- *Humanities professors*
- *Career counselors*
- *Corporate salespeople*
- *Human resources employees*
- *Therapists*
- *Social workers*
- *Journalists*
- *Television media personnel*
- *Public relations people*
- *Diplomatic service workers*
- *Politicians*
- *Ministers*
- *Mentors*

Teachers can succeed in any one of these and other related roles where they have the opportunity to inspire people on an emotional level, living a life of integrity, in a field that tells them they are indeed fulfilling their life's mission—and having fun while doing it.

Great Teachers: Do What You Love, the Money Will Follow

Joseph Campbell taught for a long time at Sarah Lawrence College. His attitude toward money is common among many teachers: "My life course is totally indifferent to money." The fact is, Teachers are often more focused on their work and on taking care of others rather than on taking of themselves.

Many Teachers make enormous sacrifices for their students. It's just part of their personality code. They're dedicated to helping people, yet they are often underpaid, working extra hours, with minimal benefits. When budgets are cut, you'll often hear stories about how they dip into their own pockets to buy school supplies. Yet in spite of the inequities in their working environment, they'll tell you they love their work.

Fortunately, many of America's teachers are employed by school districts, colleges, and universities that have pension and retirement plans. The same is true for many of the other typical careers for Teachers—in government, business, and the media. However, like most plans, they may not be sufficient.

Teachers need to become very disciplined and aggressive with their personal savings and investment programs to fill in the gaps. For many, this may not be easy because it conflicts with their tendency to put money matters on a low priority. It is important that Teachers fully recognize this natural tendency to avoid, delay, and minimize money issues and that they consciously take steps to counterbalance this. Keep in mind that this is a lifelong process.

One solution is to find a trusted financial adviser to act as a conscience and disciplinarian in matters of planning, budgeting, saving, and investing, including regularly depositing money directly from your checking account to savings. Better yet, let your spouses handle financial matters, and trust them to keep you on track to a comfortable retirement. You don't have to be an aggressive investor. Even finance professors at top schools are likely to keep their money in passive, indexed investments.

Stay in control of your money, but let someone else monitor and manage the details for you so that you can focus totally on your mission in life: Teaching and inspiring people to achieve their highest potentials.

* * * * * * *

I thought anybody who worked for money was a fool.
I took a vow never to do anything for money.
Now, that does not mean that
when I do something I don't ask for money.
I want as much as I can get,
but that's the secondary part of the game.
My life course is totally indifferent to money.
As a result a lot of money has
come in by doing what I feel
I want to do from the inside.

Joseph Campbell

CHAPTER 26

CHAMPIONS AND CAUSES (ENFP)

MAHATMA GANDHI, MOTHER TERESA, THE DALAI LAMA

Ask yourself:
How am I best suited to serve humanity?
Answer that question and put it into practice.
Discover your divinity,
find your unique talent,
serve humanity with it,
and you can generate
all the wealth you want.
When your creative expressions
match the needs of your fellow humans,
then wealth will spontaneously flow
from the unmanifest
into the manifest from
the realm of the spirit into
the world of form.

Deepak Chopra,
*The Seven Spiritual
Laws of Success*

If you take your cues from the media, you'd have to believe that Champions win Super Bowls, World Series, Olympic gold medals, and heavyweight title fights. If you're a fan of movies and novels, fairy tales and mythology, you know that the champion is a hero slaying dragons, rescuing damsels in distress, and saving the world from evil forces: Sir

Galahad and Frodo, Rambo and James Bond, Luke Skywalker and Princess Leia.

In the broader sweep of history and world affairs, however, we know the Champion is always a leader with a cause—a cause so powerful that it stirs the emotions of the masses, rallying them into action, the stuff revolutions are made of. Consider the impact of these Champions and their causes:

- *Mahatma Gandhi,* who freed a nation by advocating nonviolent change
- *Mother Teresa,* tireless champion serving the outcasts of society
- *Martin Luther King Jr.,* leader of America's civil rights movement
- *Cesar Chavez,* founder of America's first farm workers union
- *Dalai Lama,* spiritual advocate for peace and moral responsibility

There are many other champions of special causes. Religious leaders such as Billy Graham and Robert Schuller. Statesmen such as Abraham Lincoln and Nelson Mandela. Media icons such as Oprah Winfrey and Bill Moyers. Financial leaders fighting for Main Street investors, such as Jack Bogle and Charles Schwab.

The Cause: A Mystical Bond between the Champion and You

Champions are vibrant personalities. They love people, love life, love working on their projects. Most of all, they love championing a cause. And the feeling is mutual: The cause energizes the people. They fall in love with their Champion. They bond in a common goal—challenging a system that no longer works and creating a new order.

In each case, Champions feel a profound sense that they have been chosen to lead the challenge, to define it, to represent the people, to create the new order, that they have a calling. They feel passionately about the cause and believe their unique gifts are necessary for the cause to succeed.

The system under attack may be ethical, moral, spiritual, or political. It may be humanitarian, social, or economic. It may deal with issues of health, education, economics, and welfare. Most of all, the issues reflect inequities crossing many boundaries of our culture—inequities creating a gap between the haves and the have-nots, between the power elite and the underprivileged, between the greedy and the deprived.

NEW SPIRITUAL REVOLUTION ANCHORED IN THE OLD GOLDEN RULE

Although the cause acts as a powerful magnet uniting the people, the rallying point is the Champion, both as a symbol of the cause and as its leader. Often, the message and the cause are incredibly subtle.

For example, in *Ethics for the New Millennium,* the Dalai Lama challenges us—*in his words, yes, but more significantly, in his actions, by the example of his life*—to a new spiritual revolution that is simply a return to our roots in the Golden Rule of selflessness that underlies all great faiths:

> My call for a spiritual revolution is . . . a call for a radical reorientation away from our habitual preoccupation with self. It is a call to turn toward the wider community of beings with whom we are connected, and for conduct which recognizes others' interests alongside our own.

Indeed, somewhere deep within all causes and within all Champions is this universal call to live by the Golden Rule, to do unto others as you would have them do unto you—to correct social and economic inequities, to alleviate the suffering of the many, to close the gap between the privileged few and the masses in a world where a power elite of less than 10 percent controls 90 percent of the wealth, manipulating the political structure to their continued advantage, while half the people in the world go to bed hungry.

MAHATMA GANDHI: NONVIOLENCE AND THE CAUSE OF FREEDOM

In a world where wars rage on incessantly, where poverty, hunger, illiteracy, and sickness are part and parcel of the daily lives of the majority, where freedom and liberty are hollow words to most, Mahatma ("Great Soul") Gandhi became a living example of the power of a single person and their cause.

Gandhi was the ideal Champion: His life, his actions, and his words inspired a nation to rise up and demand freedom. Yet he had no political power, nor did he command an army. Gandhi ruled by the force of his character, a man of principle and integrity whose cause—gaining freedom for India through nonviolence—became the cause of millions.

Gandhi's message was simple. We have heard it many times before from the prophets of the great religions and the Champions—you are the message, be a living example, do unto others as you would have them do unto you:

> Be the change you want to see in the world. . . . The best way to find yourself is to lose yourself in the service of others. . . . There are people in the world so hungry that God cannot come to them

except in the form of bread. . . . Whatever you do will be insignif-icant, but it is very important that you do it. . . . If you want some-thing really important to be done you must not merely satisfy the reason, you must move the heart also.

Gandhi, the Champion, did indeed tap into the heart of a nation by the sheer force of his character. He is even today universally identified with the cause of nonviolent revolution. With a novel "weapon"–*unheard of in a world where power is won through military victories*–Gandhi was able to rally millions, wear down his enemies, and free his compatriots from foreign domination:

> Nonviolence is the greatest force at the disposal of mankind. It is mightier than the mightiest weapon of destruction devised by the ingenuity of man . . . the seven blunders of the world that lead to violence: wealth without work, pleasure without conscience, knowledge without character, commerce without morality, sci-ence without humanity, worship without sacrifice, politics without principle.

Gandhi was a living example of all these qualities–a man of character, of conscience, integrity, morality, humanity, sacrifice, and principles–all part of the personality code of Champions, defining them as leaders of causes.

MOTHER TERESA: CHAMPION OF COMPASSION IN ACTION

Mother Teresa was another Champion, a living example, an answer to a simple challenge: "Whatever you do for the least of my brethren, you are doing for me." In *For the Love of God,* Mother Teresa has this to say:

> God and compassion are one and the same. Compassion is the joy of sharing. It's doing small things for the love of each other–just a smile, or carrying a bucket of water, or showing some simple act of kindness . . . trying to share and understand the suffering of peo-ple . . . it's not how much we give, but how much love we put in the *doing.*

Mother Teresa often said that when she looked in the eyes of a dying leper, she saw God. Even when she was received the Nobel peace prize, this extraordinary person spoke of the joy her work gave to her:

> The poor are very wonderful people. One evening we went out and we picked up four people from the street. And one of them was in a most terrible condition–and I told the Sisters: You take

care of the other three, I take of this one that looked worse. So I did for her all that my love can do. I put her in bed, and there was such a beautiful smile on her face. She took hold of my hand, as she said one word only: Thank you—and she died . . . she gave me her grateful love. And she died with a smile on her face.

While Gandhi, Mother Teresa, the Dalai Lama, and so many other great Champions set an incredibly high standard, probably out of reach for most humans, the truth is, all people born with this unique genetic code have the same qualities. They clearly see the inequities in the world, the plight of the less unfortunate, the poor, sick, the uneducated, the enslaved, the disenfranchised, the unwanted. As Mother Teresa said,

> In these twenty years of work among the people, I have come more and more to realize that it is being unwanted that is the worst disease that any human being can ever experience.

Champions are not only aware of the inequities between people, *they feel these inequities in their soul,* and they hear a loud voice calling them to do something to correct the situation, to right the wrongs, to become Champions of the people and their causes. In answering the call, they often become possessed of great powers to great things, beyond what they considered possible.

Careers and Causes for the "Champion Next Door"

The lives of Champions can take many forms and involve all kinds of causes, each in their own unique way as meaningful as the causes of Gandhi, Mother Teresa, and the Dalai Lama, although perhaps less noticeable in newspapers and history books—people we might call the "Champion next door."

Many of the world's great Champions have full-time commitments in jobs serving people, directly or indirectly. Others are part-time volunteers working off-hours and using their business and professional skills and funds. Here are a few examples of the wide variety of careers, causes, programs, and projects that attract Champions. They may touch one life anonymously or millions with widespread notoriety. What matters is that they are giving of themselves, and doing it out of love.

- *Ministers and laypeople,* working in hospices and homeless shelters
- *Restaurateurs,* conducting food bank pickups for the indigent

- *Teachers,* organizing an international movement to outlaw land mines
- *Investigative journalists,* exposing corporate corruption
- *Public advocates,* protecting battered wives and homeless children
- *Psychotherapists,* working with trauma victims after tragedies
- *Documentary filmmakers,* exposing mistreatment of the mentally ill
- *Local politicians,* fighting for services for our aging population
- *Attorneys,* working pro bono in legal aid clinics for the poor
- *Business men and women* organizing various charitable events
- *Teachers,* working in inner city ghettos with underprivileged children
- *Chemical dependency specialists,* working with prison populations
- *Missionaries,* teaching about God and farming in underdeveloped countries
- *Advertising agency directors,* working on public-service programs
- *Philanthropists,* committed to reducing world hunger and illiteracy
- *Doctors or nurses,* providing medical services in foreign countries

What distinguishes Champions is not their specific career, profession, or business as much as their *motivation.* A philanthropist merely looking for a tax deduction is not a Champion. Mother Teresa put it simply: "It's not how much we give, but how much love we put in the doing." A smile, carrying a bucket of water, a simple act of kindness may be as defining of this personality as the leadership of a grand revolutionary movement.

Champions come in all sizes and shapes. They are leaders of a different kind. Their lives are filled with a spirit of caring and compassion for the people served, and when they lead, they lead by example more than anything, inspiring people through the power of their character and charisma to follow them and the cause that becomes their destiny.

Millionaire's Code for Passionate Champions: Extravert, Intuitive, Feeling, Perceiver (ENFP)

Yes, they are Extraverts, chameleonlike, showing strong signs of leadership and theatricality that resemble the personality traits of Commanders (ENTJ), Entrepreneurs (ESTP), and Entertainers (ESFP)—and using whatever talents and resources it takes to advance their cause with passion.

Like all *Extraverts,* Champions love people—friend and foe, confident and stranger, individuals and crowds, people energize them. Their charisma and message energize the people. They are constantly looking for opportunities to promote their cause, telling the public all about it—on the phone, in meetings, at press briefings, conferences, lunches, updates, you name it. They want a forum, an audience, a following, support for the cause, whatever it is. They go to the people and energize the power in them.

THE BATTLE BETWEEN GOOD AND EVIL DRIVES EVERY CAUSE

Not all Champions can say "my life is an open book," as Gandhi once said. Most Champions have a well-guarded private side—*perhaps rooted in a broken home, poverty, or a learning disability, often a liability turned into an asset.* Yet this secret often underlies their mission, becomes the driving engine in their personality, and the reason they are leaders of a cause.

Champions are the extraverted siblings of Introverted Mystic Heroes. Both carry the weight of the world on their shoulders. Within them rages a battle between good and evil, a battle for their soul in the secret territory of their inner world.

In time, this internal battle emerges onto the everyday world. There they can prove themselves by championing a cause, by becoming a Champion for good in its battle with evil, where a victory over the dark side will redeem them and prove they are worthy. It is the inner battle that ultimately defines their life. It is the outer battle we see. In his autobiography, Carl Jung wrote of the depth of his struggles:

> I had early taken it for granted that the split in my personality was my own purely personal affair and responsibility. Faust . . . awakened in me the problem of the opposites, of good and evil. . . . The dichotomy of Faust-Mephistopheles came together within myself into a single person, and I was that person . . . this was my fate. . . . Later I consciously linked my work to what Faust had passed over: Respect for the eternal rights of man.

Within the soul, a raging battle between good and evil. On the surface, the world sees Champions united to a cause. Jung's battle would remain secret, revealed only after his death, in his autobiography, *Memories, Dreams, Reflections.* What the world saw was a psychologist with a cause, to create a *science* of the mind:

> From my eleventh year I have been launched upon a single enterprise which is my "main business." My life has been permeated and held together by one idea and one goal: namely to penetrate *the secret of personality.* Everything can be explained from this central point, and all my works relate to this one theme.

Jung's personal struggles did remain secret until his death, and it is clear that they were the central theme, the driving force in his work. However important keeping such secrets may be to the Champion, they are probably less important (if not irrelevant) to the people served. They are attracted to the Champion's cause—*because it is also their cause!*

INSIDE THE EXTRAVERT: A WARRIOR FIGHTING GOD'S BATTLES

This pattern is extremely important in understanding the personality of Champions. They may be Extraverts, they may love people and talking and mixing it up, they may be energized by the cause that unites them, and they may feel that they cannot refuse the demands made on their time by the cause—but deep inside they still have their own personal battle going on, a battle between good and evil.

They need time alone to figure out where that battle stands. They are deeply spiritual and need to know that things are right between them and their God, that they are winning the battle for good, that they are not succumbing to evil. They often go off alone to pray, to read, to relax, to be with nature and God. They need to reexamine and recharge because they often have traits of both Extravert and Introvert.

Intuitive: The "Power of One" Who *Must* Make a Difference

Gandhi would free his nation. Mother Teresa would let no one die alone, unwanted and unloved. Champions know they are born with "the power of one" imprinted on their soul—they are the chosen ones.

Visionaries, yes, but they not only dream of a better future, they have an overwhelming need, indeed a command, to make a difference. They know they have the power to make the future happen—and they cannot let the people down. For they have been chosen to lead their cause; they have the power of one, the one who can make a difference.

Most of all, they cannot disappoint their God, for they are on a spiritual mission. Deep inside, they know they have been called to do a job by their Creator, and they know they don't have much choice in the matter. It's the right thing to do, the *only* thing they can do to bring them into harmony with their destiny, their genetic code, their God.

In a real sense, the champion is the ultimate Pathfinder, all four Pathfinder personalities wrapped into one dynamic personality—the *Inspiring Teacher,* the *Healing Counselor,* the *Mystic Hero,* and the *Champion* with a cause. They are all *Intuitives:* Facts and data, information about today and yesterday are interesting, as starting points, to get where they're going.

WHATEVER THE CHAMPION'S MIND CAN CONCEIVE, IT WILL CREATE

It is the future that possesses champions, not the present, not the past. Their thinking is always abstract, not concrete, for they know, absolutely, as so many great Intuitive minds have known throughout time, "Whatever the mind can conceive, it can create."

Gandhi and the Indian people had their eye on freedom, on tomorrow. Like every Intuitive, they were discontent with the way things were, and they united behind the one chosen. They had a vision of what could be and were inspired to go after the dream, against all odds. Their hero was able to instill in millions the *power of one*—the power to make a difference, the power to change the present, the power to transform the future, to make the vision and the dream a reality.

Until they lock onto their cause and commit to their destiny, Champions feel as though they're drifting as they search, possibly even trying out different careers and exploring various personalities. After all, even Gandhi wore the garb of a button-down lawyer before he wore the loincloth of the mahatma.

The fact is, Champions are on hold, simply awaiting instructions for the right moment, a moment not of their choosing. As frustrating as that may seem for highly energized Champions, they are not wasting their time, they are gaining necessary experiences, including a sense of humility, while being trained, prepared, and strengthened for the calling and the cause that is to come.

Feelings: Sharing a Common Cause and a Higher Purpose

The third element of a genetic code tells us which criteria a person will tend to use in making decisions. A Thinking personality uses objective, external standards, whereas the Feeling person relies on subjective, personal criteria. However, the distinction hardly does justice to Champions. They are not just *Feeling* people—they are one of the most passionate of all personalities, passionate about life, passionate about the people and their causes, passionate about their relationship with God.

When it comes to love for fellow humans, Gandhi has few equals. Indeed, Albert Einstein said, "Generations to come will scarce believe that such a one as this ever in flesh and blood walked upon this earth."

One of the last statements Gandhi made before his death in 1948 summarized his intense passion for the people he served:

> I will give you a talisman. Whenever you are in doubt, or when the self becomes too much with you, apply the following test. Recall the face of the poorest and the weakest man or woman whom you may have seen, and ask yourself, if the step you contemplate is going to be of any use to him. Will they gain anything by it? Will it restore them to a control over their own life and destiny? In other words, will it lead to freedom for the hungry and spiritually starving millions?

Gandhi the Champion walked the way he talked, filled with compassion and sharing his life completely with the people he served. His life was dedicated not just to the freedom and independence of his country, but to a much deeper and more personal task: He was dedicated to the emancipation and freedom of each and every individual soul to choose for themselves.

Together the Champion and the people share a common cause and a common passion that connects them across time and space and through eternity. There is absolutely no question in the minds of Champions that they are guided to do the will of God; theirs is not merely a nine-to-five job; they share their lives; and everyone knows of their passion to live as God would have them live, by the Golden Rule.

IT'S NOT WHAT YOU DO, BUT THE LOVE YOU GIVE IN THE DOING

Nor is the guidance reserved for grand masters such as Gandhi, Mother Teresa, and the Dalai Lama. All Champions are guided. They may be a store clerk volunteering in a hospice, a deli owner collecting leftovers for a homeless food bank, a corporate manager serving as a big brother, an attorney doing pro bono work for the homeless, a nurse or doctor traveling as a relief volunteer to foreign lands.

The name tag is unimportant. Nor how much Champions give, but how much love they put in the doing for the least of their brethren. For Champions, "Whatever you do will be insignificant, but it is very important that you do it," because Champions and their causes are guided by the will of God.

Perceiving: All You Need Is Love (and a Sense of Humor!)

Champions are also Perceivers: They are not just happy, joyful, free, and passionate about life and people and the fact that they are in sync with

God's will–they are filled with unbridled compassion and love for others, and *they must share it*. Mother Teresa put it simply: "Compassion is the joy of sharing. It's doing small things for the love of each other . . . *we have all been created for the sole purpose to love and be loved.*"

The truth is, *Perceivers* are much more relaxed and content with their lives than their opposites, Judgers, who are more uptight about life, worrying endlessly about getting things done on time, trying to control life with tools like goal setting, plans, schedules, deadlines. All that is of little importance to Perceivers, for they know there is a master scheduler at work behind the scenes.

When Champions are in their groove, when they are in harmony with their destiny, they really are happy campers. Yes, they may radiate spirituality, but you can see the dance in their step, feel the song in their heart, and hear the lightheartedness in their spirit. Like Mother Teresa, a tiny ball of energy who once remarked with a smile, "I know God never gives us more than we can handle, but I wish he didn't trust me so much."

EVEN GANDHI HAD A SENSE OF HUMOR

Gandhi is another good example: "If I had no sense of humor," he said with a twinkle in his eye, "I would long ago have committed suicide." In fact, minutes before his death he was joking about being late as he headed for the prayer grounds following a simple meal with India's deputy prime minister. He drank some goat's milk and ate some cooked vegetables and oranges.

The 79-year-old Gandhi put his forearms on the shoulders of two young girls, relatives who were helping him: "My walking sticks," he said, playfully. He mentioned the carrot juice one girl had given him that morning, laughing: "So you are serving me cattle fare," adding that his deceased wife used to call it horse fare. "Isn't it grand of me," said Gandhi, with mock humility, "to relish what no one else wants?"

He was already 10 minutes late. As they walked, the girls kidded with Gandhi: "Your watch must be feeling very neglected, you would not look at it today," one said. "Why should I, since you are my timekeepers?" replied Gandhi. "But you don't look at the timekeepers," the girl said. Gandhi laughed.

Moments later an assassin fired three shots at close range, killing him. His last words, "Hey Rama" (Oh God). He died as he lived, serving his God and his people. The night before he had said, if "somebody shot at me and I received his bullet on my bare chest without a sigh and with Rama's name on my lips, only then should you say I was a true Mahatma." And so it is.

Most people admire Gandhi and Mother Teresa, yet know they could not travel the same paths. Champions are unique. Not everyone can enjoy the life of an ascetic and care for dying lepers carried off Calcutta's streets. But when Champions are doing what they came here to do, they feel it, and they radiate joy—they are doing the will of God, and that makes them happy, joyous, and free.

Money? God Is My Source and Will Provide All I Need

Imagine Gandhi meeting with a financial adviser: "Mahatma, we need to review the budget; expenses are getting out of hand; we may have to sell off some of the portfolio." The Gandhis and Mother Teresas of this world don't really think that way, but if the question arose, they'd surely reply, "Don't worry, God will provide."

And he always does—especially for the true Champion. Actually, for every Pathfinder. And for that matter, everyone else, too. Champions, however, have total faith, never doubting they'll be cared for. If you're doing God's work, *of course* God will provide. Remember, God's delay is not God's denial. But just in case, consider working with a trusted financial expert for assistance and possibly letting them manage your financial life so you can focus on the cause.

* * * * * * * *

Remembering that God is my source, we are in the
spiritual position of having an unlimited bank account.
Most of us never consider
how powerful the Creator really is . . .
God has lots of money.
God has lots of movie ideas, novel ideas, poems,
songs, paintings, acting jobs. God has a supply of loves,
friends, houses that are all available to us.
By listening to the creator within,
we are led to our right path.
On that path we find
friends, lovers, money,
and meaningful work.

Julia Cameron,
The Artist's Way

CHAPTER 27

HEALING COUNSELORS (INFJ)

M. SCOTT PECK, WAYNE DYER, THOMAS MOORE

Each soul comes to
the Earth with gifts.
Before it incarnates,
each soul agrees to perform
certain tasks upon Earth.
It enters into a sacred agreement
with the Universe to
accomplish specific goals. . . .
Whatever the task your soul has agreed to,
whatever its contract with the Universe,
all of the experiences
of your life serve to
awaken within you
the memory of that contract,
and to prepare you to fulfill it.

Gary Zukav,
The Seat of the Soul

T he *Healing Counselors* are the one Pathfinders whose genetic code naturally leads them to counsel, mentor, guide, and advise people in one-to-one relationships and small groups. Healing Counselors are the introverted siblings of Inspiring Teachers (ENFJ), who enjoy working in the limelight and are energized by groups.

Both types have a strong desire to teach and inspire people. The difference is that Counselors prefer teaching people in a more intimate and private setting. For one thing, they're more likely to be found working in a therapy office with individual clients and families than onstage as motivational speakers. They also wear many other name tags.

You see them working as guidance counselors, advising kids on career plans. Or as tutors, math coaches, or school nurses. Or as ministers consoling grieving families, as one-on-one fitness trainers, or as human resources consultants for businesses. Perhaps as hairstylists whose advice and words of encouragement are the main reason customers keep coming back.

Yet in each instance these Counselors are teachers in a special sense—inspiring individuals to change, challenging them to go after new opportunities, to reach beyond their current limitations, bringing out the best in themselves, and encouraging them to do whatever it takes to grow personally in their own unique ways.

Yes, they are Teachers, but Introverted ones, working on a one-to-one basis—tutors of sorts. Like Zen masters, one of their major goals is to teach students to trust themselves so much that they become free and independent of the master.

Making a Difference—One Person at a Time

Unlike the more extraverted Teacher who is drawn to groups of people, Counselors tend to measure their successes in career and in life one person at a time, much as Ralph Waldo Emerson so eloquently put it in *On Success:*

> To laugh often and much; to win the respect of intelligent people and the affection of children; to earn the appreciation of honest critics and endure the betrayal of false friends; to appreciate beauty, to find the best in others; to leave the world a bit better, whether by a healthy child, a garden patch or a redeemed social condition; *to know even one has breathed easier because you have lived.* This is to have succeeded.

This shows Counselors at their best—helping one person at a time, often working tirelessly, meeting one person after another, all day long in a clinic, office, church, or other private setting, allowing others to reveal intimate secrets, to safely expose their dark side, express their pains and joys, tears and laughter, anger and love, and bring the real you into the light.

COUNSELORS EMERGING IN TIMES OF CRISIS AND SOUL-SEARCHING

Counselors help others, they advise, they teach, and their sense of accomplishment is validated one person at a time. But remember, Counselors are also Pathfinders—underneath all their tireless counseling, they are on a path, searching for the meaning of life, their own life, not merely performing some technical specialty. Because if what they are doing becomes hollow and mechanical, they are not healing the soul.

Helping people is their mission in life, true. But Counselors also have a personal need to be validated from within—*from themselves,* from the inner voice that tells them they are on track, from their spiritual core. They need to know that they are in harmony with their own life, in alignment with their mission. Yet so many do not because of society's increasing cultural angst.

Why Is Everyone So Cranky? is a great summary of the key cultural trends making us angry: compressed time demands . . . communication overload . . . electronic linkages versus personal disconnectedness . . . increasing consumerism and competition . . . depersonalized consumer contacts . . . cultural changes accelerating in pace and increasing in complexity. Witness the escalating use of antidepressants and tranquilizers to handle pressures, tensions, stress, and anxiety. The media adds to the tension all day long.

Today Counselors are in the middle—caught between a troubled soul and a troubled world—experiencing a widening gap between the traditional practices of their professions and the increasing needs of the people and society they serve.

Something is missing—a deep inner spiritual connection that people everywhere hunger for and are not getting through conventional sources that may have worked in earlier cultures and simpler times. To fill the gap, Counselors are searching for new ways to help people, and perhaps more significantly, the role of Counselor is taking on new forms and being performed by many who are not officially Counselors.

THE EMERGING NEW SPIRITUAL PSYCHOLOGY FOR SOUL-SEARCHERS

In 1933, Carl Jung first addressed the issue in *Modern Man in Search of a Soul:* "Spiritually the Western world is in a precarious situation—the danger is greater the more we blind ourselves to the merciless truth with illusions about the beauty of our soul." Technology, war, prosperity, and the shortcomings of our health care system have actually increased the illusions, further undermining the traditional role of the Counselor.

Sixty years after Jung's warning, psychologists James Hillman and Michael Ventura punctuated Jung's message in a follow-up critique: *We've*

Had a Hundred Years of Psychotherapy and the World's Getting Worse. Similar challenges have been voiced by other critics in recent years who, while recognizing different counseling specialties, share one common voice in identifying the missing element for effective counseling.

- Thomas Moore, *Care of the Soul:* "In the modern world we separate religion and psychology, spiritual practice and therapy. There is considerable interest in healing this split, but if it is going to be bridged, our very idea of what we are doing in our psychology has to be radically re-imagined. *Psychology and spirituality need to be seen as one.* In my view, this new paradigm suggests the end of psychology as we know it altogether because it is essentially modern, secular, and ego-centered. A new idea, a new language, and new traditions must be developed on which to base our theory and practice"
- Gary Zukav, *The Seat of the Soul:* "Psychology means soul knowledge. It means the study of the spirit, but it has never been that. Psychology is the study of cognitions, perceptions and affects . . . psychology seeks to heal the personality without recognizing the force of the soul that is behind the configuration and experiences of the personality, and, therefore, cannot *heal at the level of the soul.*"
- James Hillman, *The Soul's Code:* "The concept of this individualized soul-image has a long, complicated history; its appearance in cultures is diverse and widespread and the names for it are legion. Only our contemporary psychology and psychiatry omit it from their textbooks."
- Joan Borysenko, *Fire in the Soul:* "When our souls are on fire, old beliefs and opinions can be consumed, bringing us closer to our essential nature and to the heart of healing. . . . This book is about the *newness that can emerge in our souls* when that shell is broken; the freedom to be ourselves and the awakening to a whole new dimension of life–the spiritual. . . . Although psychology technically means the study of the soul, most psychological systems abandoned any interest in soul in their bid to be scientific."
- Wayne Dyer, *Real Magic:* "There is a new collective consciousness in the minds of people, and a new spiritual awareness is spreading throughout humanity. Nothing can stop it, for nothing is more powerful than an idea whose time has come. An idea is a thought–individual or collective–that, *once spread to enough souls, manifests in physical changes.* . . . Now we see a new reality, a reality that comes

from a new way of thinking, and this is the context of our spiritual revolution."

All this is a very healthy sign. Although contemporary counseling is limited by theories that ignore the soul and practices controlled by a failing health care system, our best Counselors are working to get us back on track—in contact with our soul. And this really isn't as metaphysical as it seems, it's just another way of being a teacher and coach, inspiring people.

This trend is expanding rapidly. Many traditional counselors, professionals in social work and psychotherapy, are adapting alternative approaches. More important, many others, professionals and nonprofessionals in other fields, are stepping in to fill the gap, speaking from deep in their soul, deep in the spiritual center that connects everyone, the *collective unconscious,* as Jung calls it.

Careers: A Noble Calling to Save a World on Fire

Counselors are rare in our culture, and could easily become even rarer—they have many good reasons to avoid the call, knowing it will mean sacrifice and pain if they take on the challenges ahead in today's troubled world.

"We are living in an unprecedented time. The world soul is truly on fire with hunger, pollution and hatred. Many of us are wounded," says Borysenko. Yet the world soul needs help, people who can "use the fire of their wounds consciously—to heal, to work for peace, to transform the world." And that puts Counselors in a metaphysical dilemma:

Counseling in a world on fire. On one hand, if they answer the calling and work as Counselors, they will have a sense of satisfaction from helping people. However, that means that they'll be living in the pain of a world on fire, every day sharing and healing the wounds of so many suffering individuals going through hardships, tragedies, grieving, divorces, sickness, and death, as well as the joys. It takes a very unique and dedicated personality to take on this kind of work willingly.

Fire fighting and burning out. On the other hand, if individuals with this genetic code sense the work ahead as too heavy for them and they walk away, they will experience a sense of loss from being out of sync with who they really are. Fortunately, experience shows that most individuals with this genetic code do actually embrace the call to serve people in need.

Either way, counselors will be exposed to a world filled with suffering and pain—*from people around them and from within themselves.* They need to find ways to avoid becoming wounded healers, otherwise their effectiveness as a healer will be limited. Where are Counselors likely to find career opportunities? Some will be wearing traditional name tags; many others will be wearing rather unconventional ones, disguised as something else:

- *Marriage and family therapists*
- *Psychologists and psychiatrists*
- *Ministers, priests, monks, nuns*
- *Social service workers*
- *Doctors and nurses*
- *Alternative health care practitioners*
- *Personal services providers*
- *Consultants in many fields*
- *Personal fitness trainers*
- *Twelve-Step sponsor*
- *Charity workers, Salvation Army*
- *Hospice counselors and volunteers*
- *Mediators and negotiators*
- *Career and guidance counselors*
- *Mentors and Big Brothers*
- *Private tutors and coaches*
- *Camp counselors and guides*

With the levels of crankiness, suffering, and pain increasing in the world, and with the growing need for counseling services everywhere, two things are obvious. First, traditional providers of counseling services will be modifying their methods and practices, adopting unconventional ones.

Second, in the future most Counselors probably won't be wearing "official name tags." They will simply be people helping people one-on-one, inspiring them to overcome setbacks, achieve their dreams, and do the right thing. More and more Counselors will have no official status, but will serve.

Millionaire's Code for Healing Counselors
Introvert, Intuitive, Feeling, Judger (INFJ)

Counselors are *Introverts* laboring in relative anonymity and obscurity, working on a relatively small scale, focused on the people they feel committed to help. They usually don't get (or want) a lot of public attention:

- Much of their work must be done discreetly, to protect the confidentiality of their clients, patients, and parishioners.
- People typically find them by word-of-mouth and personal referrals.
- In a successful business or practice, working on a one-to-one basis, there are only so many people Counselors can help without themselves burning out.

Every now and then, however, the American media will draw *Introverts* out of their isolated niche in the world and into media celebrity status, putting them to work "counseling" 10 or more people every hour on a talk show.

Suddenly, everybody in America knows the latest Dr. Phil or Dr. Laura, with their shows and books. Talk-show formats are typically a series of brief one-to-one sessions, with audiences acting as voyeurs, surreptitiously tuned in to an assembly line of troubled call-ins or guests, hopefully picking up a few tips.

NO QUICK FIXES ON THE ROAD LESS TRAVELED

Extraverts are energized by people in the outer world. They feed on these interactions. In a paradoxical way, Introverted Counselors are much like their Extraverted cousins, the Champions (ENTP). Introverted Counselors are also energized by working with people, but not with just anybody, anywhere, and not with large audiences. They are more likely to be energized by close, intimate, spiritual relationships nurtured over time, where their clients, patients, or parishioners relate to them on a soul level.

Talk-show counselors are creations of the American media, "reality" shows responding to a culture in search of quick fixes. They are more Teachers (ENFJ) than Counselors. They are rare and also present a rather misleading image of the counseling process. Dr. M. Scott Peck touched on this in his classic, *The Road Less Traveled: A New Psychology of Love, Traditional Values and Spiritual Growth:*

> As a psychiatrist, I feel it is important to mention at the outset two assumptions that underlie this book. One is that I make no distinction between mind and spirit, and therefore *no distinction between the process of achieving spiritual growth and achieving mental growth*. They are one and the same.

The other assumption is that *this process is a complex, arduous and lifelong task.* Psychotherapy, if it is to provide substantial assistance to the process of mental and spiritual growth, is not a quick or simple procedure. . . . I believe that *brief forms of psychotherapy may be helpful and are not to be decried, but the help they provide is inevitably superficial.*

Of course, psychotherapists and psychiatrists aren't the only Counselors. Yet Peck's two key assumptions are important in order to understand the Introverted nature of the Counselor—whether a therapist, minister, nurse, mentor, doctor, nutritionist, fitness trainer, tutor, or other.

The fact is, Counselors are *Introverts,* and they are participating in intimate one-to-one and small-group experiences that touch the souls of the people they are helping. As a result, the most effective counseling experiences will be spiritual in nature—*as well as psychological, or mental, behavioral, medical, physical, nutritional, business, or whatever primary service is provided by the counselor.* There are no quick fixes.

Intuitives: Visionaries Unlocking the Secrets of the Soul

All Pathfinders are *Intuitives* or visionaries, and Counselors are visionaries of a special kind. They have a unique gift, the ability to see deep into the mind, into the psyche, deep into very soul of people—uncovering their secrets and, in the process, freeing them from being held captive by their own secrets.

The visionary powers of Counselors come naturally. They seem to have a psychic sixth sense, an extrasensory perception that penetrates beneath the surface, often uncovering hidden secrets in those they serve, secrets about their past—and secrets of their future, at least the future their secrets are blocking. In his autobiography, *Memories, Dreams, Reflections,* Carl Jung tells us why unlocking "the secret" is so critical to mental and spiritual health:

In many cases in psychiatry, the patient who comes to us has *a story that is not told, and which as a rule no one knows of.* To my mind, therapy only really begins after the investigation of that wholly personal story. It is the patient's secret, the rock against which he is shattered. *If I knew his secret story I have a key to the treatment.*

Counselors have the power to uncover and unlock this secret in people they're helping, whether it be physical or metaphysical, secular or spiritual. The key to recovery, wholeness, and growth is unlocking the secret.

THE SECRET YOU KEEP BY GIVING IT AWAY

Why Counselors? Because Counselors have unlocked the secret to their own destiny. They know the meaning of their life, or at least they're on a path, searching. They are explorers of the inner universe, searching for the secrets of life—most especially, *the secret to their own life.*

They instinctively know the secret of their destiny. They know that as Pathfinders, they *must* make a difference—they must make a difference in the lives of the people who come to them for help, who are themselves searching for meaning in their lives.

That's the destiny of Counselors—making a difference, one person at a time, being catalysts for change in the lives of their clients. You cannot help people find their way unless you have discovered your way. More- over, Counselors are compelled to share what they have discovered, *for they have discovered a secret they can keep only by giving away.*

Conversely, Counselors become magnets, drawing people to them, because people sense that they can trust Counselors. They feel safe enough to reveal the secret "story that is not told, and which as a rule no one knows of," not even the teller.

The magnetism of Counselors is no secret. People are drawn to them because they sense their passion for life, their love, their desire to help, and their values. They see in the Counselor a person of character, a liv- ing example of a life based on values, integrity, and ethics. This draws people to the Counselor—whether the Counselor is a family therapist, career counselor, acupuncturist, mentor, nurse, monk, nun, tutor, Big Brother, AA sponsor, unusually spiritual hairstylist, or your favorite aunt or uncle who always seems to have the right take on life.

A VISION OF THE FUTURE FROM SOME MYSTERIOUS SOURCE

Counselors are born with this unique visionary power. From an early age they somehow sense that they can see and hear and know things that other people are thinking, about distant events, about the past, and about the future. If you ask them, they'll probably tell you they can't really explain how they know, they just know.

Perhaps they are psychic, perhaps naturally telepathic, or perhaps just good at reading body language—after all, as much as 80 percent of all communication is nonverbal. More often than not, Counselors really can't explain how, they just *know*—and they're usually right.

Remember, the *Intuitive* function is the second of the four elements; it tells us how people gather information about the world around them, information ultimately used in making decisions. Unlike their opposite types, Sensors, they don't need a lot of hard data; they're guided by an inner voice. If there's any disagreement between that voice and the facts, they will trust their inner voice.

Regardless of how they get their information—through body language, mind reading, telepathy, psychic radar, reading textbooks, or their genetic structure—Counselors *do* have the information, and it is the basis of their vision of the future, the one they are destined to create.

Feelings: Living by the Rules, Yours and God's

Counselors are *Feeling* personalities, the third element of the genetic code. The rules they play by are their own rules—what feels right for the people and the situation at hand. When they make decisions, they are guided by personal, subjective criteria. They are, however, clearly guided by a set of values and principles encoded in the genes and felt deeply in their heart and soul.

Subjective, but not arbitrary. They have a strong sense of right and wrong based on an internalized moral code. However, if there is a conflict between their code and an external authority—whether it's a cultural custom, the law of the land, or the Commandments—Counselors will trust their own inner voice in making their decision and choosing the right course of action.

Yet Counselors do not like conflicts, confrontations, and competitions. In fact, they prefer avoiding them at all costs, except when they are asked to compromise their values to a higher authority.

NATURAL-BORN PEACEMAKERS, NEGOTIATORS, AND MEDIATORS

The plus side of all this is that harmony and peace have a high priority in the lives of Counselors, in their own personal lives with family and friends and in their work lives.

From a career standpoint, Counselors are natural-born peacemakers, mediators, and negotiators who can be very effective in resolving conflicts, improving relationships, and creating harmony among people—*because that's exactly what Counselors want in their own lives.*

Remember, however, feelings can backfire. Counselors are passionate about their values, and they love doing what they do. Yet the sheer magnitude and intensity of their work—caring for so many troubled people in troubling situations, coupled with their low tolerance for conflict—can leave Counselors feeling drained of energy and spirit.

This makes it critical for Counselors to work hard at keeping balance in their own lives, with well-rounded family, social, fitness, and spiritual lives, plus a backup support system when things get out of whack. Otherwise, it's too easy for them to fall into a messiah complex, overdo things, overload their schedules, and overwhelm themselves to the point of burnout. If you are a Counselor, keep that in mind.

Judging: Superdisciplined, Superorganized, Superefficient

Counselor personalities need to live a well-ordered and structured life in order to handle the demands of their daily lives. They easily soak up the feelings of everyone around them. They feel a sense of pressure to do something to make things better, to save, to cure, to help, to relieve the sufferings of humankind—and there's never enough time to do everything that needs to be done.

The feelings are so intense and the pressure is so strong that a normal person might buckle under. Not Counselors. They are blessed with a *Judging* personality trait and the strength of character and can make every minute count in their daily schedule. They become superefficient at home and at work.

Counselors are masters at organizing their day, their year, people, and projects. They probably have a written statement of their life's mission (written as a kid), project completion deadlines, progress schedules, to-do lists prepared the night before—whatever it takes to gain control of their lives so they can help a few more people each day in a world on fire.

They absolutely love the work they are doing. To get everything done, they know they need to be well organized. They have a job to do, a calling from a higher source, and, by God, they will get the job done.

In short, Counselors are highly disciplined individuals with strong principles and an enormous capacity to perform on a daily basis and to achieve greatly in their lifetime—and to do it without becoming overwhelmed, as they go forth each day onto the battlefield to ease the suffering of the souls they touch.

Making Money: A Calling to Fulfill a Sacred Agreement

All Pathfinders have an overwhelming sense that they are here on earth to fulfill some special mission. Physicist Gary Zukav captured this sense of mission in *The Seat of the Soul* when he wrote: "Each soul comes to the Earth with gifts. Before it incarnates, each soul agrees to perform certain tasks upon Earth. It enters into a sacred agreement with the Universe to accomplish specific goals," although the gifts and tasks differ for each of us.

Counselors come with a strong sense of their mission, and also the sacredness of their mission. Deep in their soul they feel the pain and suffering of a world on fire, and they have a compelling need to do what they can to help people—a calling that is spiritual and cannot be denied. They are Pathfinders who truly understand that they have a sacred agreement with the universe to serve as soul-searchers, making a difference one soul at a time.

Making money? That's not why Counselors are here in this lifetime. Besides, they believe they are called, that they will be provided for, that their reward will be in heaven, so to speak.

In earlier cultures, Counselors (shamans, oracles, and high priests) were cared for by the community. Today, Counselors in many charities and religious communities are provided for, although in a modest way, when serving and later in retirement. Many other Counselors are part-time volunteers through churches and charities and have other sources of income.

Many Counselors, including social workers, marriage and family therapists, alternative health care practitioners, mediators, and others, operate as independent entrepreneurs, lacking organizational support such as ongoing financial services, retirement plans, and insurances.

RENDER UNTO CAESAR WHAT IS CAESAR'S, AND TO GOD . . .

Fortunately, Counselors are organizational experts in their work lives, so they have the right skills to manage their money. However, they may need more than an occasional nudge telling them that it's okay to be a bit more selfish and also take care of the needs of themselves and their own families. But the reality is, while they know something must be done and have the right attitude, their minds are more focused on alleviating the world's suffering, one person at a time.

Their need to help others and their selfless attitude must be recognized, accepted—and compensated for. When push comes to shove, Counselors will usually put the interests of a client, patient, or other suffering soul ahead of their own. That's the nature of their priorities—*they are Pathfinders*.

As a result, it is imperative that they lean heavily on the assistance of a spouse, friend, or professional adviser to handle money matters, budgeting, savings plans, insurance, investing for retirement—so they can focus their efforts on healing a world on fire.

* * * * * * * *

What constitutes wealth?
In worldly terms, it is the possession
of money and valuable things.
But if we were to measure wealth
in other ways, besides mere dollars,
many who are poor in possessions
are spiritually rich,
and many who own much
are spiritually impoverished.

M. Scott Peck,
The Road Less Traveled

CHAPTER 28

MYSTIC HEROES (INFP)

RICHARD BACH, RICHARD CARLSON, JULIA CAMERON

> The call to adventure signifies that
> destiny has summoned the hero and transferred
> his spiritual center of gravity from within the
> pale of society to the zone unknown.
> This fateful region of both treasure and
> danger may be variously represented
> as a distant land, a forest,
> a kingdom underground,
> beneath the skies or above the sky,
> a secret island, lofty mountaintop,
> or profound dream state,
> but is always a place of strangely
> fluid and polymorphous beings,
> unimaginable torments,
> superhuman deeds, and
> impossible delights.
>
> Joseph Campbell,
> *On His Life and His Work*

Mystic Heroes quietly carry the weight of the world on their shoulders, for within them a great battle wages—the battle between good and evil. Yet, because it is an inner conflict, the world may never hear the real story.

Instead, the inner world of these deeply spiritual people may remain unnoticed as they go forth to slay dragons and make the outer world a better place in rather quiet ways—as missionaries and ministers, as social workers and psychologists, as novelists and journalists.

Like Special Forces commandos, they are on a unique mission to battle evil and save the world. They play out their inner drama on the world's stage, always carrying with them a deep sense of a cosmic battle raging between evil and good, a grand conflict that defines their life's mission.

Into the Zone Unknown: *Memories, Dreams, Reflections*

Carl Jung is a perfect example of a mystic hero. The world knows Jung as a rational Visionary Thinker (INTP) who gave the world a new scientific approach to psychology in a couple hundred published works, all written with the logic you'd expect from an objective researcher . . . except for one book, *Memories, Dreams, Reflections,* Jung's autobiography, which was not to be published until his death and not to be included in the collected works of Carl Jung, the scientist—for the two were separate.

Beneath the public face of the rational scientist, Jung was engaged in the grand conflict between good and evil. Not just the normal temptations and qualms of conscience everyone has, but an agonizing drama that played out throughout his life—his professional, public life as a world renown scientist and psychiatrist and his personal, private life below the surface that he kept secret until late in life.

SECRETS HIDING AN UNENDURABLE LONELINESS

From early childhood, Jung spoke to no one of his deepest secrets. His father and eight uncles were ministers, skilled in theology, yet he knew they could not understand his "profound doubts about everything his father said." Most of the world did not get a peek into this secret world until his autobiography was published. Jung had many secrets, which reflected a rich inner life:

- A long secret relationship with a large stone in a field, thinking, "Am I the one sitting on this stone, or am I the stone on which *he* is sitting?"
- A symbolic manikin hidden in a forbidden attic, an "inviolable secret that must never be betrayed, for the safety of my life depended on it."
- His feigned fainting spells after an injury, which gave him hours to "plunge into the world of the mysterious," where he played fantasy games for hours.

- As a 12-year-old, he was aware he was "actually two different persons . . . the other was important, a high authority . . . powerful and influential . . . an old man . . . skeptical, mistrustful, remote from the world of men."
- Later, in his thirties, he had long conversations with his anima, the feminine alter ego in his psyche, and with Philemon, a winged centaur and wise old man: "He said things which I had not thought . . . it was he who spoke, not I."

Most of us grow up with many secrets and our own fantasy world. That's not news. Witness the popularity of Christopher Robin's Winnie the Pooh, Calvin's Hobbes, Charlie Brown's Snoopy. Movies. Video games.

The world of the Mystic Hero, however, reaches far beyond light entertainment. These individuals live in a world of perpetual spiritual conflicts between right and wrong, good and evil, God and devils, a world demanding great personal commitment and sacrifice from the chosen. For the Mystic Hero, this is no Dungeons & Dragons video game but a matter of life and death.

THE UNFORGIVABLE SIN BEFORE THE MIRACLE OF GRACE

Jung's biggest secret was the "miracle of grace," a profound event he describes in great detail–revealing much about the Mystic Hero personality. When he was 12, he was walking home from school through the cathedral square on a sunny day. His thoughts were on the vast beauty in life: "God made all this and sits above it far away in the blue sky on a golden throne."

Suddenly he was gripped with fear. Evil thoughts were overtaking him. "Don't go on thinking now. Something terrible is coming." He feared that if he gave in, he was "in terrible danger of committing the unforgivable sin and plunging myself into hell."

For three days he stayed home, tormented. Finally, he came to an awareness that "God himself was arranging a decisive test for me." God *wanted* him to sin so that he could "give me His grace and illumination." Jung finally gave in to the forbidden thought:

> I saw before me the cathedral, the blue sky. God sitting on His golden throne, high above the world–and from under the throne an enormous turd falls upon the sparkling new roof, shatters it, and breaks the walls of the cathedral asunder. So that was it! I felt an enormous, and indescribable relief. Instead of the expected damnation, grace had come upon me. . . . It was obedience which

brought me grace. . . . One must be utterly abandoned to God; nothing else matters but fulfilling his will.

Jung never did share his secrets with his family. He was convinced no one would understand. Certainly not his father and uncles, who were skilled theologians but, he was convinced, knew nothing of "the secret of grace." However, it no longer mattered, for he had "a sense of destiny . . . to do what God wanted," and his sole "duty was to explore daily the will of God," which he did for the rest of his life.

THE HERO'S JOURNEY: A QUEST TO DISCOVER THE REAL YOU

In fact, this sense of a personal calling to a divine destiny is characteristic of Mystic Heroes, paralleling the classic definition of the archetypal hero in Joseph Campbell's *Powers of Myth:*

> A legendary hero is usually the founder of something—a founder of a new age, the founder of a religion, the founder of a new city, the founder of a new way of life. In order to found something new, one has to leave behind the old and go in quest of the seed idea, a germinal idea that will have the potentiality of bringing forth the new thing.
>
> The founder of all religions have all gone on quests like that. The Buddha went into solitude and then sat beneath the bo tree, the tree of immortal knowledge, where he received an illumination that has enlightened all of Asia for twenty-five hundred years.

All Mystic Heroes share similar characteristics—a calling, a quest, the discovery of something, and the founding of the new. Buddha founded a new way of life, Jung a new psychology.

Most are not in the spotlight of history like Buddha and Jung. Still, all Mystic Heroes receive a calling to go on a quest to find a new way of life— *for themselves personally and those they touch along the way.*

Careers: Where the Secret Emerges into the Light of Day

Many Mystic Heroes are drawn to the ministry and missionary work, where their secret of grace comes out in the open and empowers them. Saint Francis and Saint Augustine come to mind, as does Mother Teresa. Others are the Trappist monk, Thomas Merton, and his friend, Buddhist monk Thich Nhat Hanh, author of *Living Buddha, Living Christ.*

Jung's experience is perhaps more revealing and significant, *because for many, the secret remains a secret!* Jung is an example of how Mystic

Heroes live in a world not easily visible to you and me. They spend a life-time living in two separate worlds—an inner world filled with secrets as well as a profound sense of destiny. And the outer world, where their inner secrets and conflicts play out in career choices ranging over a wide area:

- *Missionaries*
- *Priests and ministers*
- *Social scientists*
- *Therapists and psychologists*
- *Social services advocates*
- *Humanities teachers*
- *Writers, novelists, and poets*
- *Musicians and composers*
- *Artists and photographers*

Many Mystic Heroes enter careers that let them gradually "leak" their secrets, especially through their writings. For example, author Richard Bach gave us the fictional account of *Jonathan Livingston Seagull* in 1970, an inspiring story about a bird breaking free to teach others the joy of fly-ing and the power of a dream.

Seven years later Bach gave us *Illusions: The Adventures of a Reluctant Messiah,* a fictional story of a barnstorming pilot who discovers that when your soul has wings you don't need an airplane to soar. In 1986, *The Bridge Across Forever,* a fictional autobiography of Bach and his inner child, finally revealed some personal secrets on his spiritual journey, much like Jung's conversations with his anima, shadow, old man, and other arche-types.

Psychologist Richard Carlson, another Mystic Hero, brings a sense of peace to life's conflicts in *Don't Sweat the Small Stuff, For the Love of God,* and other books. Similarly, screenwriter Julia Cameron's *The Artist's Way* and martial artist Chuck Norris's *Secret Power Within* reveal a path to enlightenment. You can sense the mystic in many musicians—Carlos Santana, for example, or George Harrison, who said, "It doesn't matter if you're the greatest guitar player in the world, if you're not enlightened, forget it."

Watching Stephen Spielberg's films certainly leaves you with a sense of Mystic Heroes on spiritual missions: *Close Encounters of the Third Kind, E.T.,* and *Artificial Intelligence.* His work reveals the same sense of destiny that inspired Jung, hidden just below the surface. Whatever career is cho-sen, behind the scenes or in the spotlight, the Mystic Hero is a messenger of gods.

Millionaire's Code for Mystic Heroes
Introvert, Intuitive, Feeling, Perceiver (INFP)

The difference between introverted Mystic Heroes and their sibling types, the more extraverted Champions (ENFP), may be subtle, but it is nonetheless profound for Mystic Heroes and the missions they may be called to.

Champions are instinctively drawn to people. They have causes that touch the hearts and souls of people, and this energy in turn excites the Champions, encouraging them further. They have an instinctive sense of the dynamics between them and the people. They can relate to one person or to a crowd; they feel the pulse, because the cause bonds Champions to the people they serve.

Mystic Heroes are, by nature, *Introverts.* They are far more comfortable in their private inner world, away from people. Moreover, they have a much more powerful bond commanding them, in solitude, directing their life: a sacred bond with God. They may be drawn into public life, like Visionary Thinkers (INTP). But given the choice, they're rather lead quiet, contemplative lives with their books, researching, writing, and thinking, which explains why they are often in fields such as journalism and book publishing, rather than running seminars as a motivational speaker.

MEETING REMARKABLE BEINGS ON A ROAD LESS TRAVELED

Mystic Heroes tend to have a few close friends, people they feel comfortable with, often those who have a similar relationship with the spiritual world and a special calling to their field of expertise. But the truth is, the introverted Hero doesn't *need* people in the same way that the extraverted Champion needs people.

As we saw with Jung, Mystic Heroes *already have a rich dialogue going on in their heads.* Their minds are populated with people, or beings, that arise out of the archetypes of our psyche. Jung had profound relationships with God, with his feminine alter ego, with Philemon, the wise old man, and others.

In Jung's inner world, all these people and his relationships with them were real, more real than most of his relationships in the physical world. We accept it when a youngster speaks with a bear or tiger, but society worries when an adult does. Yet, as we've seen for Jung, his conversations and relationships with these people are remarkably real in a psychological and spiritual way. Moreover, such experiences may not be unusual even for hard-nosed business leaders. As Napoleon Hill tells us in his classic, *Think and Grow Rich:*

I have never entirely divested myself of this habit of hero-worship. . . . I have followed the habit of reshaping my own character, by trying to imitate the nine men whose lives and life-work had been most impressive to me. These men were Emerson, Paine, Edison, Darwin, Lincoln, Burbank, Napoleon, Ford and Carnegie. Every night, over a long period of years, I held an imaginary council meeting with this group whom I called my "Invisible Counselors."

Skeptics may dismiss such talk as New Age mumbo jumbo, or perhaps even as evidence of a personality split. Actually, most people would be a bit suspect, even Jung himself, because his family history included mental illness. And it's suspicions such as this that often encourages Mystic Heroes to keep their secrets secret.

EVENTS FORCING INTROVERTS INTO THE WORLD OF EXTRAVERTS

This distinction between *Introvert* and *Extravert* is crucial if you are a Mystic Hero—because in spite of all your efforts to protect your privacy and your inner world, your worldview may become so popular that you are drawn into the public eye as an Extravert. You may find, as Jung did, that exposure in the limelight is so draining that you need to retreat to recharge: "Solitude is for me a fount of healing which makes my life worth living. Talking is often a torment for me, and I need many days of silence to recover from the futility of words."

In fact, Jung spend much of his time withdrawing to the peacefulness of his lakeside retreat at Bollingen, out away from his home in the city of Küsnacht, to rest and recuperate, alone:

I have done without electricity, and tend the fireplace and stove myself. Evenings, I light the old lamps. There is no running water, and I pump the water from the well. I chop the wood and cook the food. These simple acts make man simple; and how difficult it is to be simple.

Away at his tower by the lake, "in the midst of my true life," he was most deeply himself, doing the simple chores that brought him back from his travels deep into the world of the soul and the psyche, helping ground him for a while in the real world of the inner senses.

Remember, Extraverts are energized by people. *Introverts,* on the other hand, though they cannot deny their calling, are likely to find that extended contacts with people drain their energy. Like Jung, they need large blocks of time to recharge in order to complete their mission in life.

Be sensitive to your genetic code if you are a Mystic Hero. You are by nature an Introvert. If your life's calling eventually draws you into the world of the Extravert, make sure you allow for a lot of downtime to retreat into your private world. Otherwise, there's a danger you could find yourself burning out.

The Intuitive: A Raging Inner Battle between Good and Evil

Like all Pathfinders, the Mystic Hero is an *Intuitive* by nature on a deep spiritual level. All Intuitives see beyond the present reality, beyond current trends and patterns in the physical world, beyond the hard data of everyday life. Intuitives have a vision of a brighter future. Unlike their counterparts, the more grounded Sensors, Intuitives see the present reality as but a starting point for a world to come, as they search for ways to make tomorrow a better place for humankind.

Like the heroes of great legends, Mystic Heroes truly do carry the weight of the world hidden in their souls and a quiet serenity on their faces. They arrive in the world with a grand vision encoded in their genes, one that goes beyond even the world of values, morals, ethics, integrity, and principles.

They sense a timeless struggle between the forces of good and evil, a conflict played out on a cosmic level, touching all people, spanning the entire history of the world and the planet—and they sense they are destined to play a significant role in the battle against the forces of evil. Somehow, they know from early childhood that they have a place in this great drama, searching for their calling and spending a lifetime fulfilling their mission.

From their calm exteriors, you get little sense that so much is going on below the surface. In fact, even they are in awe that somehow they have been chosen to follow in the footsteps of the great masters, leaders, heroes, and defenders of the faith—Mahatma Gandhi and Mother Teresa, Joan of Arc and Saint Francis, Buddha and Jesus.

Yet they know that somehow they must make a difference, they must become a leader in the battle, at a time and in a manner and place to be decided by another, much as Jung was enjoined to do what God wanted.

SURRENDERING: FIND ME WHERE YOU KNOW I NEED TO BE

Why Mystic Heroes are chosen to think and feel and be this way is as much a mystery as the mysterious drama raging in their minds. Few will understand; some will even laugh at them. But in their minds there is no doubt that this battle between good and evil is very real—they have been given a vision of things to come and they must fulfill their destiny in the grand scheme of things.

The life of a Mystic Hero is one long journey of searching for answers to the mysteries of the universe and the nature of God. They have no choice but to make the journey, because they were chosen. At the bottom, however, they are not so much searching for the meaning of life as they are for the meaning of *their own life*. Who am I? Why am I here? How may I best serve humanity? These are the ultimate questions of a Pathfinder, and most especially the Mystic Hero.

Regardless of their career choices, the intuitive visions of Mystic Heroes will dominate all their decisions along the way, no matter how profound or incidental in the overall fabric of life—though not always in a linear nor logical manner, and often understood only in retrospect. Yet they, more than any of the personalities, will come to trust the still small voice guiding them from within, much in the same sense that physicist Gary Zukav spoke in *Seat of the Soul:*

> Take your hands off the steering wheel. Be able to say to the Universe, "Thy will be done." . . . The final piece of reaching for authentic power is releasing your own to a higher form of wisdom . . . say to the Universe: "Find me where you know I need to be." Let go and trust that the Universe will provide, and so it shall. Let go of all. Let your higher self complete its task.

Mystic Heroes have a vision of the future in all its glory, with so many possibilities, full of many alternative ways to achieve the goal of a better world, and they understand their role in the drama. All they must do is surrender and let it unfold.

Feelings: Passions Guided by Uncompromising Principles

All Pathfinders are incredibly passionate, about everything, and this is especially true of Mystic Heroes. They are not, however, likely to show their emotions in any outwardly dramatic way. In fact, regardless of how much turmoil is brewing below the surface, they're likely to present a rather calm, serene face to the world—that is, until their principles are challenged, forcing them to spring into action and defend the faith.

In fact, their thoughtful manner is deceptive, suggesting to the world around them that they are a Thinking type, which is actually the opposite of the *Feeling* personality of the Mystic Heroes. They are a cauldron of emotions, not just their own, but those of everyone in their vicinity, a raging war of the gods within.

Mystic Heroes entered the world equipped with highly sensitive radar, forever scanning the world, absorbing emotions from everywhere—humans, animals, society, nations, the planet, news, photos, vibes. They are telepathic, with a keen sixth sense, extrasensory perception. They have learned from experience to trust their hunches and gut instincts more than facts.

They feel the anguish of humankind, searching for ways to heal the rift. They cannot resist a call to come to the aid of the needy, the helpless, the castaways, life's disadvantaged. In the purest sense, they reflect the true spirit of the savior and messiah, the martyr and sacrificer, for they are asked to give much of themselves throughout life. Theirs is the prayer of Saint Francis: "Lord, make me a channel of thy peace . . . for it is in giving that we receive. . . ."

For them, Emotions are the window into the soul—the soul of the world, your soul, my soul, and most of all, their own soul. They may have a commanding gift of language, great skill as a writer, and a powerful, rational mind, yet all these skills are but tools in the service of their emotional energy.

RAW EMOTIONS TURNED INTO PURE SPIRITUAL PASSION

Yet their emotions are not feelings in a conventional sense—such as cheering for the winning team, smiling at a loved one, or satisfaction from a job well done. The *Feeling* function of the Mystic Hero is an ingrained network of values, morality, and principles that are passionately felt and cannot be broken without seriously compromising the integrity of the Hero's mission.

Above all, Mystic Heroes must be true to themselves. Any breach is likely to trigger a profound sense of guilt and failure. Their sense of ethical responsibility for the world is without equal. It is the underlying force driving their emotions, their feelings, and their intense passions.

In a strict sense, the feeling function, the third of four elements in a personality's genetic code, tells us how decisions are made. Feelers use subjective criteria in making decisions, in contrast to the objective, external criteria of Thinkers.

In making their decisions, Thinkers are impartial, relying on established codes from law, science, society, religions, or the rules of logic, all separate and apart from how they personally feel about the people (including themselves) and the issues involved. In contrast, Feeling types tend to rely on a subjective and personal standard. The Mystic Hero's decisions, however, are not relative to any shifting mood, but rather are based on eternal values that come from a higher source and must be followed.

Perceivers: Perpetual Students with Beginners' Minds

In spite of the cosmic grandeur of their character, it may come as a surprise that Mystic Heroes also have a lot of fun, thanks to the playful free spirit of their Perceiver trait—especially when they're away from the noise and pressures of people and everyday life, where they can roam freely across the vast expanse of the universe they carry in their minds.

Perceivers, however, know they are outnumbered: The everyday world is overpopulated by Judgers, the polar opposite of Perceivers. Given a choice, Mystic Heroes will avoid these control freaks, with their obsessive obedience to goals, plans, organization, deadlines, rules, and regulations, all the stuff that annoys and restricts the Mystic Hero.

Mystic Heroes have enormous capacity to accomplish anything they believe in. If a project is in alignment with their goals, they instinctively know what needs to be done, when to do it, and how. Give them responsibility and minimal restrictions and and get out of their way—once committed, they will complete the job, for they are honorable and keep their word.

Jung is an obvious example of the Perceiver. He was a perpetual student, with what the Zen masters call the "beginner's mind," an infinitely curious child searching the most esoteric areas of the mind in every culture throughout history. So many of Jung's photos seem to reveal a kindly man who radiated the sense of the joy he must have felt in traveling freely in uncharted ground.

A JOURNEY INTO THE OUTER REACHES OF INNER SPACE

In addition to psychopathology, schizophrenia, dementia, manic depression, dream analysis, personality typologies, archetypes, the collective unconscious, and so many other areas of his new analytical psychology, Jung was venturing far afield into areas of personal interest that helped him better understand the human psyche: the occult . . . paranormal . . . seances . . . astrology . . . alchemy . . . fairy tales . . . mythology . . . mandalas . . . yoga . . . meditation . . . Zen . . . modern art . . . flying saucers . . .

life after death. He traveled to India, Africa, and America, including a special visit to the Pueblo Indians of New Mexico, studying religions and cultures everywhere. I'm envious of his long days off, reading and writing and resting at his lakeside retreat—it must have been pure ecstasy!

In *Powers of Mind,* financial journalist Adam Smith refers to Jung's *Memories, Dreams, Reflections* as the "Most Far-Out Autobiography." Well, Smith's (a pseudonym) autobiographical work was even "further out" (and more fun to read) when it was published in the mid-1970s.

Adam Smith is another Mystic Hero, obviously trying to outdo Carl Jung. Smith weaves together brain hemisphere research, altered states, time-space continuums, magic, stigmata, gravity, telepathy, ashrams, martial arts, biofeedback, psychedelics, reincarnation, mantras, paradigms, astronauts, the healing value of laughter, Rolfing, Zen and the *I Ching,* Satchel Paige, Ram Dass, and Carlos Castanada . . . and more. All experienced during a sabbatical!

Read *Powers of Mind* and you'll see why Mystic Heroes want to keep their secrets secret. Why? Because they are having a ball in this incarnation. Their lives are one big fabulous trip, and it's happening right there in the "outer reaches of inner space," *in their minds!*

Money: You Do Not Live by Bread Alone, Fulfill Your Destiny

Mystic Heroes are not here on earth to make money. It would be an insult to try to convince them otherwise. They are on a mission. A mission chosen by a higher power. They know they will be taken care of. They know it deep within their soul. Their life is not a simple, "Do what you love and the money will follow." They are not in a barter system where they are simply trading their skills for dollar bills.

Mystic Heroes know they have been *chosen* for a particular task. And they know they have no choice but to fulfill that destiny. They know they cannot miss because they are being guided, directed. Furthermore, they know that they will be taken care of—that the Spirit commanding them to go forth and fulfill their special task is also a shrewd financial backer.

Of course, the Spirit is also smart enough to provide help in the form of savvy spouses and financial advisers to take care of stuff in the mundane world—savings accounts, investments, mortgages, budgeting, and other easily ignored matters—while the Mystic Hero ventures forth into the world to do the work of the Spirit, slay a few dragons, and have a little fun, in secret, of course.

* * * * * * *

Why do the enlightened seem filled with
light and happiness, like children? Because they are. . . .
The masters of life know the Way,
for they listen to the voice within them,
the voice of wisdom and simplicity. . . .
Within each of us there is
an Owl, a Rabbit, an Eeyore and a Pooh. . . .
If we are smart we will choose the way of Pooh.
As if from far away,
it calls to us with the voice of a child's mind.

Benjamin Hoff,
The Tao of Pooh

GUARDIANS OF THE ESTABLISHMENT

GUARDIANS OF THE ESTABLISHMENT:
SENSOR-JUDGING (S-J)

- Chief Executive Officers (ESTJ)
- Diplomats and Peacemaker (ESFJ)
- Results-Oriented Experts (ISTJ)
- Master-Servants (ISTJ)

CHAPTER 29

CHIEF EXECUTIVE
OFFICERS (ESTJ)

WARREN BUFFETT, JACK BOGLE,
CHARLES SCHWAB

> We expected that
> good-to-great leaders would
> begin by setting
> a vision and strategy.
> We found
> instead that
> they *first* got
> the right people on the bus,
> the wrong people off the bus, and
> the right people in the right seats, *then*
> they figured out where to drive it.
>
> Jim Collins,
> *Good to Great:*
> *Why Some Companies*
> *Make the Leap, and*
> *Others Don't*

Chief Executive Officers (CEOs) are the take-charge individuals among the Guardians of the Establishment, whether that establishment is business or government, military or legal system, a high school math club, the local PTA, or a university. They are confident, no-nonsense, bottom-line leaders anchored in the realities of the day-to-day world.

CEOs want things running along smoothly and efficiently. They know exactly how to organize the system, develop a plan of attack, get into action, and, by God, they expect everybody around and under them to get with the program.

Their motto? That old familiar challenge: "Lead, follow, or get the hell out of my way." Yet CEOs are far more than tough Scrooge-like taskmasters. They are the keepers of the faith, the rock upon which the establishment was built, the guardian angel watching over and protecting us. At the core, they are leaders you respect because of what they stand for.

The CEO is the one personality who will aggressively step forward and defend the established order, whatever it is—fundamental values and principles, our customs, traditions and history, authority figures, rules and regulations, all those sometimes sentimental, sometimes dogmatic things that say, "This is what we stand for; this is the way we do things; this is the American way of life; it's my way and I will lay down my life to defend it." These leaders have the convictions first seen in the signers of the Declaration of Independence.

Moral leaders would call them *men of character*. In *The Seven Habits of Highly Effective People,* Stephen Covey says that character is "the foundation of success—things like integrity, humility, fidelity, temperance, courage, justice, patience, industry, simplicity, modesty, and the Golden Rule . . . basic principles of effective living, and that people only experience true success and enduring happiness as they learn and integrate these principles into their basic character."

Great Leaders Are Quiet, Humble . . . and Tenacious Bulldogs

In his book, *Good to Great: Why Some Companies Make the Leap, and Others Don't,* Jim Collins tells us a great leader is not a high-profile celebrity appearing on CNBC, but "self-effacing, quiet and reserved—these leaders are a paradoxical blend of personal humility and professional will. They are more like Lincoln and Socrates than Patton or Caesar."

Yes, they are determined and bullheaded, but they are always consummate team players, with enormous patience and persistence—and, above all, an absolute conviction that they will eventually win if everybody just sticks to their principles and does what's in front of them.

CEOs love to work. That's what they live for. Work turns them on and makes them feel alive. But more than that, it's the right thing to do. Dad was a hard worker, Grandpa, too, and his father, as well.

They all live by the good old-fashioned American work ethic. It's in their blood, their genetic code, drummed into their heads—a strong sense of duty, obligation, and responsibility to family, to the company, to employees and their families, to church and local community, to partners and shareholders, to buddies, and to the citizens of America.

It's not just the right thing to do, it's the only thing to do—work hard. Do your fair share, be productive, and keep the economy growing. That's the American way. Here are some examples of exceptional leaders who fit the profile and are also as nice as your favorite uncle.

WARREN BUFFETT: GETTING RICH ON
SEE'S CANDIES, COKE, AND INTEGRITY

The second richest man in America, Warren Buffett, once told a congressional committee, "I want employees to ask themselves whether they are willing to have any contemplated act appear on the front page of their local paper the next day. . . . If they follow this test, they will not fear my other message to them: Lose money for my firm and I will be understanding; lose a shred of reputation for the firm, and I will be ruthless."

Buffett is a businessman with integrity and a simple approach to buying companies: "Coke is exactly the kind of company I like. I like products I can understand. I don't know what a transistor is, but I appreciate the contents of a Coke can." Buffett loved See's Candies: "When business sags we spread the rumor that our candy acts as an aphrodisiac. Very effective. The rumor, that is; not the candy." He's brilliant; he has integrity; and he has a sense of humor. The consumate CEO.

JACK BOGLE: CHARACTER COUNTS, PEANUT BUTTER SANDWICHES, TOO

Jack Bogle is the founder of Vanguard Funds, America's largest mutual fund family. In a world of mutual funds run by self-interested individuals and companies, Bogle built Vanguard on a number of novel ideas reflecting the principles that make America great: Vanguard is the only mutual fund company actually owned by its investors. Its core funds are index funds that simply track market averages. And they are all no-load funds with no money paid to commissioned brokers. Plus the expenses are rock bottom, with the savings passed on to investors.

Saint Jack, as Bogle is affectionately known, had such an obsession with controlling costs that he brought a peanut butter sandwich and apple to work each day because he didn't want to pay for them in his own cafeteria. Read Bogle's *Character Counts: The Creation and Building of the Vanguard Group*. You'll see why character does count more than money.

CHARLES SCHWAB: SIMPLE, ETHICAL INVESTING FOR THE LITTLE GUY

Charles Schwab is the founder and chairman of one of America's most respected financial services companies. In the mid-1970s, when Wall

Street's ethics and self-interest were being challenged, Schwab's discount brokerage firm was a rarity: He was focused on helping the little guy. The mission: "Provide the most useful and *ethical* financial services in the world . . . demystifying investing . . . no sales pressure, no high commissions, no hidden fees, and no conflict of interest, [just] unbiased guidance and advice."

A revolutionary idea, and also one that has its roots in the basic ideals driving our founding fathers during the American Revolution. His private life operates the same way. Schwab's charitable foundation helps kids with learning disabilities, in part because he had one. His book, *You're Fifty, Now What,* has a long chapter on charity, treating it more in its true spirit instead of simply as a tax write-off. He encourages people to "look around you, start in your own backyard, the neighborhood you live in, the community you work in."

GREAT LEADERS CONFRONT BRUTAL FACTS—CONVINCED THEY'LL WIN

All CEO personalities share these traits. In *Good to Great,* Collins says that great leaders "channel their egos away from themselves and into the larger goal of building a great company." It's not that these "leaders have no ego or self-interest. Indeed, they are incredibly ambitious—*but their ambition is first and foremost for the institution, not themselves.*"

The path of the CEO often comes in a series of steps leading to the top, not always as rapid and direct as planned by the leader in training. Most CEO types know this instinctively, yet they need a refresher course. You'll find it in *Good to Great,* the one must-read book for every CEO. Why? Because along the way to the top—*and on a regular basis when you're up there*—every leader and every company will encounter great challenges, obstacles, and failures, often seemingly insurmountable. Here's Collins's solution:

> *Confront the Brutal Facts (Yet Never Lose Faith).* We learned that a former prisoner of war had more to teach us about what it takes to find a path to greatness than most books on corporate strategy. Every good-to-great company embraced what we came to call the Stockdale Paradox: You must maintain unwavering faith that you can and will prevail in the end, regardless of the difficulties, *and at the same time* have the discipline to confront the brutal facts of your current reality, whatever they may be.

One of the more brutal facts confronting every CEO personality is the reality of competition, specifically in regard to other aggressive men and women who are trying to move up the corporate ladder, often with questionable ethics.

Challenges like this are to be expected. They will come and they will test CEOs more than once in their careers, forcing them to confront their greatest adversary: not the competition in or out of the company, but their own dark side within and its challenge to their integrity. If you are a CEO, don't compromise. Face the brutal facts with unwavering faith that you will prevail by taking the ethical path.

NO SAVIORS WITH QUICK FIXES: GRIND IT OUT A DAY AT A TIME

Moreover, the CEO personality has incredible patience and persistence, more than enough for a lifetime. These individuals aren't quick-fix executives—the kind chosen by boards of directors, perhaps mistakenly, back in the glory days of the late 1990s, when quarterly earnings were all that mattered, however manipulated. That shortsighted attitude proved to be flawed, as Harvard Business School professor Rakesh Khurana points out in his book, *Searching for a Corporate Savior: The Irrational Quest for Charismatic CEOs.*

The CEO personality approaches life and business quite the opposite way, as we see in Collins's seventh step, "The Flywheel and the Doom Loop: Those who launch revolutions, dramatic change programs, and wrenching restructurings will almost certainly fail to make the leap from good to great."

The reason is very simple, good-to-great transformations never take place in one sudden leap: "There is no single defining action, no grand program, no one killer innovation, no solitary lucky break, no miracle movement. Rather the process resembled relentlessly pushing a giant flywheel in one direction, turn upon turn, building momentum until a point of breakthrough, and beyond." Just patience, perseverance, perspiration, and dogged stick-to-itiveness—day after day, year after year. That's the way of the CEO.

Careers: Leadership Skills, Integrity, and a Sense of Duty

This new CEO personality is in high demand, and not just in the executive suites and boardrooms of Corporate America. There are a lot of career opportunities open these people—for people with all kinds of talents in virtually every segment of the job market.

Men and women with these skills *plus* a strong sense of duty and uncompromising integrity can look forward to positions of leadership in many areas. In fact, the paths to the top are many and varied when it comes to the CEO personality type. Here are a few springboards:

- *Business:* Managers, team leaders, supervisors, executives
- *Finance and insurance:* Brokers, loan officers, managers
- *Law:* Paralegals, research assistants, attorneys
- *Education:* Teachers, principals, professors, administrators
- *Military and law enforcement:* Strategists, detectives, officers
- *Technology:* Programmers, analysts, engineers
- *Government and politics:* Civil service, elected, appointed
- *Advertising:* Account executives
- *Real estate and construction:* Brokers, managers, contractors
- *Health care:* Physicians, researchers, administrators
- *Entrepreneur:* Conservative leaders in their own business

In the CEO arena, it is not so much the particular sector of the economy or the particular skills, but rather the character traits that count. CEO types may be Marine officers, trial lawyers, college professors, surgeons, or small business owners. Most areas of endeavor have need for the traits found in these rather unique personalities.

Millionaire's Code for CEOs
Extravert, Sensor, Thinker, Judger (ESTJ)

Like all Extraverts, the CEO is a people person. CEOs draw their energy from the outside world. They love the exchange with staff at all levels, and they are as likely to be talking with the new kid in the mail room as members of the board of directors. They want to hear what you have to say, and they want to tell you what's on their mind. They are thinking out loud, working things out with associates, assistants, consultants, customers, family, investors, voters, patients, students, store clerks, you name it, CEO types are always mixing it up with others.

The CEO is unique as an *Extravert,* too. CEOs are very much team players when it comes to work, be it a business, the army, government, school, or some other establishment. They see themselves as "first among equals," similar to the kind of relationship between a chief justice and the other justices on the Supreme Court.

It's extremely important to understand this way of thinking, because it runs *counter to the conventional wisdom of management theory.* In his "First Who . . . Then What" step, Collins says that successful leaders do not start with a grand design: "We expected that good-to-great leaders would begin by setting a vision and strategy. We found instead that they *first* got the right people on the bus, the wrong people off the bus, and the right people in the right seats—*then* they figured out where to drive it."

In short, the CEO's first job is getting the right team in place, people who will work well together, then jointly figure out how to take the hill, so to speak. Once the CEO has the right team in place, there develops a sense of faith in the team as a whole, a confidence that together they can handle any situation, even the worst-case scenario—*the "brutal facts"*—and come out winners. This attitude translates into leadership for organizations in virtually any arena: business, education, law, military, government, foreign affairs.

Sensor: For the Hedgehog, Success Comes One Day at a Time

Interestingly, you often see the character of CEOs in the simplicity, the niche focus, and the little things in their careers more than any grand gestures and accomplishments. Leadership guru Jim Collins calls these leaders, "hedgehogs," after that strange little crossbreed between a porcupine and an armadillo that just minds its own business "waddles along, going about his simple day, searching for lunch and taking care of his home." When its enemies regularly attack, it just rolls up in a ball until they give up and leave, then the hedgehog goes back to its simple life, focusing on the task right in front of it.

How does the fable translate into the real world? Hedgehogs are the ones who know how to take a "complex world and simplify it." They are like Einstein, "they understand that the essence of profound insight is simplicity. What could be simpler than $e = mc^2$?" Collins continues the analogy:

> The key is to understand what your organization *can* be the best in the world at, and equally important, what it *cannot* be the best at—not what it "wants" to be best at. The Hedgehog Concept is not a goal, strategy, or intention; it is an *understanding*.

Similarly, Vanguard founder Jack Bogle wrote about his own hedgehog strategy in *Character Counts:*

> We are the lone hedgehog who knows *one great thing:* that financial success is based on long-term investing in highly diversified portfolios, grounded in investment fundamentals and operated at low cost. For the wise investor who stays the course, the hedgehop strategy is the winning strategy. For it works. It works."

This hedgehog character trait parallels the second element of the CEO four-part personality code: CEOs are *Sensors,* realists, the type of people who are more comfortable working with hard evidence about the real world, evidence that can be verified, today. No guesswork. They need to be able to use their eyes, ears, smell, taste buds, and touch, whatever they're dealing with, today, this minute. They are very much into the here and now.

NO GUESSWORK, JUST TOTAL RELIANCE ON HARD EVIDENCE

Unlike their opposite types, the Intuitives, visionaries who love speculating with grandiose mission statements and strategic plans, Sensors have their feet firmly anchored on earth. Sensors work with hard evidence, detailed, tangible data, and specific answers to specific questions: sales reports, satellite photos, blood tests, legal documents, financial statements, economic data, forensic data, credit reports, stock quotes, end-of-day production progress reports, and so on.

Abstract theories don't impress the CEO personality as much as some hard numbers from reliable authorities—the Federal Reserve Board, the *New England Journal of Medicine,* the carpenter actually working at the construction site, the forward air controller with an enemy tank in the crosshairs—hard evidence you can use right now, this minute.

Remember, this second element of the genetic code tells us how the personalities collect information about their world. CEOs are not speculative visionaries who walk into a situation with preconceived plans, grand strategies, and a quick-fix solutions. CEOs are just humble, reserved, keep-it-simple, dedicated, confident, aggressive, tenacious bull-dogs who pragmatically go about doing whatever needs to be done. And they never, never quit, no matter what the odds. They find a way to achieve their goals, somehow.

Thinking: Objective Decision Criteria . . . with a Conscience

One of the chief characteristics of CEOs is the way they make decisions, the third element of their genetic code. They are *Thinkers,* and invariably they will make final decisions based on objective criteria—what's best for the institution, the company, the university, the judicial system, the hospital, or whatever establishment is under their responsibility, using a standard other than their personal belief system, which is the subjective criteria preferred by their opposite, Feeling types.

The standard used by *Thinkers* may be the customs and rules of their industry, a code of ethics, tax regulations, state statutes, the U.S. Constitution, the Geneva Convention, the Commandments, universal law, and equally likely, their own conscience, that tough inner taskmaster, the still small voice within. Whatever it is, it's an *objective* standard that the CEO can point to as an authority when finally making a decision.

The response of the good-to-great companies identified by Collins versus the not-so-great companies is an excellent way to distinguish between the Thinking and the Feeling types. For example, one of Collins's 11 good-to-great companies was Walgreens drugstores (a Thinker).

When drugstore.com (a Feeler) went public in 1998, Walgreens lost 40 percent of its market value, around $15 billion. Wall Street analysts said the company was too stodgy and wasn't adapting to the new-economy technology fast enough. Stock market mania had quickly pushed drugstore.com's value to 398 times revenues, billions, while Walgreens was languishing at an embarrassing 1.4 times revenues.

NO CHICKEN LITTLES: GO SLOWLY, PLAN, MAKE IT WORK, THEN ACT

A Walgreens executive told *Forbes,* "We're a crawl, walk, run company," that, according to Collins, was using a "deliberate, methodical approach to the Internet. Instead of reacting like Chicken Little . . . they decided to pause and reflect. They decided to use their brains. They decided to think! Slow at first."

Instead of jumping impulsively onto the Internet—*like most feeling-type companies were doing, chasing get-rich-quick dreams as emotions ran wild*—the executive team at Walgreens stopped, put on their collective thinking caps, and asked how the new Internet technology would enhance things they were already doing—their core concept of customer convenience, inventory control, the distribution system, and other elements of their business. The strategy paid off.

In other words, they were the perfect Guardians, with their first duty being to enhance the existing establishment. They were purposely "late to the ball," but when they did come on stream later, the new technology worked for them.

In the final analysis, the CEO personality is invariably a *Thinker* rather than a Feeling type. Objectivity controls decisions. Yes, CEOs do have feelings, but they just don't let their immediate feelings control how they'll react to short-term business challenges, new technologies, competition, financial problems, the latest fads, or whatever. They'll pause and use their brains first.

Besides, you should remember that CEOs and their teams operate with a rock-hard positive conviction that no matter what, they can and will eventually solve any problem and win the game. All they have to is stick to their game plan, keep their eye on the ball, trust their principles, and do what's in front of them, right now, in a disciplined, rational way—think, think, think!

Judging: More Discipline than a Good Ol' Plow Horse

CEO personalities are *Judgers,* the fourth element of their genetic code. This doesn't mean CEOs are judgmental in the conventional sense of the term. Rather, Judgers want stability in their lives, personal, family, social—and most of all, in their work. It's a personality trait. It's in their blood. They need to feel a sense of control over their world, from morning to night, day after day, year in and year out. They want it and they will do whatever it takes to get it.

CEOs tend to be the stabilizing center of their organizations—like a rock. They insist on planning ahead methodically, working on the facts, looking at the whole picture, moving at a reasonable pace, getting everybody on the same page, or rather, on the same bus, to use Collins's analogy in *Good to Great.*

Equally important, one of the CEO's key responsibilities is creating a culture of discipline. That is not the same as acting as a top-dog disciplinarian, because that works only on a short-term basis, never for the long term. Rather, the CEO wants to create a culture of discipline with everybody on the team.

Discipline is probably the single best term to describe what it means to be a Judger, at least for the CEO personality, in a very special way. No question but that the CEO is an incredibly self-disciplined human being.

As Collins would say, they have "a workmanlike diligence—more plow horse than show horse," willing to make the tough decisions and obsessed about results. CEOs are the kind of people who will "attribute success to factors other than themselves. . . . When things go poorly, however, they look in the mirror and blame themselves, taking full responsibility."

CULTURE OF DISCIPLINE: LEADER, TEAM, COMMITMENT, THEN ACTION

The culture of discipline begins at home for a disciplined leader. From there, it ripples out, embracing everybody in the organization. As Collins says, leaders surround themselves with a team of "people who display extreme diligence and stunning intensity," disciplined individuals, all on the same bus, all heading in the same direction:

> They hired self-disciplined people who didn't need to be managed, and then managed the system, not the people . . . a culture of discipline is not just about action. It is about getting disciplined *people* who engage in disciplined *thought* and who *then* take disciplined action.

We see that CEOs are leaders who surround themselves with teams of disciplined people, committed to doing the right thing, living by the rules, acting methodically and responsibly–then they can accomplish anything, one day at a time.

Disciplined, responsible, stable, focused, organized, team player: Add up all the unique characteristics of the CEO and you have a person of character, someone who has a strong sense of morals and integrity. CEOs are guided by a set of values and principles that transcend the law–call it a conscience–they know their conduct is being judged by a higher authority, with more rigorous standards than the rules and laws of the real world they work in.

As a result, the conduct of CEOs reflects the Golden Rule, do unto others as you would have them do unto you, an awareness that they are here to serve–their family, their community, their church and friends, employees, associates, and investors, their country, everybody.

For the CEO, being a good citizen isn't just good business, it's the right thing to do. And doing the right thing makes CEOs feel good about themselves, because then they know they are living up to the high standards dictated by their own conscience. Winston Churchill's words seem natural to CEOs: "We make a living by what we get, we make a life by what we give."

Moneymaker: Voted "Most Likely to Become a Millionaire"

If there were a vote on "most likely to succeed and retire as a millionaire," it would probably be a CEO personality. These individuals not only have what it takes to make money using their unique leadership skills, their discipline, attitude, and ethics in the workplace, they also have what it takes to leverage the money they make into a solid retirement portfolio.

Making money comes natural to all four Guardians, but most especially to the CEO personality. They seem to be born with all the tools and common sense they need when it comes to personal budgeting, regular savings, and investing, using all the same skills that make them successful in their careers. They are money machines, born with integrity.

* * * * * * * *

The human beings we serve—real, honest-to-God,
down-to-earth human beings—have been the
epicenter of every business decision we have made.
Vanguard does not represent a throng of 14 million investors;
Vanguard represents 14 million souls, all of whom with *their*
own hopes and fears, *their own* financial objectives,
and *their own* trust in us.
And we have never let them down.

Jack Bogle,
Character Counts

PEACEMAKERS (ESFJ)

GEORGE SOROS, WILLIAM URY, ANDREW CARNEGIE

> Whatever you do,
> you need courage.
> Whatever course you decide upon,
> there is always someone to tell you
> that you are wrong.
> There are always difficulties arising
> that tempt you to
> believe your critics are right.
> To map out a course of action and
> follow it to an end
> requires some of the same
> courage that a soldier needs.
> Peace has its victories,
> but it takes brave men
> and women to win them.
>
> Ralph Waldo Emerson

In a world dominated by aggressive competitors engaged in endless struggles, where the game is win or lose at all costs in business and in government, *Peacemakers* come into the game with a special mission: they are ambassadors of goodwill, seekers of harmony and cooperation, diplomats, the ones most likely to create a world where everyone is a winner. And they're doing whatever they can to make it happen.

The Peacemakers may be wearing any one of a number of different hats, although the role is always the same: They may be a sales rep helping a customer, a mediator working on settling a law suit, a foreign service officer hammering out a trade agreement, a crisis negotiator in a hostage situation, a labor dispute arbitrator, perhaps even a public relations consultant, little league coach, or nutritionist, a minister, wedding planner, or marriage counselor, an office manager, receptionist, or the head of an organization.

Whatever the role, the Peacemaker sees the world quite differently, not as an arena between combatants, but as an opportunity to build new relationships where people can live in peace. The Peacemaker comes not as a champion arguing for the agenda of one side or the other, but rather as a win-win advocate, with fierce loyalty and allegiance to the established order and its authorities.

Peacemakers do not come to situations to take control of everyone and dictate the solution. Nor do they come to achieve their own personal goals. They come to serve all parties in the cause of peace, bringing a sense of order in the world shared by all the parties. Peacemakers can fulfill their personal life's mission working in many jobs, from retail sales to international treaty negotiations.

The Ultimate Guardian: Bringing Peace to the World

In this sense, the Peacemaker is the ultimate Guardian, the ultimate defender of the established order, the ultimate protector of our way of life, the ultimate keeper of the peace in a troubled world.

Indeed, when they are around you can feel the energy shift as they set about their work. People sense that Peacemakers care about them—*personally.* You somehow know they are warm, sensitive, gentle souls who will listen with an open mind and respect the interests and needs of the people, their goals and grievances, their feelings and values, even their differences.

In fact, it doesn't matter how big or small their concerns seem to others, people know that Peacemakers genuinely care and will work hard to help everyone achieve what they are looking for—even when the differences seem insurmountable. You'll find this unique personality filling many different roles in the world, all with one common trait—helping people find diplomatic solutions:

- *Mediators and negotiators.* Conflict resolution is too stressful for most people who focus on what seem like irreconcilable positions taken by opposing sides. Mediators and negotiators "separate the people from the problem," as Roger Fisher and William Ury tell us in *Getting to Yes.* They get people to "invent options for mutual gain." It takes a special personality to win the trust of both sides in a conflict and get them working jointly on problem solving. That's a Peacemaker for you.

- *Diplomatic service.* Foreign service diplomats such as secretaries of state and U.N. ambassadors walk a fine line between taking strong positions for their country and negotiating agreements with people and countries holding substantially different values. It takes a uniquely sensitive person to connect with people, bridge the gap, and win their confidence enough to work out major differences.

- *Business sales reps.* The most successful salespeople aren't selling anything: They're helping buyers solve problems and make buying decisions, acting more as management consultants than as stereotypical fast-talking hustlers. They build one-to-one personal relationships with their customers, providing information, helping them solve *their* problems, helping them find the right solution that works for *them.*

- *Health care providers.* There is a new breed of doctor in the world. The day of the doctor as an all-knowing parent are gone. Even physicians like Deepak Chopra, Dean Ornish, Larry Dossey, and Andrew Weil are telling us we're responsible for our own physical and mental well-being. The patient must take charge, in partnership with traditional doctors and healers using alternative treatments. Today, prevention and wellness are as important as healing.

- *Youth sports coaching.* All those volunteer dads and other coaches are teaching the next generation some of life's most valuable lessons: Good sportsmanship, teamwork, confidence, training, competition, being the best you can be, how to win and lose with dignity. In *Coaching Kids for Dummies,* Rick Wolff's top two great coaching tips are to "be sensitive to every child's needs" and to "get the kids to believe in themselves." In fact, you can find Peacemakers doing all kinds of volunteer work, not just youth sports, and very often turning this avocation into a full-time vocation.

- *"Warm, fuzzy" executives.* That's how *SmartMoney* magazine described Aaron Feuerstein, the 70-year-old owner and CEO of New England's largest textile mill and manufacturer of Polartec. When fire destroyed its factories, rather than shut down permanently, the "mensch of Malden Mills" not only decided to rebuild, he continued paying all 3,000 employees for the three months it took to do so, because it was "the right thing to do."

- *Receptionists and hostesses.* There is no hierarchy in the world of diplomacy, where some, such as international diplomats (the

U.N. secretary-general, or the Dalai Lama) are more important than others. Emerson once wrote that success is "to know even one has breathed easier because you have lived." True Peacemakers live to make the world breath in peace, one person at a time, regardless of the job or position, regardless of whether they receive any press coverage for their work. It's in their blood.

Beneath the various roles that Peacemakers play in the outside world is an inner personal integrity. In *Living a Life That Matters,* Harold Kushner focuses on this trait that lights the character of Peacemakers and draws us to them.

Integrity means being whole, unbroken, undivided. . . . Like the karate expert who can break a board with his bare hand by focusing all his strength in one spot, the person of integrity, the person whose soul is not fragmented, can do great things by concentrating all his energies on a single goal. For the person of integrity, life may not be easy but it is simple: Figure out what is right and do it. All other considerations come in second."

There are many more examples of Peacemakers. They go about bringing harmony and goodwill to a troubled world, working from a wide variety of positions.

The Diplomat's Mind at Work in a Negotiation

The Peacemaker is very much a negotiator. In perhaps one of the best books on the subject of conflict resolution and negotiations, *Getting Past No,* William Ury of the Program for Negotiation at Harvard Law School spells out the five key steps that lead to successful negotiation.

The Peacemaker often begins as a negotiator identified more with one side than as a totally neutral third-party mediator. This situation is quite realistic since more often than not, the negotiator is, in fact, identified more with one side than the other—for example, our secretary of state negotiating a U.N. resolution that must satisfy a group made up of 190 nations.

Most people with a Peacemaker's genetic code will instinctively understand Ury's following five steps to successful negotiation as a natural part of their thinking process in many life situations, from working with angry siblings to heads of state:

1. *When attacked, don't react.* Remember, you can't control what other people do. You can, however, control your own emotions and behavior. What if your offer is rejected or you're attacked. "Go to the balcony" says Ury, "buy yourself time to think." Instead of counterattacking or giving in, instead of "getting mad or getting even, focus on getting what you want."

2. *Step to the other side.* While you're getting your own emotions under control, remember, your opponents expect you to resist, react, or counterattack. Surprise them. Do the opposite. "Listen to them, acknowledge their points, and agree with them wherever you can." Avoid arguing, which is the normal reaction.

3. *Change the game.* Never reject their offers, even when they take a hard-line position. They'll just dig in further. Reframe all challenges until the game changes from one of positional bargaining to joint problem solving and you have a win-win negotiation.

4. *Build a golden bridge.* Ury says you're now ready to negotiate. In other words, until you reach this point, everyone is still jockeying for position. Again, if they continue stalling, don't push or resist. Do the opposite: Entice them. Take the role of a mediator. "Make it easy for them to say yes." Involve them, include their ideas, answer their personal needs. "Help them save face and make the outcome appear as a victory for them."

5. *Use power to educate.* Even at this point they may resist, believing they can win without compromising their position. Now "you need to make it hard for them to say no." Threats and force will backfire. "Educate them about the costs of not agreeing . . . reassuring them that your goal is mutual satisfaction, not victory."

Of course, many Peacemakers gravitate into careers that naturally minimize or even avoid conflict. They want peace *in their own lives,* choosing jobs where the possibility for conflict, and the opportunities for cooperation, are built in, such as corporate sales rep, motivational trainer, or receptionist. Others, for example, a hostage negotiator or foreign service officer, actually seek out opportunities to use their special skills as a diplomat.

Conflicts are a part of life. Eventually, everyone must face them, and the real test is how you handle them. William Ury's bottom line is simple—convert adversaries into partners. "It takes two to tangle, but only one to begin to untangle a knotty situation," says Ury. "Your greatest power is the power to change the game—from face-to-face confrontation to side-by-side joint problem-solving." The Peacemaker understands this and will be the first to act and take on the role of the untangler!

Millionaire's Code for Peacemakers
Extravert, Sensor, Feeling, Judger (ESFJ)

The Peacemaker is a consummate *Extravert*. One thing you immediately notice about Peacemakers is their presence. They have a graciousness about them that draws people to them, a mystique, an aura. You feel they're on your side. They have a unique ability to make you feel that you are the only one in the crowd they truly care about. Their eyes seem to penetrate directly into your soul, communicating with you at a deep level. This bond makes them incredibly effective statesmen, diplomats, negotiators, and mediators.

Peacemakers have mesmerizing voices. They can charm anyone, from a crying baby to a hostile dictator—they have the gift of the orator and the schmoozer. They are masters of the art of conversation, anytime, any-where, and all the time: fireside chats or working a room . . . one-minute managing . . . muffled whispers in a cell phone or at a TelePromptTer deliv-ering a speech in an arena . . . analyzing a staff research study or rumors in the press . . . trading smiles with a great-grandmother or inspiring a teenage honor student . . . one-on-one meetings with customers and clients, large and small . . . photo ops with foreign dignitaries . . . late-night sessions with an energetic assistant or joking with the office cleaning lady . . . always talking, telling stories, networking, questioning, compli-menting, debating, and arguing. They love to talk because they love peo-ple. People energize them and make them feel alive.

THE POWER TO PREVENT WAR AND SAVE THE WORLD

Yes, even arguing is handled artfully by Peacemakers. By nature they are incredibly positive people. They believe in the power of positive thinking and see arguments as opportunities that open the door to agreement, because they are master negotiators. Gerry Spence is one of America's most successful attorneys; he's never lost a criminal case. You regularly see his gentle, calm, reassuring style on NBC or *Larry King*. In *How to Argue and Win Every Time,* Spence offers this perspective on the critical importance of arguing:

> Why argue? Why experience the pain? Why take the risk of los-ing? . . . In important ways argument is a gift—a gift of ourselves to the *Other*. Without the gift of ourselves we can never succeed. . . . The magic comes when, by argument, we unearth a bit of ourselves,

and, thereby, we likely discover something about all others who inhabit the universe. . . .

The art of argument is the art of living. If we are successful in our arguments we will bloom and grow. We can accomplish massive good and experience endless joy. We can prevent war and save the earth. Our success in life, our cultural immortality depends on our ability to argue.

Peacemakers like this are constantly looking for opportunities to bring peace and harmony into a contentious world. They know how easy it is to communicate with people we like and avoid dealing with people we dislike.

What sets Peacemakers apart is that they not only understand the consequences of avoiding dialogue, with even our most contentious adversaries, they understand the advantages of keeping the lines of communication open *and welcome the opportunity to act as a bridge to peace.* They are living examples of what Hill and Stone meant in their best-seller, *Success Through a Positive Mental Attitude,* and they will take every opportunity to express their thoughts and ideas to anyone—a hopeful message of peace in a troubled world.

Sensor: Masters at Reading People

One of the greatest assets of Peacemakers is their keen sense of observation, a trait common to Sensors, although particularly heightened in the Peacemaker. All *Sensors* focus on the immediate, the facts, the hard evidence in front of them that they can see, touch, feel, smell, and taste. Moreover, they have excellent memories and go out of their way to record details they observe, possibly with a lot of note taking or by memory.

Peacemakers are also especially gifted in multitasking, that is, using all their senses at one time, like a highly sensitive radar system tapping into different information sources. For example, while they're doing what they love most, talking, their other sensory channels are scanning people for hints and clues that confirm or contradict the verbal reality.

In fact, the Peacemaker has a near-psychic ability to read people, both this multitasking sensory perception and an extrasensory ability that penetrates beneath the public persona of people like a mental X ray. All people do this to some extent, but the Peacemaker's ability is extraordinary.

Psychologists and language specialists tell us that more than two-thirds of all communication is *nonverbal*—reading body language, eye movements, voice modulation. The Peacemaker is a master at going beyond the spoken word and picking up the contradictions and hidden meanings in what is being said.

This talent, which comes rather natural to Peacemakers, is especially valuable in negotiations of all kinds, because more often than not the people on the other side are, in fact, concealing something—consciously or unconsciously, intentionally or accidentally—information that could be valuable for both sides, whether it's an issue in a dispute that is central to a large organization or some personal information about the individual actual handling the negotiation.

For example, a corporate sales rep, maître d', real estate agent, or government trade negotiator might just improve their edge by remembering personal information about their clientele—perhaps children's names and birthdates, favorite sports teams, flowers—as well as the rather impersonal data tools, equipment, supplier referrals, sales discounts.

Feeling: Transforming Emotions into Peaceful Solutions

This third element of the Peacemakers' genetic code refers to the way they make decisions. Their opposite type, the Thinker, relies on objective standards and criteria—rules and regulations, laws and commandments, moral edicts and universal principles, something impersonal and impartial. On the other hand, *Feeling* personalities rely heavily on subjective standards and criteria when they make their decisions.

Of course this doesn't mean Peacemakers ignore the law. Quite the opposite. Like all Guardians they are firmly committed to maintaining the established order, in peace and free of conflict. Indeed, they need to know they are have a part in creating a stable society. They can certainly be as moralistic and dogmatic about their convictions and value systems as Thinkers. Nor are they any less logical or rational.

The difference is that the primary consideration for Peacemakers is doing what's right for the people, not some abstract morality, but what's right and good for the people in their community. That may mean a particular person or group of people whose rights are being affected, but it boils down to a subjective choice relative to the merits of the individual case rather than an impartial decision based on impersonal rules and external standards.

THE CHARACTER OF THE PEACEMAKER: LEADER, TEACHER, AND COACH

Peacemakers (ESFJ) have some key personality traits in common with their cousins, Teachers (ENFJ). Each of them has a high emotional quotient

(E-Q), which Daniel Goleman reviews in his book *Emotional Intelligence,* abilities essential to effective leadership. Goleman identifies five factors that make up the emotional quotient and also reflect the personality of the Peacemaker:

1. *Self-awareness* (of your feelings, strengths, and weaknesses)
2. *Self-control* (manages own feelings of anxiety, fears, and anger)
3. *Self-motivation* (converts emotions into positive goals)
4. *Empathy* (sensitive to others' feelings and points of view)
5. *Diplomacy* (team builder, teacher, inspiring, integrity, character)

Great Peacemakers are born with a naturally high E-Q, with all five of these factors as part of their Feeling function, with diplomacy the bottom line.

For example, self-awareness, self-control, self-motivation, and empathy are obviously important for inner personal growth. Ultimately, however, the role of the Peacemaker is as an Extravert, helping people—*working to resolve conflicts, inspiring teamwork, acting as a coach and teacher, and encouraging everybody to live a principled life*—and along the way showing, *by example,* what it means to have good character and integrity, the essential ingredients of a Peacemaker.

Judger: Negotiating Peace in a Contentious World

In the world of sales there's a big difference between the *door opener* (who generates leads, screens prospects, and maintains long-term relationships with customers) and the *deal closer* (the one who can get the customer to make the final decision). The Peacemaker has both qualities.

We know that Peacemakers have the soft touch, the glad hand, the smooth talk, the charm. They also have a powerful presence, they mean business, they want results. Even when they're gentle, they are forceful. All four Guardians have a combination of the Sensor and Judger traits. It's part of their genetic code.

This is an unusually powerful combination for Peacemakers. They are effective door openers *and also effective closers*—of the sale, the deal, the project, the assignment, the commission, the agreement, the treaty—of whatever goal they are responsible for negotiating.

Well before the first handshake and introduction, the Peacemaker has the endgame specifically planned in their mind. They know exactly what they want, whether it's a sale, a treaty, or some other goal. Remember, a *Judger* wants a well-structured lifestyle, planned well in advance, with no surprises, complete with contingency plans to handle the unpredictable and expected.

Judgers are unlikely to show it, but they get quite uncomfortable when they can't control events using their diplomatic skills. If things do start spinning out of control, they then redouble their efforts and work even harder to bring things back under control.

They need stability, safety, and security in their own personal lives, and they often step forward and take on the responsibility of making the world a safe, secure, stable, and peaceful place to live in.

Remember, Peacemakers, like all Guardians, are committed to maintaining the existing order and preserving the traditional way of life. As a result, they are likely to be slow in accepting change or trying new, untested technologies, preferring to stick with the good old-fashioned tried-and-true solutions that worked in the past.

Careers: Many Great Opportunities to Find Peaceful Solutions

Here's a summary of the various kinds of roles and positions that Peacemakers are likely to find personally gratifying, careers that offer substantial opportunities to work with a lot of people on a daily basis, to use their unusually creative skills as successful negotiators, and at the same time to add to the level of peace and harmony in a troubled world:

- *Business:* Trainers, salespeople, human resources, project leaders
- *Finance:* Bankers, real estate agents, office managers, financial planners
- *Personal services:* Home decorators, hostesses, caterers, PR consultants
- *Social services:* Social workers, spiritual counselors, family therapists
- *Health care providers:* Nurses, medical assistants, family doctors
- *Charities:* Directors, organizers, contributors, fund-raisers, volunteers
- *Education:* Career advisers, day-care providers, teachers, coaches

The particular career or position or job title worn by the Peacemaker is not the important factor here. The unique character of Peacemakers will come through in virtually any role they play in achieving harmony.

What really counts is what's in the heart and soul of Peacemakers, in their character. For each of these roles offers them an opportunity to carry a positive message of goodwill and peace, to their family, community, and society, to their business, government, and culture—and that applies as much to a hostage negotiator in action or a wartime general negotiating a truce as it does to the everyday business relationships of a corporate sales rep, caterer, nurse, office receptionist, or a professional financial adviser working with a client on a total lifestyle plan.

DUAL PERSONALITIES: THE BILLIONAIRE AS A DIPLOMAT

Being a Peacemaker is more a state of mind than a name tag, as Peacemakers often gain power in one way, and then an alternative personality emerges, such as *philanthropist*. Andrew Carnegie is one of the best examples of this dual personality. He immigrated to America from Scotland with very little and became the richest man in the world, building the U.S. Steel empire. Then he gave away his billions, most notably for the creation of a national public library system at a time when few Americans were literate.

Another example of a diplomat-billionaire is George Soros, a wealthy financier whom one biographer called a "messianic billionaire" because he was the "only private citizen with a foreign policy." Soros left Hungary after surviving the Nazi occupation. He studied at the London School of Economics and later immigrated to America, where he built his $12 billion Quantum Fund in the international currency business.

Today, the Soros network of philanthropic organizations is active in more than 50 countries, giving away hundreds of millions annually. The stated mission of his Open Society Institute is certainly the voice of a Peacemaker at its best: "Working to strengthen public discourse in areas where one view of an issue dominates all others, precluding alternative approaches."

Making Money: The High Price of Peace on Earth

Carnegie and Soros may be unusual given the size of the fortunes they accumulated. Yet they have much in common with Peacemakers at all economic levels. At a core level, most people are peacemakers at heart. They are willing to share what they have materially through donations, contributions, and volunteering. As Mother Teresa once said, "It's not how much we give, but how much love we put in the *doing*."

The world has a great need for Peacemakers, to bring calm into a troubled world. Fortunately, people are inexorably drawn to Peacemakers. They have a magnetic quality about them, a special warmth, a sense of compassion; they are kind, gentle souls.

They also have enormous energy, passion, and dedication to their work, which makes them incredibly effective and powerful in any job and organization that fits their personality—whether in business and finance, in government affairs, in charitable, educational, and health care fields, in personal services of all kinds, they are always working to promote peace and harmony among people.

As a result, Peacemakers are one of those rare and talented beings who are likely to make more than enough money working in the material world—for themselves, their families, and their nonprofit efforts for peace. If things are tight or there's a shortfall, it won't matter, they'll still pitch in for the cause of peace because that's why they came here this lifetime.

THE UNIVERSE ALWAYS TAKES CARE OF THE PEACEMAKER

Like their cousins the Champions (ENFP), Peacemakers have faith that the universe will provide for them somehow. And the fact is, the universe always does take care of Peacemakers . . . through comfortable incomes . . . wealth creation (which they're likely to give away) . . . and enormous personal satisfaction knowing their mission was accomplished, peace achieved.

In the final analysis, Peacemakers, like all Guardians, have such a healthy respect for money and a need for safety, security, and stability in their own lives that they can also be counted to protect their own establishment, the family, with a regular savings and investment plans for their retirement years.

* * * * * * * *

We are going to have to find ways of organizing ourselves cooperatively,
sanely, scientifically, harmonically and in regenerative spontaneity with
the rest of humanity
around the earth. . . .
We are not going to be able to operate our spaceship earth successfully
nor for much longer unless we see it
as a whole spaceship and our fate as common.
It has to be
everybody or nobody.

Buckminster Fuller

31

RESULTS-ORIENTED EXPERTS (ISTJ)

PETER DRUCKER, JAMES LOEHR, CHUCK NORRIS

> You are the
> most important living person.
> Stop and think about yourself:
> In all the history of the world,
> there has never been anyone
> exactly like you,
> and in all the infinity
> of time to come,
> there will never be another. . . .
> You can direct your thoughts,
> control your emotions and
> ordain your destiny with PMA. . . .
> Think with a
> positive mental attitude.
>
> Napoleon Hill and
> Clement Stone,
> *Success Through a*
> *Positive Mental Attitude*

All four of the Guardians of the Establishment are masters of the bottom line, regardless of the type of organization or institution they serve. The *Results-Oriented Expert* is the one that is most focused on the establishment, a living machine guided by pragmatic realism.

Experts have several identifiable character traits. They are extremely disciplined, with a strong sense of personal integrity. Their work ethic is one of the most intense. They have great pride of accomplishment in their particular area of expertise, whatever that may be—*business management, medicine, finance, real estate, school administration, law, military.*

Moreover, they are fierce competitors, wanting recognition and respect from their peers. Similarly, they have great respect for authority and a strong sense of duty to maintain the established way of life, whether it's related to family heritage, church, community, country, or the American way of life.

The Expert's commitment is reflected, for example, in the guiding principles, traditions, and creeds of the West Point Military Academy ("Duty, Honor, Country"), Los Angeles Police Department ("To Protect and to Serve") or the physicians' Hippocratic oath.

Their fierce sense of loyalty to the existing order is reflected everywhere in their personal and social lives as well as at work. Look for them hosting church events, being active in community events, PTA, local sports, volunteering, and holding fast to the principles and traditions that make America great.

Laser-Focused Formula Targeting Bottom-Line Results

Discipline, integrity, diligence, pride, respect, duty, service, excellence. Put all of these powerful character traits together and you have a supercharged formula creating a personality type that is laser-focused on the bottom line, on solving problems, on getting results.

Focus comes naturally to Experts, born in their genetic code. They think logically and automatically about mission statements, project goals, strategic plans, team assignments, tasks, performance standards, schedules, deadlines, and results. Whether they are management Experts, professional Experts, or technical Experts, Experts look at their establishment, business, institution, or organization as a productive machine designed to achieve results—*measurable results.*

THEORIES AND PLANS ARE NICE, BUT ONLY THE FINAL SCORE COUNTS

Experts may be successful specialists in any one of many different disciplines, but the one characteristic that best defines Experts is their single-minded focus on the bottom line: Everything they do focuses on the results, tangible, concrete, specific results.

Organizational theories are interesting, and all those fancy goals, mission statements, and strategic plans may look great on paper, but when the chips are down, the theories and paper are of little value to the

Expert. They mean nothing unless you get results—*positive results*—in one form or another for the establishment. Check these examples of the kind of results measured in a number of sectors of the economy:

- *Business:* Production output, labor costs, sales, net income, profits
- *Finance:* Assets under management, fees, public offerings, returns
- *Military:* Ordnance delivered, direct hits, damage reports, casualties
- *Law:* New clients, billable hours, judgments, convictions
- *Education:* Student-teacher ratios, state test scores, SAT results
- *Technology:* Lines of code, killer apps, new sales, market share
- *Medical:* Patient load, hospitalizations, procedures, transplants

The fact is, the Expert is measuring the results—*keeping score*—and it seems, at times, that everyone else is, too: competitors, enemies, supervisors, boards of directors, generals, program directors, rating agencies, journalists, and other members of the establishment.

The score is all-important to Experts. They live and breath results. They don't like losing the battle, the patient, the case, the sale, the test, the contract, the deal, the promotion. And they know the only way to win is to be in top shape, ready to go on a moment's notice, to work hard all the time, using all their skills, training, and experiences, and, when the time comes, to fight hard in order to score a win in a highly competitive world.

Experts not only play a win-lose game every day, they *hate to lose*. They need to excel, to score, to come out a winner. They hate to lose. They are similar to their cousins, the Master Craftsman (ISTP) because both take enormous pride in their expertise. All experts come into the game with some unique skills, talents, and training—but to prove how good they are they must have a *winning record*, much like Lombardi's win-loss coaching record and Michael Jordan's NBA championships and MVP awards.

MONEY IS THE BIGGEST SCOREKEEPER, BUT NOT THE ONLY ONE

For many Experts, the biggest scorecard is the money they make: a large jury verdict, a big commission on an investment or real estate deal, or perhaps regular income from working a 70-hour week to handle a big load of clients or patients—for example, in the professions of medicine, law, tax accounting, real estate, or securities investing.

In fact, for many Experts, especially those in the business and financial worlds, money is the only way they can keep score. It's the main benchmark proving they really are experts in their field; it's a primary source of personal satisfaction at the end of the day.

Yes, there is a sense of personal pride in a job well done, which becomes easier to focus on after Experts have established a reputation and their income is comfortably steady. But fortunately or unfortunately, in the commercial and financial worlds, money *is* the bottom-line benchmark, the measuring stick, the score.

For other Experts, especially when the money they make isn't as directly tied to performance, the results they focus on may be various intangibles: Winning a conviction in a drug deal case, reporting that their school ranked highest in the state in the SAT scores, knocking out an enemy aircraft installation, performing another successful heart bypass surgery, or setting up a new inventory control system in their company.

PRESSURES TO WIN AT ALL COSTS

Whether the scorecard measuring the Expert's performance is money or some intangible benchmark, making the right career choice is particularly important for someone with the Expert's genetic code.

Why? Because, ultimately, Experts come to realize that the journey is more important than the destination—that the bottom-line results, no matter how important they seem at the beginning of the game, don't matter much if they're not enjoying the trip, if they're not doing their job with integrity, and if they're not being of service to people, community, and country. Playing the game well really is more important than the final score to the Expert.

Yet in today's highly commercialized world, Experts are especially vulnerable when it comes to picking a career. Not only is the external world pressuring them for results, Experts are naturally driven, even haunted, by *inner* pressures to perform, to achieve, to accomplish, to get results; it's in their blood.

As a result, Experts often sacrifice too much, picking a career based more on perceived tangible results—often at the expense of enjoying the ride, of pride in their work, of being of service, and even at times of compromising their integrity. In short, both external and internal pressures can result in an Expert picking a career primarily because it looks like a moneymaker or solely as a way of looking like a hero.

Remember, do what you love and the money will follow. Experts cannot avoid their unique calling and must honor the pressure for results. But at the same time, they must work equally hard to find a balance between the destination and the journey.

YOUR #1 DECISION: PICKING THE RIGHT CAREER

This problem cannot be understated, because the Expert, more than all the other personality types, is being hit from both sides, so to speak. By the outer world, with all its money pressures. And by the Expert's own natural instincts to produce results. This is why Thomas Stanley's advice in *The Millionaire Mind* is especially crucial to the Expert, not just as a way of becoming a millionaire, but as a way to live a happy and fulfilling life:

> If you make one major decision correctly, you can become economically productive. If you are creative enough to select the ideal vocation, you can win, win big-time.... As most millionaires report, stress is a direct result of devoting a lot of effort to a task that's not in line with one's abilities. It's more difficult, more demanding mentally and physically, to work at a vocation that's unsuitable to your aptitude.

The message is clear. Your chances for success are higher, and the stress factor will be lower, if your career choice matches your interests and abilities—*if you're doing something you really love doing on a day-to-day basis.*

Yet so many Experts (and other personality types, too) make choices for other reasons, succumbing to external (family, friends, cultural, counselors) and internal (genetic code) pressures that nudge you to go for the money because, of all tangible results, money seems to be the best way to measure your success in today's materialistic culture.

DOES MONEY MEASURE YOUR SELF-WORTH OR JUST NET WORTH?

In addition to the pressure to achieve results, there is yet a third challenge for Experts—a challenge that they will not confront until later in life, when backtracking or shifting into the right career may not only be difficult, but is likely to add considerable stress.

Here's why. In his work on the stages of life, the psychologist Carl Jung observed that so many highly successful people lost their zest for life and work in their midyears, around age 40. For 20 or 30 years before that they had invested most of their energy and efforts in achieving results in the outside world—career recognition and financial independence. But after achieving their goals, with the race won, the thrill was gone, life lost its meaning, they felt empty and depressed.

This tendency can affect anybody, but it is particularly challenging for the high-performance Experts in the business and financial worlds, who tend to measure their *self-worth,* as well as their *net worth,* by the amount of money in the bank and other assets (the size of their home, clothes, cars, awards, trophies, number of employees, and other external rewards accumulated by chasing results for decades. *In the process of focusing so exclusively on money, they miss their true calling.* Joseph Campbell offers sage advice about money and your life's calling:

A lot of money has come in by doing what I feel I want to do from the inside. If you do that, you are doing things that attract money, because you are giving life and life responds in the way of its counterpart in hard coin. If you follow your bliss, you will always have your bliss, money or not. If you follow money, you may lose it, and you will have nothing.

The same caveat applies to chasing *any* results—*not just money.* If you focus too narrowly on just the results and get caught up in running up the score, you may win the battle and lose the war. As a result, when picking a career, the natural instincts of Experts may lead them to place too much emphasis on money and results.

Careers with High Payoff for Results-Oriented Experts

If you are an Expert making career decisions, you might consider counterbalancing the natural pressure for results: Consider going *against* your natural instincts. Go more with your heart than your head. *For the moment, forget about the money;* don't focus on the results.

Instead, make absolutely sure you love the process, the discipline, the daily grind, the opportunities for service and working with authorities, and everything else that goes into the day-to-day action in the business, trade, or profession selected. This is your life's work, make certain the job matches your interests and abilities that you really are doing something you really love:

- *Business:* Managers, supervisors, accountants, production analysts
- *Finance:* Portfolio managers, bankers, brokers, loan underwriters
- *Military:* Officers in intelligence, logistics, strategy, and combat
- *Criminal justice:* Police officers, detectives, investigators, prosecutors
- *Education:* Administrators, principals, librarians, business teachers
- *Law:* Litigators, corporate lawyers, estate and tax planners, judges
- *Technology:* Programmers, systems engineers, product specialists
- *Medical:* Hospital administrators, surgeons, lab techs, pharmacists

In general, the opportunities for Experts are considerably broader than for other personality types, in part because of their fierce obsession with results, but also because of their specialized education, training, and experiences. They have expertise that is usually transferable to other fields, which makes them a valuable resource to many establishments, companies, and organizations and also opens opportunities for promotion into management positions in their fields.

Management guru Peter Drucker likely had Experts in mind when he offered this advice to people considering a new career or facing a career change:

> There are a few elemental things you can do: First, you know what you don't want to do, but what you do want to do is still a mystery. There is no way of finding out but trying. Second, one doesn't get married to a job. A job is your opportunity to find out, that's all it is. . . . Don't try to reason out things that one can only learn by experience.

Then Drucker added one key observation: "Do you know enough about yourself . . . one of the most important things would be to know if you like pressure." Very important, especially because a great deal is usually on the line for the Expert—life-and-death struggles in a jury trial, open-heart surgery, a military attack, a drug bust, a multi-million-dollar real estate transaction, even the curriculum redesign of a school system.

This pressure to get results—*positive results*—is never-ending for all Experts. Their clients, customers, investors, competitors, and family are constantly making demands, keeping the pressure on. Not everyone can handle the stress that goes along with being an Expert, especially since the outcome is often risky, requiring intense preparation at high cost over a long period of time before the final results are in.

Millionaire's Code for Results-Oriented Experts
Introvert, Sensor, Thinker, Judger (ISTJ)

The Expert has characteristics in common with other personalities that need to be emphasized. First, the expert is the *Introverted* sibling of the Extraverted CEO (ESTJ). Experts are often members of the CEO's team, on staff or as a consultant, and for that very reason they are often not only part of the key decision-making teams, they may be groomed for promotion to a more senior management position.

Real Introverts, of course, must think twice about such a switch, because it will pull them out of their private world and demand a lot of interaction with people. Remember, Extraverts draw their energy from people. They love talking and thinking out loud, schmoozing, one-to-one updates, large staff meetings, walking around the production floor, striking up conversations with strangers, investors, bankers, customers—they love exchanging ideas with people.

In contrast, *Introverts* tend to be more self-contained, more like the lone wolves portrayed by movie heroes such as Schwarzenegger, Stallone, Norris, and Cruise. They tend to say little, talk softly, and carry a big stick. They may defend the establishment, respect authority, and serve the public, but their energy comes from deep within themselves.

Inside the brains of Introverts is an inner world operating like a computer command center, constantly storing and processing vast amounts of specialized information necessary for them to function as Experts. Even those who are Experts in administrative and management systems tend to see staff as impersonal elements in an organizational machine.

HEROES COMMITTED TO DEFENDING THE AMERICAN WAY OF LIFE

It is worth noting that a large percentage of military and police officers fit this profile. Obviously, the armed forces and law enforcement best represent the establishment. The main job of Experts in the military and the police is to protect, defend, and maintain the established order.

It should come as no surprise that many Experts are drawn to these fields. There is a clearly a mutual identity here between the organization and the personality; both are committed to maintaining the stability of the existing way of life. The recruiting poster message that identifies a soldier as "an army of one" captures the spirit of this Expert to a tee—each individual soldier carries the spirit of the entire organization.

In this way, Experts also have personality traits similar to their cousins, the Master Craftsmen (ISTP). Where Craftsmen are more like freelance heroes mystically bonded to their physical tools of the trade, Experts have a rock-solid bond between their inner intelligence and the establishment itself—whether in business, finance, military, medical, education, or any other organization.

Beyond that, the two are siblings, both with heroic tendencies. Inside, both personalities are programmed as archetypal heroes, the one "who has given his or her life to something bigger than oneself," as Joseph Campbell put it. Craftsmen are more likely to engage their hero's journey with a big physical stick, while the Experts prefer brains and instruments, but their journeys are still heroic, still with an eye to the *results*.

Paradoxically, many Experts do rise to senior management and leadership positions, largely because of their expertise in their field. When they do, it is important that they continue to honor their needs as Introverts. Put on the game face in the public arena, play the game, but give yourself lots of private time with family, friends, and whatever your favorite diversion might be—fly-fishing, coaching soccer, golf, reading. Seek balance.

Sensor: Calm, Cool Problem Solvers in the Midst of Chaos

Remember, *Sensors* are like Sergeant Friday in *Dragnet* ("The facts, ma'am, just the facts"), concrete thinkers, interested in specific, detailed, hard evidence, not a lot of what-ifs, maybes, speculations, and conjectures that are part of the Intuitive's way of collecting information about the world. But Friday's deadpan demeanor is deceptive.

In fact, Sensors may appear to be the calm center in a chaotic storm, but inside, their heart beats fast, their breathing quickens, the adrenaline is rushing—*and all that makes them feel very much alive!* They go through life looking for thrills.

This is especially true for the Expert. They feel most alive when they're in the moment, in the action, experiencing life—cross-examining a witness, cutting into a patient with a scalpel, responding to a bank robbery, buying and selling blocks of stocks, launching Tomcats off the deck of an aircraft carrier. Sports psychologist James Loehr was clearly speaking to the Expert in *The Mental Game* when he said:

> You feel that the problems you face in competition are not threatening but stimulating. You've gone well beyond simply loving to win. You have clearly come to *love the battle.* As a result of this emotional response, you have become an excellent problem solver. When everyone else is heading for the trenches as the problems start mounting, you smile inside because you know you have the emotional edge.

The *Sensing* function serves Experts well—they love playing the game, whatever it may be, because they love solving problems. In fact, the Sensing function is critical to Experts because they know that once they have the right information, the problem practically solves itself. The results become obvious, which is why they are such thorough, detailed researchers and investigators.

In order to feel fully alive they need to jump in and experience the action, get their hands dirty, and kick the tires, so to speak. They live to touch the evidence, rough or smooth, hear the roar of the engines, see the expression on their opponent's face, smell the damage, taste the spoils of victory—today, now, this moment.

PEAK EXPERIENCES: AT ONE WITH THE CENTER OF THE UNIVERSE

For the Expert, being alive is an immediate, concrete, materialistic, sensual experience. It is also a subtle and yet profound spiritual experience in the Eastern tradition, one that Experts are likely to avoid discussing because it's metaphysical, something Intuitives are more likely to verbalize than Sensors. For example, in *The Secret Power Within,* martial arts champion Chuck Norris speaks directly to this natural ability of getting into alignment with the source:

> Ki: The Universal Power. The Zen masters believe that the way of the universe is a way of remaining in balance and in harmony with nature. Moving with and not against energy can open the creative paths of the mind. You will then be at one with the universe. In the truest Zen sense, you will be the center of the universe, no matter where you are or the circumstances you find yourself in. This source of inner power, called *ki,* is an invisible life force that flows throughout the universe. . . . By being "centered"–being focused and in touch with that "one point"–we can make use of this universal energy.

The labels, *Zen* and *ki,* are unimportant. Only the experience matters–and the experience can occur anywhere, anytime, for anyone. What is important is the experience of getting your life in alignment–*your personality type, your inner soul, your career, and your experiences in the present moment*–all operating as one in you. This is the kind of peak experience the Expert lives for. It is the kind of spiritual experience Veronique Vienne is talking about in *The Art of Imperfection,* when she says, "You are enlightened, though you don't know what it means . . . let alone care about it."

Thinking: Follow the Rules, Go by the Book, You'll Win

Of all the Guardians, the Expert is perhaps the single most objective and focused in making decisions. Experts are *Thinkers,* the third element of their genetic code. When Experts make decisions they focus their minds like laser beams on very specific projects, using very specific logical and rational processes to get very specific results.

Thinkers, especially Experts, invariably make decisions using proven research techniques, traditional analytical methodologies, standard operating procedures, and practices that are the accepted customs of their professions. Portfolio managers use fundamental and technical analysis; trial attorneys are bound by the rules of evidence; doctors use well-established protocols; soldiers and police all have set routines established by their authorities.

When Experts make a decision, there is nothing personal involved in the decision. It's virtually mechanical, a slam dunk. They have formulas, equations, calculations, and standards that, when applied in a professional way, will objectively determine the answer. The cop registers your speed; your doctor runs an EKG; a forward observer locks on the enemy's coordinates; an appraiser has comps; a librarian identifies the book's number; your broker sells when the stock hits a stop-order price; a judge rules that the evidence is inadmissible.

In every case, Experts are going by the book, following the rules set by some authority in the establishment. There really is nothing personal about it. They are working within the existing system, working to maintain and stabilize the established order of things.

They are totally committed to following the rules, because that's the right thing to do, and they've sworn to do the right thing according to their code of conduct, their authorities, and law of the land. It's the American way, has been for over two centuries. And the Experts are, in their own way, defending, protecting, and preserving their way of life by obeying all the rules.

Judging: The Perfect Soldier in an Army of One

The Expert personality is also a Judger, the fourth element of the genetic code. Experts are conservative and traditional in their values and work hard at creating a stable, structured, well-organized lifestyle, not only at work, but in their family, social, and community lives. They have a full plate of activities, and their appointment book will prove it, with every day being well planned in advance. They get to meetings early, probably arrive fully prepared to make a presentation, take notes, and keep everything in logical order.

Experts, perhaps more than all the other personalities, are among the most dependable humans in any establishment. They fit well as part of the whole, and yet, paradoxically, while operating within the structure of the organization, they are among the keenest, most rational, independent, and aggressive problem solvers—*an army of one*. They want results, and by God, within the confines of the existing establishment, *they will get the desired results*.

Experts in every field have this insatiable focus on the bottom line, on being a success, on solutions, on achieving positive results. Chuck Norris addresses this singular focus in *The Secret Power Within:*

If you really want something, you must go after it yourself, and with all your dedication: No one is going to give it to you, and if you waver or doubt, you're sure to fail. And what could be a better imitation of life than finding yourself faced with the responsibility for performing a series of chores, things you've never done before, without advance warning, without prior instruction, and without guidance or help?

Experts really are the perfect Guardians of the Establishment. They are absolutely committed to defending and preserving the establishment. At the same time, they have such an independent spirit that they are able to work within the system on new problems and unknowns, as troubleshooters and problem solvers. In fact, they thrive on working in challenging environments where there are loads of opportunities to score points, generate positive results, and make money.

Making Money: A Positive Mental Attitude Spells Success

Experts are laser-focused on results, and money is one of the biggest results crossing their radar screens on a daily basis. They have a keen eye for financial opportunities and will aggressively pursue them. Perhaps of all their traits, the strongest is a will to win and a belief that, yes, they *will* win because they will work their butts off doing all the necessary research and analysis well in advance, and, in the end, they will come out a winner.

You can call it self-confidence or a strong ego—they have it. Long ago, two great success gurus, Napoleon Hill and Clement Stone, identified this one single, simple, most important secret to financial success:

> After years spent studying successful men, the authors of *Success Through a Positive Mental Attitude* have come to the conclusion that a positive mental attitude is the one simple secret shared by them all.

A positive mental attitude—the secret ingredient that separates successful people from the rest of the pack—is one ingredient that the Expert personality has in abundance. It's all part of the genetic code of Experts, the formula for their success: Discipline, hard work, integrity, duty, commitment, pride, service, excellence, and results add up to one thing—a *positive mental attitude*—and that translates into success and money.

Experts tend to gravitate toward work in established companies, businesses, professions, and institutions, where their expertise is needed and where they have opportunities to produce results, solve challenging problems, and troubleshoot, and for which they are usually well compensated.

Moreover, these traditional organizations are likely to have well-established bonus, pension, and retirement plans, health benefits, and other services to help the Expert budget, save, and invest assets for various personal and family goals, including accumulating a nest egg for retirement. Experts are the one personality most likely to capitalize on every opportunity to make and save money and retire successfully, thanks in a large measure to their positive mental attitude.

* * * * * * * *

The desire of most people today for quick, sure, and highly visible results
is perhaps the deadliest enemy of mastery.
It's fine to have ambitious goals, but the best way to reach them is to
cultivate modest expectations at every step along the way. When you're
climbing a mountain, in other words, be aware that the peak is ahead, but
don't keep looking up at it.
Keep your eyes on the path. And when you reach the top,
as the old Zen saying goes, keep on climbing.

George Leonard,
*Mastery, the Keys to Success
and Long-Term Fulfillment*

32

MASTER-SERVANTS (ISFJ)

THOMAS MERTON, THICH NHAT HANH, JESUS, BUDDHA

> Which is more important;
> to attain enlightenment,
> or to attain enlightenment
> before you attain enlightenment;
> to make a million dollars,
> or to enjoy your life
> in your effort,
> little by little,
> even though it is
> impossible to
> make a million;
> to be successful, or
> to find some
> meaning in
> your effort to
> be successful.
>
> Shunryu Suzuki,
> *Zen Mind,*
> *Beginner's Mind*

All Guardians are fierce defenders of the established order in the world—family, church and community, company and country. The *Master-Servant* personalities are the ultimate self-sacrificers, guardian angels whose sense of duty is so strong they will do virtually anything for others—work long hours alone to complete assignments, donate countless hours and dollars to charities, serve endlessly as caregivers for sick loved ones, even lay down their lives for others, as a fireman, cop, or citizen in an emergency. They *need* to protect and nurture the world.

Martyr and hero, the Master-Servant personality has some of the best of what Buddha and Jesus inspire in human beings. They are masters of a life of service, here and now, in the real world of everyday work and living.

Yet there is an air of mystery surrounding Master-Servants. They are a paradox at work—they say little, do much, are frugal with language and money, yet are generous with their time and caring for others. They ask little for themselves, they simply go about their work quietly doing what needs to be done. In their noble serenity, you sense they have mastered the secret of life. If they are overlooked by tough-minded, insensitive bosses when the rewards are being passed out, they often rationalize that their true reward comes from a higher source. And for these gentle, humble souls, it does.

Keep It Simple: When Hungry, Eat, When Tired, Sleep

Master-Servants are in the ancient tradition of the Zen masters, appearing mysterious, yet for them there is no mystery. Life is simple, obvious, and practical: As the Zen masters put it, "When you are hungry, eat, when tired, sleep." And when working, focus on the work. When playing, just play. When loving, just love. When you hurt, feel the pain. When you suffer loss, grieve. *Life is in the living.*

Master-Servants are gentle, kind souls who don't talk much about the meaning of life—it just is. There is no talk of a cosmic plan, no grand conflict between good and evil, no grand philosophy to figure out, no grand mission to fulfill during this incarnation, no surrendering to a universal power—you just do what's in front of you. When asked about the meaning of life, like the ancient Zen masters, they may point to the wind blowing in the tall grass, or a bird in flight, or they may stare silently with a knowing smile.

Yet the Master-Servants know we are guided by a mysterious force, one that no one can understand, ever. So, while they say little, their quiet simplicity speaks volumes, reminding us of the words of the ancient *Tao Te Ching,* "Those who know do not speak, those who speak do not know." The Master-Servant is one who knows.

NO IDEA WHERE I AM GOING, BUT KNOW I'M GUIDED

Western mystics echo the same message, such as the prayer of Thomas Merton, a Trappist monk. His prayer begins: "My Lord God, I have no idea where I am going. I do not see the road ahead of me. Nor do I really know myself." Yet he had absolute faith: "You will lead me by the right road, though I may know nothing about it."

Master-Servants are those who do not speak, but know, do not see the way, yet the way opens for them. And along the way, they eat, sleep, work, laugh, play, love, hurt, grieve—live life on life's terms, one day at a time. As Merton once put it: "Life is not a problem to be solved, but a mystery to be lived." And in that sense, Master-Servants are very much alive, much more so than most people—noticeably reserved, yet silently and fully aware of the secret meaning of life in the little things they see in each moment.

INSTRUCTIONS TO THE COOK: MASTERY TAKES A LITTLE LONGER

There is a wonderful old story about a young boy who came from a poor family seeking admittance to a Zen monastery. The head monk immediately saw the boy's wisdom and put him to work as a cook's apprentice in the kitchen rather than with the sons of the wealthy who came to study the ancient scriptures.

Many years later, when the head monk was dying, he set up this test to choose his successor: A stone jug filled with water was placed in the center of the temple and he asked, "What is its meaning?" The most learned students came forward one at a time, offering eloquent philosophic and poetic descriptions.

The cook watched this ritual from the kitchen, growing impatient with all the pompous talk. Finally, he wiped his hands on a towel, lumbered into the temple still wearing his apron, strolled up to the jar—and said nothing as he kicked it over with his foot. Water spilled everywhere. That night the master visited the cook in his cell, left the robes of the head-master, and told him to go into the woods until the hurt feelings of the other monks calmed down.

IF YOU CAN'T COOK, MASTER OPENING AND CLOSING DOORS

Life truly is that simple. Merton became friends with Thich Nhat Hanh, the Vietnamese Zen master who wrote *Living Buddha, Living Christ* and so many other wonderful books about this simple life:

> The Buddha always told his disciples not to waste their time and energy in metaphysical speculation. Whenever he was asked a metaphysical question he remained silent. Instead, he directed his disciples toward practical efforts.

And so it is with the Master-Servant. For them, the kitchen may be a cathedral. Life really is very simple to understand, simple even for those who cannot cook. In *Merton as Zen Clown,* biographer Belden Lane wrote:

Once he met a Zen novice who had just finished his first year of living in a monastery. Merton asked the novice what he learned during the course of his novitiate, half expecting to hear of encounters with enlightenment, discoveries of the spirit, perhaps altered states of consciousness. But the novice replied that during his first year in the contemplative life he had simply learned to open and close doors.

Like the Zen masters before them, Master-Servants care little about grand theories—such as enlightenment, spirit, and consciousness—they focus on practical matters, and for them, the most practical is the every-day world of working, jobs, careers, earning money, helping others. It's about doing things, not talking or reading about doing things, but actually *doing them.*

Millionaire's Code for Master-Servants
Introvert, Sensor, Feeling, Judger (ISFJ)

Although the Master-Servant has a lot in common with its extraverted sibling, the Peacemaker (ESFJ), the fact is that the *Introverted* Master-Servant works behind the scenes and, as a result, tends to get much less recognition and therefore remains relatively anonymous.

And yet, they actually prefer it that way. They're often shy in public settings and uncomfortable around strangers, even business associates, sensing they are under constant scrutiny. So they prefer working alone, out of the spotlight, doing their job—giving, giving, giving.

They will often work extralong shifts, giving up their own time with family and personal matters for the sake of the company, the public interest, or a needy individual. In fact, they can never seem to give enough and will often continue giving to their own detriment, suffering in silence, even when they know they are being taken advantage of.

YES, LIFE IS DIFFICULT: NOW GET BUSY AND SOLVE THE PROBLEM

While this trait could be counterproductive for others, as when the personal sacrifice and suffering far outweigh the service done working to help others, many Master-Servants seem to have a saintly air about how they handle this, as if they truly do understand what the great masters (Jesus and Buddha, Saint Francis and Dogen, Thomas Merton and Thich Nhat Hanh) understood about life, that for some of us, much is asked, and for all of us, life can be filled with suffering and frustration.

This paradoxical truth is eloquently captured in Dr. M. Scott Peck's classic, *The Road Less Traveled.* Peck speaks to all of us of the Buddha's

Noble Truths, yet his words seem to specifically describe the master-servant's view of reality:

> Life is difficult. This is a great truth, one of the greatest truths. It is a great truth because once we see the truth, we transcend it. Once we truly know that life is difficult–once we truly understand and accept it–then life is no longer difficult. Because once it is accepted, the fact that life is difficult no longer matters.
>
> Most do not fully see that life is difficult. Instead they moan more or less incessantly, noisily or subtly, about their problems, their burdens, and their difficulties as if life were generally easy, as if life *should* be easy. Life is a series of problems. Do we want to moan about them or solve them?

Of all the personalities, Master-Servants are probably the most aware of this truth–*that life is difficult, full of frustrations*–and yet, knowing and accepting that reality, they are also the ones most likely to get out there and solve the problem, put their backs to the wheel, their noses to the grindstone, and simply do whatever it takes to get the job done, without the incessant moaning, and probably with a knowing smile and hum.

Sensor: Ultimate Data Processor for New Information Age

When it comes to collecting information, the second element of the Master-Servant's code, these individuals are certainly one of the best of all the personality types, true master collectors of facts, numbers, data, statistics, information. It almost seems as if they were born to handle the growing workload of the information revolution, the online technology age, the computer generation. They are the ultimate Sensors–the ultimate collectors of information.

This trait originates in their natural abilities as *observers,* in the Western scientific tradition, or as *mindful ones,* in the Eastern metaphysical tradition. they are the ones with a snapshot of the total reality as it is today, without judging or analyzing, simply taking an accurate picture of life as it is in fact. Master-Servants act as cameras, microscopes, and telescopes to Westerners. In the East, they live in a state of total awareness of the world around them. No wonder they are hard to read, they are the "readers," the ones doing the reading.

We know, for example, that Master-Servants are Introverts and therefore naturally tough to read. Their siblings, the Peacemakers (ESFJ), are Extraverts and much easier to read because they're always talking and telling us what they're thinking, planning, and doing. The two share one thing in common, however: Both are highly skilled at *reading other people.* In fact, Master-Servants are even better, because they are not distracted by all the talking.

RARE LOVER OF NUMBERS, STATISTICS, AND INFORMATION PROCESSING

The Master-Servant is a *Sensor,* with incredible powers of observation and the memory of an elephant, long and accurate. These people see, hear, touch, taste, and smell with incredibly accuracy, like a high-tech radar scanning the horizon and recording their observations in a powerful memory bank.

Moreover, this ability to observe and remember large quantities of information accurately makes Master-Servants extremely valuable in a business and financial setting. They are among those rare beings who actually love numbers, facts, data, and statistics for their own sake.

Once they are involved in a complex task dealing with large amounts of information, Master-Servants will simply dig in, methodically tackle the job, organize the pieces, and get the job done, often doing the entire job themselves. Maybe even doing it in record time, much like Scotty, the engineer on the original *Star Trek,* who was always being pressed by Captain Kirk to do yet one more impossible repair job on a tight schedule, yet he invariably finished it on time or ahead of schedule.

RIGHT PLACE AT THE RIGHT TIME FOR TODAY'S NEW TECHNOLOGIES

As a result, Master-Servants are perfect in one of the fastest-growing industries around—analysis and data processing operations of all kinds. For example, they do well as sports statisticians, librarians, pollsters, mortgage and securities analysts, insurance actuaries, administrative assistants, tax accountants, bank officers, medical technicians, crime scene investigators, production schedulers, inventory controllers, engineering draftsmen, market researchers, museum curators, math tutors. All of these jobs entail enormous demands for identifying, storing, and processing highly specialized information, a function that can often bore other personalities.

We live in a world overloaded with information, where the amount of data accelerates daily. *Sensors* are naturally interested hard data, in its collection, organization, and processing, and their skills put them in a perfect position as the economy expands.

This is especially advantageous for the Master-Servant because so many other personalities simply lack the patience, discipline, talents, and powers of concentration necessary to deal with the huge, multiple-terabyte (1 trillion bytes!) databases that are currently being managed by so many large and small organizations—multinational corporations, hospitals and HMOs, government agencies, securities exchanges, military, and police and national intelligence organizations. Even small entrepreneurial operations can be perfect for Master-Servants who would feel boxed in by large and less personal organizations.

Being Sensors, Master-Servants are more interested in the operations and maintenance of systems than in the design and development of new systems. Stated another way, they are more interested in the here and now than in all the abstract planning that goes into creating something new for the future. They need jobs and projects that keep them active in the present moment, where they feel safe, secure, and content being involved in real-time mental processes that resemble fast-paced sporting events.

Feeling: Going the Extra Mile and Winning the Race

The third element of the code tells us how a person makes decisions. Both Feeling and Thinking types process information logically and rationally. The difference is that Thinkers base their decisions on external objective standards when making their decisions, while Feelers rely on subject criteria. One takes a more distant perspective, the other relies more on the one-to-one personal touch and an inner sense of what's right.

The Master-Servant is a *Feeling* personality, which creates an extraordinary sense of duty and loyalty to the external world, to people and groups, to projects and organizations. Master-Servants have a strong need to please authorities, a need for approval, and a tendency to put others' needs ahead of their own needs, even when they make crucial decisions about their life and their work.

Obviously, some people will take advantage of their good nature and sense of duty, and Master-Servants need to be alert in this regard. But this personality trait also makes them the ultimate workhorses of business, the totally reliable ones who will see the task through to the end, no matter how tedious, boring, exacting, and arduous. In the end, they are the perfect example of the classic fairy tale in which the slow, plodding tortoise wins the race against the hare, which moves in spurts, lacks discipline, and is easily bored.

BLENDING BORING NUMBERS WITH REAL PEOPLE, ONE AT A TIME

Their subjectivity often leads Master-Servants into fields as professional caretakers and nurturers, where their powers of observation and information processing are great assets. The health care field is a natural and, like data processing, a growth area filled with enormous opportunities spelled out in economist Paul Zane Pilzer's book, *The Wellness Revolution: How to Make a Fortune in the Next Trillion Dollar Industry.*

Even today you'll find Master-Servants working in hospitals, home nursing, family or medical practices, for example, and working in many other areas that satisfy their need for one-to-one contact—as nurses, doctors, technicians, therapists, nutritionists, administration, even part-time volunteers.

These same talents also draw Master-Servants into a host of other fields that allow them to nurture and care for people, especially in education and social work with younger children, as teachers, and as counselors. Plus all kinds of personal service businesses, where one-to-one contacts are the order of the day, solving problems, tending to personal needs, making people happy, and lightening their burdens, such as in retail sales in gift and clothing shops, home improvements, repairs, and decoration, maybe even a bed-and-breakfast—as long as they have an opportunity to serve, help, nurture, protect, and care for people, preferably on a one-to-one basis where they can get some feedback that tells them they're doing the job right.

Judging: Frugality Makes Us Healthy, Wealthy, and Wise

In sharp contrast to Perceivers, who prefer to hang loose and enjoy a more spontaneous lifestyle, Judgers like the Master-Servants want tight control over their lives. For them, a good day is a day well organized and well planned in advance, with everything running smoothly, according to schedule, no surprises. They become uneasy when life is off balance; they are disciplined people and will work hard to restore a balanced lifestyle when things go off course.

Sayings such as "Early to bed and early to rise makes a man healthy, wealthy, and wise" and "The early bird gets the worm" capture the life spirit of Master-Servants. They are low-key, the opposite of flashy, often living a simple lifestyle reminiscent of the monastic life of a monk, disciplined, frugal, dutiful, and totally responsible in all their obligations, an attitude that actually builds wealth the good old-fashioned way, according to Stanley and Danko in *The Millionaire Next Door:*

> Wealth is more often the result of a lifestyle of hard work, perseverance, planning, and most of all, self-discipline ... they live below their means. ... Being frugal is the cornerstone of wealth-building.

This attitude comes naturally to Master-Servants as part of their genetic personality code as *Judgers*.

THE MORALITY OF CONFRONTING LIFE HEAD-ON AND WITH INTEGRITY

The tendency of Master-Servants to put others' needs ahead of their own is counterbalanced by their ability to knuckle down and do the impossible when it comes to any task, job, or project. They have the discipline to "just do it," no matter what, blocking out the frustrations, difficulties, and pain while focusing on the goal, somewhat like their cousins, the Experts (ISTJ). Scott Peck spoke of this rare wisdom that so few possess in *The Road Less Traveled:*

> What makes life difficult is that the process of confronting and solving problems is a painful one. . . . Yet it is in this whole process of meeting and solving problems that life has its meaning. Problems are the cutting edge that distinguishes success and failure. . . . Wise people learn not to dread but actually to welcome problems and actually to welcome the pain of problems. Most of us are not so wise. Facing the pain involved, almost all of us, to a greater of lesser degree, attempt to avoid problems.

The Master-Servant personality is one of the rare few who actually can see problems as challenges and then face them head-on, focusing with great intensity on one specific project or task at a time until completion. And when they do, in the end, like the tortoise, they will win the wealth-building race.

All Guardians are *Judgers*. They work hard to gain control over their lives at work and at home. It's an inner thing, a personality quirk that makes them who they are. They become anxious when things slip beyond their control.

However, this isn't merely an emotional hang-up for Master-Servants. They are highly moral people with a strong sense of integrity. They may not talk much about it, but they do have their beliefs and see little need to get into debates over them. Being in control of their emotions and their lives in general is proof to them that they are indeed living in harmony with moral values.

Careers: Great Opportunities in Today's New World Order

Because of their unique talents and special interests in the expanding areas of data processing and care giving, in the information technology revolution and the wellness revolution, Master-Servants have a vast array of specific opportunities open to those with their unique skills and interests.

While some career counselors have a rather limited view of the opportunities available to the Master-Servant, the fact is that the global economy is expanding so rapidly with new technologies in many areas that anyone with this profile should scan the horizon, holding out for the perfect opportunity—and never compromise. Here is a sampling of the possibilities:

- *Education:* Grade school teachers, librarians, math tutors, counselors
- *Medicine:* Doctors, nurses, lab techs, nutritionists, physical therapists
- *Social services:* Family therapists, social workers, spiritual counselors
- *Government:* Firefighters, police officers, crime scene investigators
- *Professionals:* Accountants, draftsmen, museum curators, actuaries
- *Charities:* Directors, organizers, contributors, fund-raisers, volunteers
- *Personal services:* Home decorators, hostesses, caterers, PR consultants
- *Business:* Retail salespeople, administrative assistants, retail gift sales
- *Finance:* Securities analysts, mortgage escrow agents, financial planners
- *Data processing:* Inventory controllers, market researchers, pollsters

Let's underscore this key career issue again for the Master-Servant: The economy is exploding with all kinds of new job opportunities, many of which are a perfect fit with your particular talents, skills, and interests.

Making Money: Positive Mental Attitude = Millionaire Mind

Master-Servants have excellent moneymaking potentials due to their special skills and a sense of duty that will make them incredible assets to so many organizations. If there is one concern, it is that they tend to love what they're doing so much and feel such a strong commitment and loyalty to their job and the establishment that they often minimize the value of their contributions. As a result, they may not seek full recompense in return for their services.

If you are a Master-Servant personality, you deserve much more than you realize, especially in today's world. Never sell yourself short. Get some direction from a professional, a trusted mentor, or your sibling personality, the Expert (ISTJ), who usually has an abundance of this trait and can offer excellent guidance. Speak up; demand more; you *are* worth it. Build the kind of self-confidence that Napoleon Hill and Clement Stone say is the single most important ingredient to financial success:

> After years spent studying successful men, the authors of *Success Through a Positive Mental Attitude* have come to the conclusion that a positive mental attitude is the one simple secret shared by them all.

The Master-Servant need never get stuck in a back corner, hidden out of sight in a dull word processing job. There are so many exciting new technologies in the fields of data processing, care giving, and wellness that offer virtually unlimited opportunities for someone motivated to get the necessary training.

YOU HAVE THE TALENT: PICK A CAREER THAT'LL MAKE YOU HAPPY

Here's a tidbit of advice: Instead of focusing on the skills and talents necessary (because that's easy, you're a perfectionist!), *pick the field that makes you happiest and organizations that you respect*—then go for it. Get the basic training. Get the job, give it all you have, and you will come out a winner, earning a comfortable income, living the life you were meant to live.

Once you choose a field that satisfies you personally, focus on maximizing your income and you'll then have the necessary assets to build wealth and become a millionaire, just like all Guardians—in a slow, steady, methodical way, with your eye focused on the goal, making money, saving regularly, and investing in a retirement nest egg that's growing steadily. Do this and you will become a millionaire in fact as well as in spirit!

* * * * * * * *

Millionaire investors, by society's standards,
are boring people . . .
boring breeds stability.
Stability breeds consistency.
Consistency builds wealth.

Millionaire investors limit the shocks to their finances.
They create stable lifestyles . . .
invest consistently for twenty years or more . . .
month after month after month.

Charles Carlson,
Eight $teps to $even Figures

DISCOVER THE SECRET CODE, UNLEASH THE MILLIONAIRE WITHIN YOU, AND GET RICH IN SPIRIT AND IN FACT

Writing this book has turned into an unexpected adventure in *self-discovery.* That wasn't my original purpose. I thought I understood life well enough to write a book like this. But as it happened, I was in for a pleasant surprise. I began learning more and more about myself in *every one of these sixteen personalities!*

I hope you have the same experience. In fact, if I have one wish, it is that *you read the entire book.* That's right, I am encouraging you to read the book cover-to-cover—because if you don't, *you might miss some very important secret clues about yourself that you would never discover otherwise!*

Most people who pick up a book about personality types limit themselves by focusing on only the one or two personality types that best fit the four-letter code from their test—they never read about the other 14 or 15 personalities.

Read All 16 Profiles and Discover the Secret Clues

By exploring the other personalities for *hidden narrative clues,* you might just learn something about the "real you" that your four-letter code cannot reveal. Equally important, you might miss out on some clues that will help you in your relationships with the important people in your life, *and better appreciate their uniqueness!*

In writing about these personality types, I have tried to enliven each of them by adding a touch of celebrity journalism—short stories, lyrics, scenes, vignettes, anecdotes, and quotes from famous people and their philosophies of life—as a way of encouraging you to read the entire book.

I urge you to take the time, go back, and reread everything about *all* 16 personalities. I promise you that somewhere in the remote corners of one of the other personalities you might otherwise have ignored, *where you least expect it,* you will discover something about the real you that will send you off in a new direction, down the road less traveled.

Being a Millionaire Is a State of Mind

It may be an avocation, maybe a new career, or maybe just a subtle yet profound inner transformation as you continue what you are doing, with no external change but with new awareness about your life. You will never regret the search.

As for the money, the hard cash, know this: You, me, all of us are already rich. Besides, we already know the average millionaire is at least 52 years old and that there are only 8 million American millionaires out of 289 million people. So, technically, most of us probably don't have the actual cash, *yet.* But by now, you also know that the cash is secondary to something higher.

And what's that? The truth is that being a millionaire is a state of mind, a unique spirit *within* you, not a statement from your bank or broker. When you are in this state of mind, when you are in tune with the spirit within you—*the money is irrelevant.* Yes, irrelevant.

The New Reality, Where the Search Begins

What *is* relevant? Discovering your mission in life. Awareness of your true identity. Tapping into the secret power within you. Fulfilling your destiny. Sound familiar? Of course, we hear these messages over and over again from the great masters of all ages, ancient and modern.

Joseph Campbell was one of them—and one of the two most important influences in my life. When I met him I was on Wall Street, about 40 years old, a left-brained clone in a world populated by uptight bankers, brokers, attorneys, and investment analysts in three-piece suits toting leather lunch bags.

A friend dragged me reluctantly to Campbell's workshop titled "Mythical Meditation." Campbell introduced me to a strange new right-brained world of mythology and Jungian psychology, Zen Buddhism, Christian mysticism, and Hopi shamanism, psychics, astrology, and the tarot. I had walked through a time warp into a new reality, and the searching began.

Why Are You Here? Look Inside, Then Get into Action

Campbell certainly understood the paradox of money when he said: "My life course is totally indifferent to money. As a result, a lot of money has come in by doing what I feel I want to do from the inside."

Get it? *Totally indifferent.* Money was irrelevant. Of course, that doesn't mean you can sit on your butt waiting for money to magically come to you. Quite the opposite. *Look inside, then get into action!*

Go on a search. *Discover what's really inside.* What *is* your bliss? What *is* your mission in life? Find the secret power within you, the real you, your dreams, your calling, your destiny—*whatever you choose to call it.* What *is* it?

Follow Your Bliss and You Will Always Be Rich

The searching is the key. "If you follow your bliss, you will always have your bliss, money or not," says Campbell, but "if you follow money, you may lose it, and you will have nothing."

If you are truly fortunate, this search will never end. Your life will unfold, endlessly revealing ever newer dimensions of your purpose in life. Although not always in a straight line (in fact, never).

My search took me away from Wall Street, to Hollywood on the first stop, into various businesses, newspaper publishing, television and film production, and later, into career and chemical dependency counseling, then financial journalism. Always on the path, always searching.

Jung Spent a Lifetime Searching for the Secret Code

Campbell led me to the other great mentor in my life, Carl Jung, a man who spent his entire life searching: "My life has been permeated and held together by one idea and one goal, namely, to penetrate the secret of personality. Everything can be explained from this central point, and all my works relate to this one theme."

Imagine, his entire life—searching for the secret of the personality. Interesting. That's what Jung was doing, what I'm doing, and what you are doing, by choice or default, consciously or unconsciously.

In the final analysis, my goal in writing this book has been to continue searching with the same passion and spirit I saw in the lives and works of Campbell and Jung, Myers and Briggs, Keirsey, and others who were also searching for the secret code to the human personality. In doing so, I invite and encourage you to join us in the search.

Never Stop Searching: The Best Is Yet to Come!

It is my hope that in this process, *you will discover the secret code to your personality* so that you can fulfill your mission in life, your destiny, the special reason you are here in this lifetime—for in your discovery, you will become rich in spirit and in fact.

Keep searching—the best is yet to come!

THE MILLIONAIRE'S
BASIC TRAINING LIBRARY

In spite of the incredible diversity among the 16 personality types, the individuals who distinguish themselves have one thing in common—deep within they know who they are, they are their code, they are rich in spirit. Ask any one of them and you will see that being rich in spirit is far more important than being rich in fact. They understand the distinction made by psychiatrist M. Scott Peck in *The Road Less Traveled:*

> What constitutes wealth? In worldly terms, it is the possession of money and valuable things. But if we were to measure wealth in other ways, besides mere dollars, many who are poor in possessions are spiritually rich, and many who own much are spiritually impoverished.

Of course, you want both, but first and foremost, you must be rich in spirit, passionate about life, and fulfilling your destiny. That is fundamental to all 16 personalities: Those who are richest are rich in spirit first. Being rich is a state of mind. Being rich *in fact* is the frosting on the cake, so to speak, secondary, even irrelevant.

Personal Finance Is 90 Percent Personal and 10 Percent Finance

Money managers and financial advisers also understand this personality trait. The wise ones will tell you that personal finance is 90 percent personal and 10 percent finance. That is, 90 percent in spirit and 10 percent in fact. A study of 5,000 millionaires by financial adviser Ric Edelman actually concluded that millionaires spend an average of just six minutes a day on personal finance.

That's right, just six minutes! More than that is a waste of their time. They know there are more important things in life. They know that personal finance and investing are not as complicated as Wall Street would have you believe. Here's how Nobel prize–winning economist Paul Samuelson puts it:

> Investing should be dull. It shouldn't be exciting. Investing should be more like watching paint dry or watching grass grow. If you want excitement, take $800 and go to Las Vegas. [However] it is not easy to get rich in Las Vegas, at Churchill Downs, or at the local Merrill Lynch office.

Warren Buffett: Tap-Dance into Work and Do What You Love!

If all this seems a bit too cavalier, it's not. Here's another example: In *One Up On Wall Street,* legendary fund manager Peter Lynch of Fidelity Magellan fame offers individual investors this advice:

> Rule number one, in my book, is: Stop listening to professionals. Twenty years in this business convinces me that any normal person using the customary three percent of the brain can pick stocks just as well, if not better, than the average Wall Street expert. . . . Think like an amateur. If you invest like an institution, you're doomed to perform like one, which in most cases isn't very well. If you're a surfer, a truck driver, a high school dropout, or an eccentric retiree, then you've got an edge already.

Still not sure you really got what it takes to become a millionaire? Here's the really big secret—listen very closely to what Warren Buffett, the second richest man in America, told a group of college students about how to get rich:

> I am really no different from any of you. I may have more money than you, but money doesn't make the difference. Sure, I can buy the most luxurious handmade suit, but I put it on and it just looks cheap. I would rather have a cheeseburger from Dairy Queen than a hundred-dollar meal. . . . If there is any difference between you and me it may simply be that I get up every day and have a chance *to do what I love to do,* every day. If you learn anything from me, this is the best advice I can give you.

Elsewhere he says he does a little tap dance every day when he walks into work. Whatever your code, your personality type, this message comes across loud and clear, over and over again from all the great personalities, regardless of their code: Do what you love! Do what you *love!* Do what *you* love!

Millionaire's Single Most Important Decision

Whether it's Einstein or Springsteen, Gandhi or Trump, Jordan or Jung, Kennedy or Spielberg, whoever your heroes are, I guarantee you, as different as they are, they share one common passion—doing what they love. In *The Millionaire Mind,* Thomas Stanley boils decades of research down to one rule for getting rich:

> If you make one major decision correctly, you can become economically productive. If you are creative enough to select the ideal vocation, you can win, win big-time. The really brilliant million aires are those who selected a vocation they love.

Do what you love with passion, everything else is secondary. Joseph Campbell says, "If you follow your bliss, you will always have your bliss, money or not. If you follow money, you may lose it, and you will have nothing." That's the secret to success, echoed by Warren Buffett, Peter Lynch, Scott Peck, Joseph Campbell, Thomas Stanley, everyone—*trust the spirit within you and do what you love.*

[handwritten: NOT YOURS …… GOD'S! PRAY, ACT W/O FEAR; ASK FOR FEEDBACK!]

The Secret: Live Like a Millionaire, Today

Anyone can become a millionaire, in spirit and in fact. The key is very simple: Live like a millionaire every step of the way *until you get there!* Live as a millionaire in spirit, today and every day, until you become a millionaire in fact. That way, it doesn't matter. That way, you have the best of both worlds, with the money and without it, before and after you get it, today and every day. *That way, you can't lose!*

Here's your "Millionaire's Basic Training Library" to help you along the way, to help you discover and enjoy the richness of your journey. Much you already know instinctively. So take your time, enjoy the trip. Here are 22 books. Read one a week over the next six months or so. In fact, I believe you'll get all you need just by scanning one of them each time you visit your local bookstore, relaxing over a latte and muffin:

Basic Mind-Set of the Millionaire in Training

- *The Millionaire Next Door,* Thomas Stanley & William Danko
A shift in mind-set: "Most people have it all wrong about wealth in America. Wealth is not the same as income. If you make a good income each year and spend it all, you are not getting wealthier. You are living high. Wealth is what you accumulate, not what you spend. . . . Wealth is more often the result of a lifestyle of hard work, perseverance, planning, and most of all, self-discipline."
- *The Millionaire Mind,* Thomas Stanley
An overview of American millionaires: "What do most millionaires tell me they learned. . . . They learned to: Think differently from the crowd. Much of this book has been designed around a central theme: It pays to be different."
- *Getting Rich in America,* Dwight Lee and Richard McKenzie
"All you have to do is recognize the opportunities that abound around you and work to seize a share of those opportunities; develop a long-term perspective; work and study hard; be reasonably frugal and judicious in your purchases; get married and stay married; take care of yourself; accept prudent risks and invest wisely—but above all, be patient."
- *Ordinary People, Extraordinary Wealth,* Ric Edelman
How's this for simplicity? "You're not in a horse race, you're playing horseshoes. Therefore, you don't need to pick the winner . . . merely being close is good enough to win." See also Edelman's other books, *The Truth about Money* and *Discover the Wealth Within You.*
- *Eight $teps to $even Figures,* Charles Carlson
Listen closely here: "Start Saving Now . . . It's the most important of all. You can't get to the other seven steps without starting. Oftentimes it is the most difficult step. You may have to break old habits and start new ones. . . . Buy and hold. . . . Millionaire investors never sell . . . buying and holding stocks makes you rich. . . . Buy with the idea that you cannot sell."
- *The 9 Steps to Financial Freedom,* Suze Orman
Become a do-it-yourselfer: "Whether you want to believe it or not—you and you alone have the best judgment when it comes to your money. You must do what makes you feel safe, sound, comfortable. You must trust yourself more than you trust others, and that inner voice will tell you when it is time to take action. You have more than it takes to manage your money on your own."

Investment Strategies for the Millionaire in Training

- *The Four Pillars of Investing,* William Bernstein
  Here is the basic rule: "Since you cannot successfully time the market or select individual stocks, asset allocation should be the major focus of your investment strategy, because it is the only thing you can control." You control your risks by buying the whole market—with indexes.
- *Bogle on Mutual Funds,* John Bogle
  The father of the American mutual fund offers the world's best description of the no-load, low-cost index fund investment strategy, which he used to create Vanguard, now one of the largest fund families in America. A must-read: "The idea is to own the stock market, own every company in America, and hold it for Warren Buffett's favorite holding period—forever. And that's the secret: Own everything, and hold it forever." Simple, powerful, essential.
- *Millionaire,* Wayne Wagner and Al Winnikoff
  The subtitle calls it "the best explanation of how an index fund can turn your lunch money into a fortune." Wagner and Winnikoff offer 12 steps to get you to a million bucks using index funds. A quick read for the basic fundamentals.
- *The Warren Buffett Way,* Robert Hagstrom
  A billionaire because he understands the simple magic of compounding, like the fact that putting just $16,000 into an IRA before you're 27 will grow to a million bucks by age 65. It is not much more complicated than that.
- *A Random Walk Down Wall Street,* Burton Malkiel
  "Many people say that the individual investor has scarcely a chance today against Wall Street's pros," says Malkiel. "Nothing could be further from the truth. You can do it as well as the experts, perhaps even better.... The point is rather that a simple 'buy-and-hold' strategy (that is, buying a stock or group of stocks and holding on to them for a long period of time) typically makes as much or more money."

The Millionaire's Spirit: Do What You Love, Today

- *Do What You Love: The Money Will Follow,* Marsha Sinetar
  This is an easy read: "The individual usually will not identify what he really wants because he is aiming for what he thinks is possible,

rather than what he genuinely desires. Thus, he limits his goal-setting. If he wants to be a contractor, let's say, he may feel he cannot achieve that goal, and will settle for being a carpenter instead." Never settle. Do what you really, really love.

- *Success Through a Positive Mental Attitude,* Napoleon Hill and W. Clement Stone

  Billionaire Andrew Carnegie taught young Napoleon Hill his "Science of Success," which was published as Hill's classic, *Think and Grow Rich.* Later, Hill coauthored another classic, *Success Through a Positive Mental Attitude,* with W. Clement Stone, urging people to "awaken the sleeping giant within you! How? Think. Think with a positive mental attitude. The starting point of all achievement is definiteness of purpose with positive mental attitude."

- *Don't Worry, Make Money,* Richard Carlson

  "A major mistake made by many is to give away one's power to perceived experts," we're told by this popular psychologist. "We do it all the time—to our doctors, financial planners, insurance salesmen. Always remember, if you're going to make money, you must take charge. Abundance and joy come from within you, not from other people."

- *The Secret Power Within,* Chuck Norris

  "If you really want something, you must go after it yourself, and with all your dedication: No one is going to give it to you, and if you waver or doubt, you're sure to fail," says this world champion martial artist and filmmaker. "If the bottom line is against you, remember that today is only one day, no matter how hard, and tomorrow is always more than a promise: It's a guarantee."

- *The Seat of the Soul,* Gary Zukav

  Here's a physicist with a clear metaphysical vision: "Let go. Trust. Create. Be who you are. Take your hands off the wheel. Be able to say to the Universe, 'Thy will be done,' and allow your life to go into the hands of the Universe completely. The final piece of reaching for authentic power is releasing your own to a higher form of wisdom." And trusting in that spirit.

- *Real Magic,* Wayne Dyer

  Another respected psychologist urges you to "develop a trust in your intuitive voices. If you feel a strong inner inclination to change jobs, or locations, or to be around new people, or to try a particular investment, then place more trust in that hunch. This is your divine guidance encouraging you to take a risk, to ignore the ways of the herd, to be the unique individual that you are."

The Millionaire's Saboteur:
The Enemy Within

- *Investment Madness,* John Nofsinger
  Here's a great review of the little saboteurs roaming around in your brain. Every investor should know about them. The biggest one blocking success is overconfidence. We trade too much, paying high commissions and taxes, believing we can beat the market, taking big risks, drifting into bigger losses.
- *Mind Over Money,* John Schott
  This psychiatrist/investment adviser asks: "If it's true that investing is so simple, then why do people wind up losing money on stocks, view the market as a major gamble, or feel too intimidated to invest in the first place? . . . Because every emotional drive associated with money gets played out in investing [and] the result can be financially dangerous." See his solutions.

The Millionaire in Transition:
The Path to New Wealth

- *Transitions: Making Sense of Life's Changes,* William Bridges
  This is perhaps the single best book for someone making a major career or life transition. Bridges is a psychologist with an uncanny gift of describing exactly where you are going during life's great turning points: "In the transition process, we come to beginnings only at the end. It is when the endings and the time of fallow neutrality are finished that we can launch ourselves out anew, changed and renewed by the destruction of the old life-phase and the journey through the nowhere." In fact, you should probably read this first.
- *The Artist's Way,* Julia Cameron
  Making a change" Try this 12-week course designed for anyone who wants to get rich: "God has lots of money. God has lots of movie ideas, novel ideas, poems, songs, paintings, acting jobs. God has a supply of loves, friends, houses that are all available to us. By listening to the creator within, we are led to our right path. On that path we find friends, lovers, money, and meaningful work." It works for bankers, attorneys, and accountants, too.
- *Powers of Mind,* Adam Smith
  An incredibly entertaining tale about a Wall Streeter's sabbatical into new paradigms of cosmic consciousness and adventures with psychic healers, gurus, yogis, *I Ching,* tarot cards, Zen, out-of-body

experiences, Rolfing, transcendental meditation, psychedelics, chakras, aromatherapy, chanting, whirling dervishes, and lots more. When I read it I was in the "spin-dry cycle" of life, working on Wall Street, disenchanted, seeing a shrink, attending 12-step meetings, taking acting lessons, writing screen plays, and secretly attending a dance-yoga mediation class in a Soho loft. After five years, I quit Wall Street and went to Hollywood on yet a new adventure!

PERSONALITY TYPES

Baron, Renee, *What Type Am I? Discover Who You Really Are* (Penguin, 1998).

Barron-Tieger, Barbara, and Paul D. Tieger, *Do What You Are: Discover the Perfect Career for You Through the Secrets of Personality Type* (Little Brown & Co., 1995).

Briggs-Myers, Isabel and Peter B. Myers, *Gifts Differing, Understanding Personality Types* (Consulting Psychologists Press, 1995).

Jung, Carl Gustav, and H. G. Baynes (translator), *Psychological Types* (Bollingen Series, Princeton, 1971).

Keirsey, David, *Please Understand Me II: Temperament, Character, and Intelligence* (Prometheus Nemesis, 1998).

Kroeger, Otto, and Janet M. Thuesen, *Type Talk: The 16 Personality Types That Determine How We Live, Love and Work* (Dell, 1989).

Kroeger, Otto, and Janet M. Thuesen, *Type Talk at Work: How the 16 Personality Types Determine Your Success on the Job* (Dell, 1993).

Thomson, Lenore, *Personality Type. An Owner's Manual* (Shambhala, 1998).

Quenk, Naomi L., *Essentials of Myers-Briggs Type Indicator Assessment* (Wiley, 2000).

INDEX

ABOUT THE AUTHOR

Paul B. Farrell began writing *The Millionaire Code* in the early 1970s while on Wall Street with the investment banking firm of Morgan Stanley. He already had degrees in law, architecture, and city planning. He wore three-piece suits, worked on hundred-million-dollar deals, and thought he had it made. Then something happened. After that, nothing was the same.

A friend took Dr. Farrell to a Soho loft for a Joseph Campbell workshop on "Mythical Meditation." Campbell's mysterious world looked nothing like Wall Street. It was filled with a strange network of highways and byways linking Jungian psychology, Taoism, Zen, Sufism, Christian mysticism, Hopi shamanism, alchemy, astrology, the paranormal, tarot, and much more. Campbell said "follow your bliss," so Dr. Farrell left Wall Street for Hollywood!

The trip resulted in several great opportunities: as an executive vice president of a motion picture production company; a cable television executive in charge of production for about a thousand hours of live financial news; an associate editor of a major metropolitan newspaper; and a chemical dependency counselor helping executives, attorneys, physicians, athletes, politicians, rock stars, celebrities, and royalty. He was also awarded a doctorate in psychology.

Since 1997, Dr. Farrell has been a personal finance and investing columnist with CBS *MarketWatch,* where he frequently writes about the psychology, ethics, and spirituality of money, as well as how to make it. He has also written four other books, including the best-seller, *The Winning Portfolio,* and frequently appears on radio and television.

Today, Dr. Farrell lives on the central coast of California with his wife, Dorothy Boyce, a psychotherapist who, along with Joseph Campbell, Carl Jung, and Bill Wilson, taught him everything he knows about human nature—which seemed like a lot when he began writing this book, but never quite seems like enough when he's running late for a meeting and can't figure out why the car won't start, or wondering what the ancient Zen masters would say about getting rid of a spider in the most spiritual way.

As a young man, Dr. Farrell served in Korea with the United States Marine Corps. He was a staff sergeant and an aviation radar and computer technician.